# WILL YOU WALK

# A  LITTLE  FASTER

## Michael Hanson

Printed in Victoria, Canada

**Note for Librarians:** a cataloguing record for this book that includes Dewey Classification and US Library of Congress numbers is available from the National Library of Canada. The complete cataloguing record can be obtained from the National Library's online database at:
www.nlc-bnc.ca/amicus/index-e.html
ISBN 1-4120-0934-0

**This book was published *on-demand* in cooperation with Trafford Publishing.**
On-demand publishing is a unique process and service of making a book available for retail sale to the public taking advantage of on-demand manufacturing and Internet marketing.
**On-demand publishing** includes promotions, retail sales, manufacturing, order fulfilment, accounting and collecting royalties on behalf of the author.

Suite 6E, 2333 Government St., Victoria, B.C. V8T 4P4, CANADA

| | | | |
|---|---|---|---|
| Phone | 250-383-6864 | Toll-free | 1-888-232-4444 (Canada & US) |
| Fax | 250-383-6804 | E-mail | sales@trafford.com |
| Web site | www.trafford.com | TRAFFORD PUBLISHING IS A DIVISION OF TRAFFORD HOLDINGS LTD. | |
| Trafford Catalogue #03-1303 | | www.trafford.com/robots/03-1303.html | |

10      9      8      7      6      5

# CONTENTS

This book is dedicated to someonewho made everything worthwhile. The one who is, and will always be, my lady, my wife Patricia.

I also express my thanks to the many friends, colleagues and staff through the years, and two ladies, Emma Mae Robinson and Linda Hembruff who encouraged me to write. They guided the steps of someone who found great difficulty in mastering present day technology.

Finally I must thank my son Neil, who spent many hours applying his graphic and word processing magic to create the finished book and his unfailing patience in doing so.

Michael Hanson
North Saanich. 2003.

# PREFACE

In responding to society's demands to live life faster, many people rush through the present to reach the future and are then surprised when they cannot remember many of the events or circumstances which should have registered as turning points in their life or career. They hear but they don't listen and they see but they do not take the time to understand.

Walking a beat in London as a Police Constable sees you continually observing and assessing the things which are going on around you and when dealing with an incident you resist the urge to......walk a little faster. You have to listen, question, then decide what to do and must very often remember everything in detail for a Court proceeding.

As a result I have a rich store of memories to call on. Growing up in Sheffield, which was visited twice by German bombers, through a number of career changes until retiring in Victoria, British Columbia, after emigrating to Canada.

Sitting in the back seat of an early R.A.F. jet aircraft being thrown around as a Squadron leader puts student pilots through their paces, or trying to help a Detective Inspector arrest a violent criminal in a pub, where the glasses and chairs are flying are just a few of these memories together with the challenges of bringing a young family to Canada when the Immigration Department had said that they would not lift a finger to help us.

A policeman, a detective, a farmer and a short stint working for Pinkertons before an appointment as British Columbia's first Consumer Affairs Officer are all departures from the British practice of following one career from leaving school until retirement.

In living through an exciting era which has seen another World War and substantial changes in living standards and human attitudes, I have always had the good fortune to work at something I enjoyed. Like Omar Khayam I acknowledge that the past cannot be changed and in a life which has been at times exciting, never predictable and seldom dull, I find that there is little that I would wish to.

# CHAPTER ONE

## BEGINNINGS

The war came to Sheffield on a Thursday night in December 1940. My mother had taken my sister Gillian and I to a local cinema, and when the sirens stopped their wailing about 7 pm, as we walked home on a cold clear night, you could hear the thrumming of the German planes overhead. I cannot remember much gunfire and although there was a red glow from the direction of the City some miles away, there was still an absence of explosions, which as an eight year old I suppose I anticipated would accompany bombing.

We took up the trap door just inside the back door of our house on Stephen Hill in Crosspool on the outskirts of the City, and laid on blankets on the earth floor under the kitchen, wondering if any bombs would fall on the suburbs, but on that first night the bombing concentrated on the City Centre with a great deal of damage and loss of life. We were anxious because father was a policeman and on duty that night, but he came home eventually to everyone's relief.

When the bombers came again on Sunday night, however, it was different. A large gun was firing on the other side of the valley, causing vibrations in the earth floor, and then there was a loud explosion, the back door flew open and back shut again and all the front windows were blown in.

For some reason on the Monday morning, I took the back way from Stephen Hill to Lydgate Lane School which took me past the cemetery, and when I came home in the afternoon, there was a warden standing by a barrier across the road because they had found unexploded bombs in the cemetery!

The war had seemed remote up to that point, although I can remember the family and neighbours listening to the Prime Minister's solemn radio announcement on September 3rd 1939, that we were at war with Germany, and the training squads of soldiers labouring up the hill, sweating in the summer heat in their full kit, rifle and helmet. There have often been times when I have wondered whether any of them survived the war to enjoy more peaceful summers.

My childhood was perhaps unremarkable and much the same as the other children of the day, school then homework and games in the cricket field in the summer. I was born in the Sheffield District called Crookes, a little ironic because both my parents were in the police. I was reading before I went to school as a result of mother's efforts, however being a lazy pupil I sometimes received the cane across the palm of the hand for inattention, and contrary to present thinking I sincerely thank those old teachers because in my view most children will not learn from choice and they made sure that you learned the three 'R's with the cane where necessary or writing out spelling mistakes fifty times.

Daydreaming sometimes happened outside school. I would trip over the proverbial matchstick, and the results were often extremely painful At an early age after a fall I nearly bit my tongue off, and the wound turned septic. There was a risk of the infection spreading I suppose, anyway mother scrubbed it several times with some form of antiseptic and a toothbrush and it eventually healed. On a bilberry expedition to the Moors, I jumped over a stone and fell on the remains of a broken bottle. That meant a trip to the hospital standing up in a neighbours car in case there was still glass in the wound, and stitches which were so deep that they left their own scars leaving a "Scarab" effect. Painful as these episodes were they paled in comparison to the misery caused by inner ear infections or 'gatherings' as they were called then. The pressure built up inside the ear until the ear drum burst and I was to pay for this in later life when the scarring led to inevitable hearing loss.

At this point it should be remembered that antibiotics had not been discovered and apart from disinfectants like iodine and the early days of vaccination and immunization there was little to be done for serious illnesses although there were homespun treatments of one kind or another. Despite the benefits to come from the invention of television and improved radio reception I am distinctly grateful that my boyhood was spent without these distractions and that I had to find other things to keep me busy including reading, model making, marquetry, and active participation in sports, Boy Scouts and Youth Clubs.

As a child I was expected to spend time reading after tea, and if father was there it would sometimes mean that I was unnoticed and could listen to some interesting insights into police work. The difference between murder and manslaughter for example and the arrest of the first criminal to use celluloid to slip back a yale lock so that there was no evidence of entry. It was talked about then and thought about later in life, that the general public become caught up in the arguments surrounding capital punishment and become preoccupied with what will happen to the murderer and details of the relationship with the victim. They do not realise the effect that it can have on the people who catch and try the individual and are connected with the execution. This is particularly true on the day that the execution takes place.

During the war the Sheffield Police were tipped off about the arrival in the City of allied agents in training for insertion into occupied countries, who were picked up and very strenuously questioned to see if they were up to the task.

My mother was probably  one of the first Police Women outside the London Metropolitan area and although she gave this up after marriage and I came along she had some interesting experiences too. At the time fortune telling was illegal, and she would go into pubs and have her fortune told and then arrest the fortune teller. I know this affected her strongly because although she did not say too much she was impressed by the accuracy of some of the readings.

As a Policewoman she was unlikely to have provided any details that could have helped them. There were several methods used , including cards, palm reading, tea leaves and one old lady who made a strong impression who saw different individuals in a kind of halo around a persons head. In my mother's case one of the people was said to be a little old lady in a Spanish mantilla.

Father was born in Derby into a large family which had lived in that area for some years as the gravestones in the local churchyard would testify. He served as an apprentice in the  railway yards until joining the Police, and attributed his ability to sit on his heels for a long time, to having to squat by the Engineer with the heavy leaf springs across his knees as they were fitted above the main drive wheels of the huge steam locomotives which were being built. The name of the locality I think was Alveston.

Mother was born in London into a large family and I am unsure of details of her early childhood or how she came to join the Sheffield Police.

I was born on the 29th, June 1932, at a time when starting and raising a family must have seemed precarious because it was the time of the Great Depression, which seemed to be getting worse. It was probably unremarkable to those people thrown out of work that Amelia Earhart had just flown the Atlantic.

The thousands whose main concern was where the next meal was coming from would not recognise the growing menace of Germany's Hitler and the start of his persecution of the Jews. or have been impressed by Roosevelt's declaration that the only thing we have to fear is fear itself.

Sheffield Police Constable
William Thomas Hanson

Sheffield Woman Police Constable
Irene May Hanson

Sheffield City Grammar School, Fourth Form
M. Hanson, middle row, extreme left

My maternal Grandmother still lived in London, and my Grandfather Harris who hailed from the Northeast of England and I think had served in the Boer War, was badly injured in the First World War by a shell burst which blinded him. He was apparently able to work pieces of shrapnel out of his head years later. He was a redhead and a strong minded individual to all accounts because he was returned from France directly to St. Dunstans for treatment and training to cope with his blindness, but he walked out on the first day and found his way all across London to his home.

A gift for drawing, sketching or any form of visual art did not seem to be part of my make up but I heard my parents discuss some cousins on my father's side who were incredibly gifted and were some of the only remaining people who were trusted to do the very ornate work on the outside and the ceilings of gypsy caravans, typical of the angels and cherubs to be found in old French and Italian buildings.

I was too young to appreciate the militarism which was alarming knowledgeable newspaper correspondents, the start of the Civil War in Spain which was to afford a training opportunity for German pilots and their coming tactics of Blitzkrieg. Their alarm seemed to be justified when in 1938 and 1939 Hitler stormed into Austria followed by Czechoslovakia and Poland.

The examinations which you took in your eleventh year decided which school you would qualify for, and if you did well you would go to a Grammar School. I must have been fortunate because I ended up starting at Sheffield City Grammar in the September of 1943, although it meant a bus ride into the City and back .

The school was in the centre of the City on Orchard Street and you did not have a year or a grade but there were 'Forms.' The first year was the First Form and so on. From the outset you were placed in a 'House' and the School's were named after different tribes. Mine was Maori as I remember. We were co-educational.

There I reverted to my lazy ways and just did enough to get by in most subjects except French where I seemed to pick it up very quickly particularly spoken French. This all caught up with me when instead of going into the fifth year from year three which they claimed was within my capabilities, I dropped into year four and that was a shock to the ego!

Without the student realising it a school does a great deal to shape an individuals character and the way he or she deals with life. The sports teams if you were good enough and Houses, to which everyone belonged produced the elements of team spirit and working towards a common purpose in competition with other teams. I really enjoyed team sports and played in goal at football, but did not qualify for the first school cricket team so

I played for the second team and kept wicket. The Sports Master became annoyed with the distance that I stood behind the stumps for the fast bowler and when I declined to reduce the distance he gave the gloves to another boy who did not last one over before a ball came 'right through' the batsman and hit him flush on the nose. I took the gloves back without further criticism.

I appeared in some of the school plays although not in a starring capacity, and in some cases developing the part in unexpected fashion. On one occasion I was dressed in a cloak and had to carry a large sword attached to a belt around the waist. The part called for me to walk to the front of the stage where there was a drop to the hall floor and fall to my knees saying "Let us pray" and then my two companions were to follow one at a time saying "Do not rise ... hear me." For all the practices the footlights were attached to the front of the stage, and although you had difficulty seeing beyond them they formed a useful reference point for me to kneel down. On the first night of the play someone had moved them several feet in front of the seats and my strangled "let us pray" as I went over the front was echoed by the words of the other two who fell on top of me. We clambered back up and carried on but it seemed to turn a serious effort into unintended farce.

There were other social activities of one kind or another which I generally managed to evade, however, there was something called an 'E isteddfod' which everyone had to take part in and I searched for something innocuous ending up eventually in something called 'The Impromptu Speech Competition.' This proved to be a situation where you were called out on to the stage and the master would say "Your subject is..................." and you had to start talking straight away and keep it up for either three or five minutes I forget which. Surprisingly I sailed through the heats and found myself in the final with three others. The finals along with other events were to be held in front of the whole school, Masters and Mistresses sitting in the front seats of course.

When our competition started, the two girls both dried up and were eliminated and that left another boy and yours truly. He went first and his subject was 'What I want to be.' He was quite small, and when he opened his jacket and pushed his colourful braces out with both thumbs, saying "my ambition is to be a man....." I could only watch and realise that he had his audience in the palm of his hand. When my subject was read 'Famous dictators you have known,' I felt my chances to win had sunk without trace, but started by saying that I would be expected to talk about Hitler and Mussolini, and felt that it would be more interesting to talk about dictators that we met in the ordinary course of life. I started at one end of the row and described the teachers most obvious habits and idiosyncrasies, and had not even reached half way when I was stopped for time.

To my surprise I won, and someone told me later that despite strong opposition from some of my 'victims' the English teacher had decided that I had scored highest for originality and difficulty of subject.

There were other more serious moments, and when someone came to the classroom, interrupted the teacher, and a student was asked to go to the Head Master's Office it was generally because the dreaded telegram had been received at home and a father or uncle had been killed in action. There were several like that after the parachute drop at Arnhem, because Midland Regiments were involved.

Before moving on to Grammar School, there was not the appreciation of world events and the progress of the war, and its effects were limited to air raid drills when we trooped out to brick shelters and sat on wooden forms for a while. The significance of the sinking of the Hood followed by that of the Bismarck, and the battles of Stalingrad and El Alamein did not mean a great deal to Elementary students.

At Grammar School, the Battle of the Atlantic was reflected in the content of school meals and the progress of the Allied armies in Europe was followed with keen patriotism. It was hard for anyone to understand the inhuman treatment of the Jewish inmates of Dachau and Auschwitz when they were liberated and the shocking photographs appeared in the newspapers.

The school arranged field trips for the older students, and the ones which stay in my mind are the visit to a steel mill where we saw the huge ingots walled up in furnaces, the gantries which carry them and the spectacular explosions and sparks when they pass through the first set of rollers and green branches are thrown on to break off the outer coat of impurities or 'slag.' Overall there was a lasting memory of the heat especially near the crucibles and I remember being impressed by two remarks made by the guide for our group; the prodigious amounts of beer that the workers could drink during their mid day break without any noticeable effect and that the perfect murder might be possible if the body was thrown into the molten metal because never the slightest trace of it would ever be found.

It was perhaps to be expected that during the war, references would be made to England's successes throughout a history of battles  and the tactics which had been employed, especially the discipline of outnumbered Armies and Navies who waited to fire until the moment of maximum effect. This was brought home to me when the boys were taken to see Henry Vth and the girls the Red Shoes. The way that Henry, with a seriously outnumbered army, having only the choice of when and where to fight, chose a hill and disposed his archers so that they would face the charge of the French Knights, and then with them both standing and kneeling for practical purposes, how they waited until it seemed suicidally late to fire and got in two or three murderous volleys before melting into the trees. The music background was particularly effective, building up to a loud pounding roar as the French closed on the English lines and a split second of silence as the Master Bowman dropped his arm and then the hissing of the first volley of arrows.

Although school uniforms were an added expense, they did tend to make each boy and girl the same in everyday terms. The green jacket had the school badge which was a red phoenix rising from the flames.

Wartime was the era of school meals and although these were probably nutritious they were certainly not attractive. There was a particularly watery custard I remember. Being partial to my mother's teacakes when they were hot from the oven and I was cautioned probably indigestible, some of the boys that I joined in the street for some soccer with a tennis ball would use their dinner money to buy hot bread buns, almost certainly indigestible from a bakery where the lady would split them and add what passed for butter. One lad that joined in seemed to be very gifted in the way that he handled and controlled the small ball. His name was Albert Quixall and he went on to make a name for himself in professional football in later years.

Mother's bread making was something to be watched closely and with anticipation. The yeast had that singular smell and was purchased in blocks and crumbled into the warm milk and then there was the ritual of kneading, leave to rise, punch down and leave to rise in the tins until they went into the oven. Woe betide anyone who opened a door or caused any kind of a draft when the bread was rising or the oven door was open.

Wartime rationing meant that items like butter were very scarce. When bread was a day or two old, then 'doorsteps' were cut from the loaf and toasted close to the fire using a brass toasting fork. Beef or pork dripping was then substituted for butter giving rise to the humorous greeting "How's your Mother off for dripping."

A small commentary here on English houses. They were built to last rather than for personal comfort. Insulation consisted of an air space between bricks in the wall and wooden windows and doors which soon lost their fit and became draft producers. The open fire which sent most of its heat up the chimney and any supplemental heat in the shape of a domestic boiler or paraffin heaters could not compete with Yorkshire winters. Baths were something to be dreaded.

Our physical education classes were held in the Sheffield Y.M.C.A. and this was easy walking distance from the school. In the closing days of one school year the Sports Master decided that there would be something different to our usual exercise routine and arranged an impromptu boxing ring. He called for volunteers and a boy called Ratcliffe stepped forward because his father boxed and he was reputed to be able to do the same. When nobody else came forward he told me to put on the gloves I suppose because I was one of the biggest and perhaps looked gormless. The first couple of rounds saw him dancing around me and peppering my head with his straight left which I could not seem to avoid and my two seconds made no secret of their disdain. I then started to anticipate his punches and ducked underneath them landing some of my own. The end of the 'fight ' came when I had ducked and was about to land one, when he brought his fist down on top of my head and started dancing around shaking his fist and yelling. He came back to the school that afternoon with a plaster cast up to his elbow having broken his thumb and you can guess the remarks afterwards about the kind of head which produced this result.

Homework was supposed to occupy the evening hours, but the Youth Club in the Church at the top of the road became a meeting spot for most of the local boys, and in the summer Blacktin's tennis courts near the elementary school was a popular spot for those who liked tennis, which I certainly did and it was an opportunity to meet girls, something that comes with adolescence along with spots and gawkiness.

The Fish and Chip shop in Crosspool was also a favourite with youngsters although I do not think their business profited very much as a result. Three pennyworth of chips was the usual order and in my case I used to like scraps as well which were free. Salt and vinegar were generously applied. If the chips were not ready it was an opportunity to watch the activity behind the counter. Peeled potatoes were brought in a bucket to a piece of equipment with an arm which brought a metal pad down on the spud and forced it through a cubed cutter depositing the raw pieces into another bucket from which they were tipped into the frier making a lot of noise in the process. There was always some suspense as the fingers placed the potato on the cutter and just managed to remove themselves before the ram came down. The fat in the frier was extremely hot but this did not seem to bother the proprietor when he picked up some chips on the slice and broke one with his fingers to see if they were done. The favourite and cheapest fish was rock cod and fillets were coated with a batter mixture which gave rise to the scraps as surplus small pieces left behind after the frying.

Although the Yorkshire Cricket team used to play in the City either against other Counties or teams from other Countries, they were not followed with the same kind of enthusiasm as the football teams Sheffield Wednesday and United. I do remember however going to see the Australians play Yorkshire in a cricket match which was supposed to predict England's fortunes in the forthcoming test matches because it pitted the great fast bowlers Lindwall and Miller against Len Hutton and other good batsmen. On a gloomy day several batsmen were dismissed before lunch falling to the very fast Australian bowlers. There was a little buzz of interest when a 'caretaker batsman' was sent in just before lunch. Instead of the ritual pulling on of gloves with the bat under his arm, he went down the pavilion steps, and marched to the wicket with the bat on his shoulder. It was the spin bowler Wardle, who was already making a bit of a reputation as a rebel. He took guard and as one of the Australians resumed his over he waited until he was almost at the wicket before dancing down the pitch and driving the ball to the boundary. He went on to score a respectable number of runs leading to sarcastic press comments about the established batsmen learning from his example.

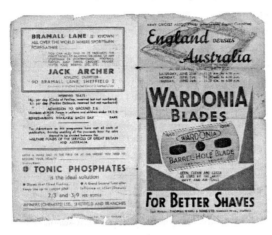

Batsmen have very fast reflexes and when Hutton was fielding in his favourite fine leg slip position and a batsman glanced the ball the crowd and the batsman could not see the ball and so he started out of the crease as if to run. Hutton brought the ball from behind his back and the batsman quickly regained the crease. Apparently the ball at great speed had bounced at Hutton's feet and in one movement he had scooped it up and put it behind his back. Another cricket moment I remember was a match against Middlesex who had Compton in their side. Sports figures advertising different things was in its infancy and Compton had started to be used in Brylcream's efforts to show that the male appearance could be enhanced by the right hair treatment. It was fashionable in those days for the better batsmen to go forward to the fast bowlers when they started their innings and play a dead bat without intending to score until 'they got their eye in.' This proved irksome to a crowd which generally observed complete silence unless there was some fine play or batsmen coming in or out when clapping showed their appreciation. There is of course a particular kind of humour in the English Midlands and when Compton had gone forward for the umpteenth time and let the ball

hit his bat, holding the position for a long time, a Yorkshire voice broke the silence to say, "It's all right Dennis, they've got thy picture now."

In 1947 at the age of fifteen, I went to stay with a French family who lived in the Seine et Oise district of Paris as part of a School Exchange Programme. For three or perhaps four weeks, in addition to making my way in French, with local idioms totally different to text book French, there were other significant changes to my usual way of life. England still experienced strict food rationing, so it was a distinct pleasure to take one of the baguettes that Madame Bourdin brought in each morning and smother it in butter, for there seemed to be no food restrictions in France. Coffee was served in a bowl, not a cup, and with lunch and dinner there was wine or something stronger.... and I never had anything like that to drink before! This meant that on occasions I was 'flapping my wings' and probably a little incoherent although I seemed to be extraordinarily cheerful. My favourite was a drink called Quinquina, and looking back it was probably a kind of sweet sherry. The family took me to the Palais De Versailles where I saw the gardens famous in history and the beautiful paintings particularly on the ceilings. There was a visit to a play which was a kind of situation comedy and two visits to the Opera to see Carmen at the Opera Comique and Faust at the Grand Opera. I went to the top of the Eiffel Tower and was impressed by the shrinking size of people as you changed from one elevator car to another, and the wind on the top platform. I did the usual silly things... sat on the rail and bought a ring which quickly turned my finger green. I seem to remember that I was smoking by then, and I brought home some packets of the Gauloise Jaune which were very similar to the English Woodbine. The most popular French cigarette with it's distinctive smell on the under ground or other confined spaces was the Gauloise Bleu and it seemed to be the cheapest and the strongest. I have to confess that I was not overly impressed with their toilet system which seemed to have a hinged metal door at the bottom of the bowl.

When Jean paid his visit to us we tried to return the hospitality, however as he wanted to be an Engineer his interests certainly seemed to centre on the industries of Sheffield. He was particularly impressed by a visit to a cutlery factory where he followed the raw metal and handles through the whole process and eventually was handed the carving knife and fork in a presentation box to take home with him.

Childhood is a time when you are most aware of sight, sound and smell, with lasting impressions for the rest of your life. My paternal grandfather had a pub in Derby, The Coronation on Baker Street, and although I was not allowed into the licensed area during drinking hours I did go into the bar areas when they were closed during the day. The patina of beer and spirits on the different surfaces coupled with cigarette and pipe smoke left a delightful aroma which was stronger near the bar area even though everything had been washed and cleaned. Another treat was to watch the beer delivery. The kegs were rolled off the wagon over to the cellar door and to the head of two long beams which led down into the cellar with bent iron rungs spaced along their length. Ropes were attached and each keg reverently lowered down the beam guides to the bottom where they were rolled into position. When the delivery men had left there was the traditional 'tapping' when grandfather would insert the connection to the pumps in the bar above and sample the keg to ensure it's quality.

The back yard was also an interesting playground with its many empty bottles of different size shape and colour, and that was my undoing because I discovered a small residue in some of the spirit bottles and when this was carefully poured into one bottle I ended up with perhaps half an inch of combined spirits. Suffice it to say that when I emptied this at one go on a hot summer's day in a fairly short time I began to feel decidedly odd and this condition quickly became apparent to my kin who, on establishing the cause administered corporal punishment. However the smarting was tempered a few days later when in the bar one early morning grandfather found a sailor's black 'rope' of tobacco and used his knife to shave off pieces and put them in his pipe which he then lit. It did not take long before he felt an unusual state of euphoria and was severely chided. From listening to the conversation later I learned that sailors take tobacco leaf and roll this with layers of rum and other substances picked up at their various ports of call until it is a black sweet smelling rope which can be carried in the pocket and small shavings used in the pipe as grandfather had done. Somehow one of the more exotic Middle Eastern substances had been used by this particular sailor.

Scout camp near to forest areas brought an awareness of the individual smell of conifers and those other smells of grass and wildflowers which always strengthen in the morning and evening hours just before and after dark when the dew seems to heighten every scent. I was to confirm this when we farmed for a brief interlude in the sixties.

Even as a youngster before I came into contact with group singing in the church choir I can remember being moved by the spontaneous singing of the Welsh at sporting events and gatherings and their natural ability to separate into their different voices to achieve beautiful harmony.

Another scent or smell which, if you came into contact with it with your eyes closed, was immediately identifiable was that of the cinemas of the day. That mixture of smoke, lysol or some other cleaner and much used seating could not be mistaken.

A more pleasant memory was of the tomatoes grown in an unheated greenhouse which father built with blitzed timber which I helped to rebate for the glass with many sharpenings of the plane required after contact with nails, shrapnel or imbedded brick or stone. When you brought them into the house freshly picked, they filled it with their distinctive smell and their taste was infinitely superior to the shop bought variety.

St.John's Ranmoor was a large Church with splendid pillars, carvings and stained glass, and it had a very big pipe organ behind the choir area. There was a small harmonium in the vestry which the Choirmaster, a Mr. Hornby, used for our weekly practices and I used to watch to see if the end joint of the little finger on his left hand which had a decided inward angle, would ever hit a wrong note ... but it never did. He sat with his back towards us when he was playing and seemed to have eyes in the back of his head if there was any mischief. One of his comments that I do remember, rising above the psalm or hymn was " Hanson, how many times do I have to tell you boy, quality not quantity ... quality!"

There was a trip to the church one evening a week for practice and then once or sometimes twice on Sunday. Boys and men were on either side in the church close to the altar and behind the pulpit and were divided into Cantoris or Decani. The men occupied a strategic position behind the boys and did not hesitate to clip the offending ear if a boy was reading during the service or otherwise not paying attention. My means of transport was a Co-op bicycle known in those days as a 'sit up and beg' with upright handlebars and after a while no back mudguard because it was all downhill to the church and my brakes were always suspect and had to be supplemented by the sole of my shoe or sandal on the back tire next to the forks. As I was always late and at high speed the friction produced near burning conditions coupled with premature wear on the shoe.

We were paid quarterly, and although it was not a large sum it provided an earning experience which was tempered by the fines levied during the quarter for misbehaviour. The fines were separated from your pay and a procession marched down the church to deposit this in the Poor Box. One enterprising boy had access to a large number of farthings which he sold to the miscreants at a halfpenny apiece. These were substituted in the march down the church and The Vicar bless him never referred to the large number of farthings in the poor box after quarterly pay day. All of us looked forward to weddings, because they meant half a crown apiece which was paid on the dot for what really amounted to a short service on a Saturday morning.The morning service and evensong followed a regular pattern of hymns and psalms except for high days and holidays like Harvest Festival and Remembrance Day when more specific ones were chosen and seemed to produce more enthusiastic accompaniment from the Congregation. There were also times when some pieces included a descant for the treble voices or a solo and I really enjoyed the way that the church seemed to contain and enhance the voices combined with the organ to provide a kind of resonance. This was particularly so when we sang the Hallelujah Chorus, however this needed concentration to perform, particularly at the end when six hallelujahs are followed by about three beats of complete silence before the final hallelujah ... and someone always manages an abbreviated squeak to spoil the silence and earn the immediate hatred of his peers.

One of the landmarks in growing up is when you exchange home haircuts for a visit to the barbers and that is something which I found I really enjoyed. Sitting waiting your turn you could read old magazines and watch the different rituals performed in shaving and haircutting. The individual would be reclined almost to a horizontal position for a shave, the sheet wrapped around and hot cloths applied before the shaving mug and brush would apply an astonishing amount of soapy lather. The cutthroat razor would be stropped a few times on a strap hanging from the counter. As the razor moved in long strokes or the face would be pulled into various positions to ensure all the stubble was removed the lather that built up on the blade would be flipped into a bowl, and then finally another hot towel to remove the last traces.

When it was my turn in the chair, I would ask for a short back and sides and would have the cotton wool pushed around the back of my collar and the sheet wrapped around and under the chin but there would be no lowering of the chair. The clippers and comb would go to work and there was a pleasant heat from the appliance. When the cutting was finished a mirror was held behind your head which allowed you to admire it in the large counter mirror and then the cutthroat razor was stropped again and used to make an even hairline at the back and straighten the sideburns. Then at no extra charge the barber would light a long wax taper and singe your hair, following with the comb and finish everything off with a spray which settled on your hair and was probably a scented lacquer of some kind. There is probably no substance to it, but there was a widely held belief that cutting the hair made it 'bleed' and you were therefore susceptible to a head cold, hence the singe to seal up the ends. The cutting winds and raw cold in the winter months gave rise to many colds and miserable head conditions. The hairdressers was another example of a combination of aromas which with a keen young sense of smell you never forget.

We had moved from Stephen Hill to Coldwell Lane before I finished school, both turnings off the Manchester Road. It was in the farm a little bit further up the Lane that I started to help on weekends. The farmer relied on a young carthorse 'Bonnie' for all those things that a tractor would do on more modern farms, and more often than not, because he made a fair amount of money from selling manure to eager gardeners, I would have to bring her out of her stall and harness her to the big two wheeled cart with big wooden wheels and metal rims and then fill up the cart with manure. Although young , she was huge, and a little temperamental! In her stall when bothered by flies she would lift a back leg and bring the hoof down with the kind of force which seemed to shake the old building and had made a crater in the cobbled floor. She also had teeth like  chisels, and if you took your eye off her for half a second, she could give you a nip that left bruises for days.

There was an elderly gentleman who loved the horse and would arrive at the weekends in a brown overall coat, and spend some time grooming her and giving her treats. This was not always a good thing for if you were using her to plough or mow or otherwise pull equipment and someone came to the top of the field, the horse would remember ... apple ... and take off with you hanging on for dear life. On another occasion he had watched me harness her up to the cart, fill up with manure and then walked with me as we negotiated a very busy main road and then down a road of new houses which had not yet been paved where the cart creaked and yawed over rocks and holes until we came to a house and unloaded. We got up into the cart which still showed evidence of its last contents and he asked to have the reins and drive home. After a few yards our speed began to pick up as Bonnie realised that we were on our way home, and when I asked him to slow her down I realised that he couldn't because the horse had the bit between her teeth. The cart was beginning to lurch and jar over the unmade road and there was a busy main road coming up, so I took the reins, sawed to one side and then yanked to the other. The bit was freed and the horse stopped and climbed with me hanging on to the reins and not going to let go, but with nothing to hold on to my companion ended up in the back of the cart covered from head to foot with manure. When he had recovered I got him to hold her and used my old trilby hat to dust her around the face, to ensure that she realised that she had misbehaved. It did not seem to affect his treatment of the horse however.

Another hazardous incident came at milking time, something which was not my favourite chore because I was not good at it and it tied you to a routine early morning and again at night. The farmer had several milking buckets but was particularly proud of a recent acquisition which was seamless. As I was milking the first cow a rat or mouse fell into it's feeding trough from the granary above the ceiling. A cow can kick you in two ways, one being a kind of roundhouse swing which gives you a bit of warning and the other by lifting its foot straight up with no warning at all and mine used the latter method. It drove the bucket up into what is euphemistically called the lower abdomen and I rolled into the aisle to see the bucket being back heeled along the row of probably amused sisters. I was not particularly pleased when the farmer seemed to be a lot more interested in the dent in the bucket than he was about the state of my ... health.

Sometimes during the morning milking an old black tomcat would come down from the granary, and although I was told never to feed him as he had to subsist on the vermin he found, there was an old saucer with a candle stub that held a little milk when I knew that we were not going to be observed. Some mornings his hide had bloody scratches, and an ear would be half hanging off where, on his own, he had been silently fighting against things that may have been bigger than him. I sometimes thought of that old tomcat in similar circumstances later in life.

The farmer had some things which he preferred to do himself, and when the hay was brought in from the field stacked high on the cart between the high ends or ames, he used to build the stack, building a little bit wider and longer all the time and teasing down the sides until he started to build up the apex at the top. He would then use straw to thatch it with binder twine and wooden pegs, and would sometimes hang ropes over it with large stones on the ends in case of strong winds. There was a hard to use hay knife which looked like a very large scythe which was used to cut blocks out of the stack when summer grazing was finished.

There was also the threshing which used to take place at the end of the summer when the thresher made its way around the various farms with all the nearby farms sending workers to service and feed the machine. The corn stack in the yard would diminish as the corn bunches were fed into the machine and the grain would pour into sacks while the straw would either remain straw to be restacked or chopped up to make bedding . Whichever method was used, if there had been grass in the bottom of the stook it would be picked over by the stock when it was thrown in as bedding and then with their droppings provide the best kind of manure for growing anything in the garden. The farmer also used to claim that by stacking and then threshing, the grain matured a lot better than the new combines which did everything at once. To save a year in crop rotation some farmers would include grass and clover seed with the corn sowing, and this increased the feed content left in the straw.

It was certainly a very dusty operation, and provided some excitement when the base of the stack was reached and rats and mice ran everywhere. It was dangerous to corner a rat, because I saw one lad chase one into a corner with a hay fork and the rat leapt over his shoulder to make its escape.

Threshing was also an occasion for the farmer's wife to show what she could do to feed the large number of hungry men and lads when they stopped at midday for a meal. Pies were the order of the day and each farms wife tried to outdo the others in the amount supplied and the quality of the pastry and contents both of the meat pies, and the fruit pies for dessert with real farm cream. There would also be tea and tarts or buns during the afternoon because unless the weather was bad the thresher only stayed for one day before moving on to its next farm.

Generally at the age of fifteen years you took an examination called School Certificate or Matriculation which is the equivalent of High School Graduation and which set the seal on your school years if you were going straight into the workforce or confirmed your entry into a further two years before Higher School Certificate which would qualify you for higher education, But you had to do well in the examination.

A few months before the School Certificate Examination. we were given a trial examination which was really one of the old exams. When those results were tabulated I failed in every subject except one ... Art... and I was a really bad artist. In an immediate post mortem of the results nearly all the teachers told me that I would fail their subject in the School Certificate ... not could fail or might fail,...... but would fail! Pride would not allow me to let people know what I was doing, but I started to hit the books hard, and every night before each exam I sat up going through as much of the work as I could and perhaps with a great deal of luck I found a lot of the last night's material in the questions.

When the results were posted in the summer I found that in the nine subjects I had a Distinction in French and a Credit in seven subjects with one failure ... in Art. Credits meant marks which were over seventy or seventy five per cent.

The reaction from the teachers was mixed, most showed a certain degree of puzzlement except one teacher in Biology who told me it had to be an absolute fluke. That made me march straight out of her class and up to the Headmaster's office where I suggested that an apology was in order, and to his credit he took me back to her class, called her outside, and I got my apology.

The whole thing however taught me two things. The first was that when anyone told me that I would not or could not do something... and I wanted to do it ... then I would find a way to do it. The other was that when you did not really understand a subject, and Chemistry and Physics were completely beyond me, then by memorizing the theorems or data you could not only pass examinations , but pass them well ... and still not understand the subject! This was to stand me in very good stead in my early Police days.

I was to spend almost another couple of years at school, however there was a distinct difference between my parents and I about an eventual career. They wanted me to go to Durham University and study Agricultural Science and I had ideas about studying Law, and as there was no likelihood of much financial assistance for either I found myself working at the farm full time for an Insurance Stamp on my Card while I still lived at home until the long arm of His Majesty reached out to claim me for National Service.

# CHAPTER 2

# R.A.F. NATIONAL SERVICE

After the usual medical which obviously did not find any problems, I was told to report to Padgate in Lancashire one cold November morning in 1951 to begin two years in the R.A.F..

Outside the gate I found a dark haired lad who was obviously about to report like me, so we went in together, his name was Hughes from Wales and I was Hanson from Yorkshire , and we received Service Numbers with only a difference of two or three  between them.

Before starting out I had what I thought was a fairly short haircut, but I suspect regardless of how short each recruits hair was we were all required to have it cut again and pay a shilling for the privilege.

We were assigned to a Flight  and a specific hut which was going to be our home for a few weeks and which had to be cleaned and polished in every way the same as our uniforms. In the first instance however we were issued overalls, a belt with webbing and gaiters for everyday drill. The uniform issue was a line parading before a long desk with quartermasters throwing different items at you as you passed along before them. They obviously had the ability to gauge the size appropriate to the trousers, beret, boots etc. that they were issuing to each recruit.

Blanco and brasso were   still in use and however dirty your belt, webbing or brasses became, they still had to be spotlessly cleaned each night or attract the sarcastic comments of the Drill Instructors on the following day. Boots had to have their toe caps carefully polished until they became ebony mirrors.

Mornings began bright and early with the tannoy sounding in each hut to rouse you out of bed and into the ablutions to wash and shave with a blade in cold water, then parade outside your hut holding your mug and 'irons' or knife, fork and spoon to be marched down for breakfast. Then back to the hut to prepare for P.E. or drill or whatever delights the Instructors had in store.

Padgate it was rumoured had been condemned some years before, and it was certainly extremely cold and damp.

Some of the rules applied in training defied commonsense, but I later found that this could be said of most rules and regulations throughout the Services. One day we reported to the running track in freezing weather wearing the prescribed shorts and singlet with gym shoes. After the first lap it started to sleet so we were told to put our ground sheets on and continue running.

Drill consisted of marching and counter marching at various speeds, forming lines and using your arm to dress against the next man and so forth. There was also rifle drill with and without bayonet using the good old 303 rifle. It was here that time honoured sarcasm from the Instructors was used to highlight real or imaginary errors.

Keeping the uniform, rifle and webbing cleaned to exacting standards was not always easy, particularly after a trip around the obstacle course. Climbing obstacles and falling into mud baths certainly did not help matters.

The firing range provided a little bit of relief, and we all looked forward to seeing whether we could score well using the targets at different distances. We used both the 303 rifle and the Bren gun on single fire and automatic. I seem to remember that my score was not particularly good and that my shoulder was sore from the recoil, however the thing that really sticks in my mind was the recruit next to me who could only fire his rifle by holding it in the middle of his chest, and each time he fired his helmet fell over his eyes. This gave rise to a profane but clear description by the Range Sergeant of what was likely to happen to him if the enemy charged his position and he still had his helmet over his eyes.

Fatigue week as it was called was when we supplied the camp guards and carried out any other chores that were necessary, and it also gave an insight into the character of some of the individuals in our Flight.

One of our night guards was Tommy, a member of Plymouth Brethren who as far as we could learn did not lie, drink or commit any of the usual sins or indulge in any vices. He had proved this when someone from our hut climbed on the neighbouring roof and stuffed toilet rolls down the chimney, smoking them out very satisfactorily. When an irate D.I. came into our billet and asked who had done it Tommy pointed out the offender without any hesitation. Being very small it was decided that Tommy would not stand guard on the main gate but would do guard duty on his own at the back gate which was nothing more but a gap in a hedge into a field.

When the Duty Officer turned out the guard at two in the morning, those of us not actually standing guard poured out and shuffled into line. He complained about the fact that we were all wearing pyjamas under our uniforms for a little warmth, and then set off with a Sergeant to inspect the perimeter guards. After about twenty minutes he was back with Tommy who was obviously upset and claimed another individual to take his place. The full story came out later. When the Duty Officer reached the back gate there was no sign of Tommy, and they eventually found him sitting by the path a bit further inside the camp. The Sergeant told him that is was a very serious offence to leave his post, and why had he done this. Tommy told him that there were cows in the field, and he could not abide cows. The Duty Officer tried to lay it on a bit thicker and told Tommy that in wartime he could be shot for deserting his post, but all that Tommy would say was that he could not abide cows. So in the face of this unshakable logic, they brought him back to the guard hut and replaced him.

At various times throughout the training we were given tests to detect tuberculosis etc. and shots to immunize us against typhoid, paratyphoid and a multitude of other ills. The accepted wisdom was that your arm would swell and become extremely hot and painful on either the first or second occasion. In my case it was on the second occasion immediately before we got our 48 hour pass, and there were a lot of uniformed bodies trying to protect their right arms during the train journey.

As many of us had volunteered for National Service Aircrew, a large contingent traveled to Hornchurch where we were pushed and prodded and given the ink blot, aptitude, coordination and other tests before we found that out of a hundred of us who had all been pronounced fit by civilian doctors and then the Padgate doctor, ninety nine were considered unfit.

One of the group that traveled back to Padgate to continue training was Jack, who could probably qualify for the description 'accident prone.' Most of us kept the cartridge clip with it's five dummy rounds, in a webbing pouch. Because I suspect some keen types put coins in their rifle magazine to make it rattle during rifle drill, Jack put his in the rifle magazine. When we went through the procedure of open breech prior to having the rifle inspected for cleanliness, Jack obviously did not do it to the satisfaction of the Drill Instructor, who told him to do it again and stood over him as he did it. By closing the bolt and then opening the breech, a dummy round was loaded, and then ejected hitting the Corporal who practically danced with rage.

When we had our passing out parade, all shined and polished and practically tiptoeing with fixed bayonets on an icy square, after being dismissed, we raced for the billet which had also been shined and polished and carefully tended during our stay and the first man in threw his rifle up the billet towards the rack in which it was normally kept. Each man kept doing the same and managed to dodge the flying rifles until Jack came in and managed to hit the stove chimney and detach it from the stove. No one was going to complain because Jack's father was 'Jack London' who had won the British and Empire Heavyweight boxing title and one day his brother fighting as Brian London  would do the same, besides he was one of our Flight wasn't he?

Training Flight, R.A.F. Padgate - November 1951

Jack Harper: back row, far right
Self: front row, second from left
David Hughes: standing behind me

When we came to the end of our basic training , it was time for some kind of trade training and we all waited expectantly to find what the rest of the two years had in store for us. Although we had nearly all failed the aircrew requirements including Jack, it seemed that practically everyone was going into a trade connected to aircraft and flying, and the cynical said the this would mean that we could be recalled to be trained as aircrew if hostilities broke out and would then know one end from the other. So what was it going to be airframes, engines or instruments? The Welsh lad Hughes who had walked into camp with me got instruments and I got airframes, which meant a few months for me at St. Athans in Wales.

The next little while was spent in filing metal, studying hydraulics and pneumatics and getting used to the perpetual Welsh rain. When we did get the opportunity to go into Cardiff the name Sofia Gardens sticks in my memory but there was sometimes trouble between the Welsh youths and servicemen. To get back home to Sheffield was not very easy even if I did get an early start on Friday afternoon with a forty eight hour pass. In a mistaken effort to save money I rode pillion on a motorbike to the Great North Road where I expected to thumb a lift quite easily. After several hours I abandoned the try and caught a train in the morning. Going back I used to get a train about 10 p.m. from Sheffield and get off at Gloucester where I had to wait a couple of hours for a connecting train to Cardiff. I then caught a milk train to the camp and the porter used to walk up and down the platform calling Barry and Llantwit ( being Llantwit Major.)

During the Sunday night travel I never used to get any sleep and everyone was going to breakfast when I got to camp. So the Service thought it quite reasonable to schedule football for Monday afternoon. I used to love to play although I could not claim to be very skilled I probably made up for this with enthusiasm.

Early in 1952 when the time came to be posted, I was relieved to find that I was going to Finningley, an Advanced Flying School near Doncaster in Yorkshire. I found myself in 'B' Flight, and the aircraft were the first jet aircraft, Gloucester Meteors, the 4 which was a single seater and the 7 which was a two seater and the student's first jet aircraft because they came straight from flying Harvards. At that time the Meteor 8 was our front line aircraft, and it was identical to the 4 except that it had an ejection seat and guns which were armed. A weekend squadron stationed at Finningley used to fly them and had their own fitters and riggers. In addition to servicing the jets we had an elderly Airspeed Oxford which had been one of the bombers early in the war, and as it flew so slowly I would think that it would have been very vulnerable to anti-aircraft fire.

Unless there was fog or some other weather conditions which socked us in, the planes were flying all the time and none of the aircraft were allowed to remain unserviceable for long. This meant hurrying service and repairs, and as you signed the Form 700 or the Log Book of the aircraft to say that it was serviceable after a pre-flight or a wheel change it meant that you were generally held to be responsible if anything went wrong.

We started pulling the aircraft out of the hangars early in the morning and they flew until late at night. Apart from the pre-flights and more simple repairs, our time was taken up with refueling, starting and marshaling. You needed a screwdriver to twist the opener on the fuel opening and other inspection panels, so this was stuck in the belt making you look like an old time pirate. We were supposed to wear kerosene suits of a type of thick green material because the fuel did not agree with everyone. We were also supposed to rub a cream called Rosalex into our hands before we started. If we could get away with it we preferred to wear the cloth overalls and runners instead of the protective garb. Once you had learned the arm signals you could bring a taxiing aircraft down the painted line and stop it exactly where you wanted it even when it was night flying and you were using lighted wands.

Starting could be an adventure because you plugged in the trolley accumulator, gave thumbs up to the pilot after you had switched on and had a green light. You stood by the nacelle on the port side. There were sundry clicking noises as the pilot went through his cockpit startup, and if all went well there would be a 'whumph' as the fuel ignited and a deepening roar as the

engine spooled up. However when the fuel did not ignite you made frantic throat cutting signs to the pilot to shut itdown and start again after the engine had been dried out, because if he pressed the emergency re-light on the high pressure cock and it ignited all the fuel in the engine there was sometimes quite an explosion. This generally went out of the back... which is why we stood at the front

Gloucester Meteor Mark 7

... but if it did come out of the front you were likely to lose your eyebrows besides being deafened.

There was a standing rule that if a pilot was sick in the cockpit, he cleaned it up or deposited a reasonable sum in the flight fund which went towards a beer up now and then.

The individuals who shared the billet were a mixed lot and included two or three Scotsmen. It was my first acquaintance with Hibernian gentlemen and it did not take long for me to form the opinion that they were never happier than when they were running around naked and making inarticulate noises which nobody could understand. On the rare occasions when we had a church parade, we always put them in the centre of the file and hoped that people could not hear the words which they were singing to well known marching tunes. These words were a form of gaelic but anyone hearing them would be in no doubt of their unfortunate meaning.

The king of the billet was a large individual who played rugby league for St. Helens, was built like a brick outhouse and completely lacked any humour. He had the bed in the corner of the room. One of the Scots we called 'Baggy' because he was small and round so that his trousers fitted him round the waist but flapped around his ankles. In contrast he was full of humour and had absolutely no fear. One of his favourite tricks was to wait until our rugby player was fast asleep, crawl across the floor on his hands and knees and rub his stubbly chin in his neck saying "Gey us a kiss George." After a noisy eruption of flying sheets, the chase would be on around the barrack block, until with muttered threats and imprecations peace was eventually restored .

The tractor which pulled out the aircraft had very utility seating arrangements and when driven at speed would leave the ground and come down with a jarring crash which rattled your teeth. At one stage I was troubled with boils in an unfortunate location but after a memorable ride to bring in a plane which was sitting on the end of the runway I did not have that problem again.

In the morning and afternoon the N.A.A.F.I. truck would come round to dispense tea and a large cartwheel of a biscuit which at times was my staple diet in view of the R.A.F. meals. As the flight line had to be manned at all times when planes were flying, we used to go for our mid-day meal in two sittings, early and late. If you were early the cooks issued very small portions being always worried that their calculations would not be enough, and if you were late and the meals had been kept hot they were generally welded to the plate. Once or twice a week we had bacon for breakfast, and then I would take a sliced loaf and distribute slices in the emptied bacon pans which still contained a lot of bacon fat. My theory was that a really good feed would last me for a day or two but it never did.

The object of careful servicing and repair is to ensure the safety of the pilot in the air, and our Flight Commander had some useful ideas in this area. He would walk into our crew room holding the Form 700 for one of the two seaters and ask who had done the last pre-flight or repair. If it was you he would say "Go and get a parachute" so you would go down to the pilot's section and draw a parachute, strap it on and get in the back seat. It was then you started wondering if you had locked everything up tight, and hoped he was not going to do hesitation rolls and aerobatics with his wing men.

The hesitation roll saw the pilot flip the ailerons and then centre them causing the plane to fly with its wings vertical, then again and you would be upside down, again and wings are vertical then a final flip to bring you back to the usual position. Remember you are flying forward all the time and this combined with an involuntary sideways somersault is not for the faint hearted or a weak stomach. In any aerobatics there would be high speed climbs and dives where the effect on the head and stomach is similar to an exaggerated fairground roller coaster.

One day I was billet orderly and sweeping and cleaning up when an Airframe Mechanic like myself came panting in and told me I had to report to the Flight right away and that I was in deep trouble. When I finally arrived in front of an irate Flight Lieutenant I was told that one of the aircraft that I had pre-flighted the night before had been stopped by the Control Tower as it was taxiing to take off because most of the inspection panels were hanging off. I refrained from mentioning that the student pilot had not done his own pre-flight walk around which should have alerted him, but did say that there was no way that I could have left the aircraft in that condition. It was Chiefy who came to the rescue. The same Flight Sergeant who had told me on my arrival "you know all the stuff they taught you at the School? well you can forget all that and we will show you how to really do the job." He quickly established that the manufacturer had people on the base who were doing modifications at night and who had collared the aircraft and were working on it. An enthusiastic tractor driver finding the aircraft missing for the morning's flying had found it in their hangar and pulled it out without noticing that there was work in progress. Now what would have happened if the plane had tried to take off? Pilots were always cavalier in their inspections particularly the students. One day there was a large pool of hydraulic oil under the front wheel and the pilot was going to ignore it. I explained that the oil dashport system in the front leg relied on the oil to make the wheel self centering during taxiing, take off and landing, but he would have still climbed in if I had let him.

The Meteor and for that matter any jet flies like a brick, and with so little wingspan, if it loses engine speed it comes down just like that piece of building material. When that happened someone had to do crash guard and it was a dismal duty to stand by a crater with some tangled metal where one and perhaps two men had died.

We also had to spend some time at Blyton, a satellite station which was deserted and used for circuits and bumps when the pilots practiced touch and go landings. There was an old Wellington on the boundary which was little more than a skeleton but you could still see its geodetic construction.

The jet aircraft could not only get from one place to another much quicker than conventional aircraft but also changed altitude at speed, which led to an interesting problem with the hydraulics. They rely on an enclosed system to work, with a reservoir of hydraulic fluid which in the case of the Meteor is in a circular shaped container at the back of the cockpit. This incorporated some kind of compensation valve which was supposed to equalise the pressures on the system brought into play by high speed climbs or dives. Unfortunately this sometimes did not do its job, and you had a trainee pilot coming into circuit with a canopy covered in red fluid and a nervous enquiry for the Duty Instructor. I have no undercarriage, no flaps and no drive brakes ... what do I do?

A callous suggestion silently offered by its ground crew would be ... "Repeat after me, Our Father......".

Because the stalling speed of a landing aircraft is so much higher without flaps, the pilot had to bring the jet in at a much higher speed in a nose up angle and touch down on the grass alongside the runway as close to the beginning as possible after burning off his fuel.

The results were always spectacular, because the tail touched, the nose thumped down and as it carved its way along the grass, canopies and cowlings flew off with other debris.

Despite being alerted and getting a flying start the Crash Tender and Ambulance never reached the plane before the Flight Engineer on his bicycle, who was busy pulling the pilot out, who had usually not come to much harm if he had fastened his straps tight.

The Airspeed Oxford was still a fabric covered machine and the W.A.A.F.S. had to repair that material if it became necessary. It did have an unhappy knack of pushing its tail wheel into the fuselage if the landing was too heavy. We had a Flight Sergeant Instructor who had flown them early in the war and would plead with us to put the old aircraft unserviceable so that he could test fly it after it was cleared. We were only happy to oblige because we would go up with him and dive bomb the pea pickers in Lincolnshire. When the fuel bowser came to fill up the Oxford with high octane there were always a couple of cans filled up for Chiefy's old Austin which must have been converted because it seemed to run quite well on it. The doors on the Bellman Hangars were huge things and difficult to start moving to open or close, and Chiefy would often put the bumper on the edge of the door and get us started. The cry of 'two six' was always used when someone needed a hand.

Shortly after I got to Finningley and much against the wishes of my parents I bought a 350 cc W.D. Matchless motorcycle to travel backwards and forwards from Sheffield to the camp. I had started to play football for the Old Boys of the City Grammar School on Saturdays. The team was called The Holly Guild and played in the South Yorkshire Amateur League. We only got a pass every other weekend which meant that after a morning of playing soldiers on a non pass weekend I would hop on the bike and quietly start up when I was too far away to be heard. I never got caught but was in mortal fear at one stage because I was sent off in a game for being unpleasant to the opposing centre forward and the league used to inform any league or team that you might play for, so if the R.A.F.. were notified they would have wanted to know how that had happened on a non pass weekend.

When I had a bona fide pass I would go out on the airfield before flying started on a Friday and gather mushrooms to take home. If I had missed some of the soil on the stems they would be a little gritty but you cannot beat fresh mushrooms.

When I traveled to and from the camp I tried to make sure that it was daylight because the headlamp on the bike gave such a feeble glow that it was next to useless, and if I did travel at night I used to pick up a car following the same road and use his lights. Perhaps this made me particularly careful because one night at an intersection near the camp the local authority had done something right in the middle and fenced it round with some old hurricane lights hanging from it with the glass well and truly smoked up. I pulled up in time and thought that someone else might be so lucky, and was not surprised when another Yorkshire lad named Goodall walked into the billet quite shaken up because he had somehow slid through the planks and his pillion passenger had flown over the top. He was an interesting individual because his family owned a Mill which manufactured wool or cotton products I forget which. In any event he described an old family way of teaching a youngster because his father would take him into the factory and standing with a piece of material held in each hand behind his back he would ask his son to reach around and handle each piece, then ask questions about them. If any of the answers were wrong then the lad got a hefty clipped ear. This I suppose was the traditional way of learning a family business.

That motorcycle certainly challenged my new  amount of mechanical knowledge. At Easter when I came home from camp with three or four days leave I decided to tackle the kick start which hung down because the spring inside had broken. When I loosened the nuts and bolts and removed the cover the wheels from the gear box fell out and it took me all the leave by a system of trial and error to get them back into the proper position. The spring itself was a matter of a few minutes work, just heating up the end and forming a hook so that it would fit over a spindle. I had an American twill flying suit which I used to wear on the bike and it eventually saved me when I was traveling down a hill during a forty eight hour pass in icy conditions, revved up to put it in a lower gear to keep my speed down.... and automatically touched the brakes to help the gear change. The camber on the hill sloped the wrong way and I flew off the bike which headed for one of the big trees at the side of the road and hit it with a sickening noise. I hit and rolled, but was shaking like a leaf and when a householder came out in a dressing gown as I was trying to get the bike up on its kickstand. I told him that it had just fallen over which in view of the damage was a little stupid. With his help I put it in his driveway and eventually had it picked up and taken to camp where some charitable souls in Workshops straightened out the front end.

That was enough of motor bikes for me because it had earlier skidded sideways on tram lines in the City and deposited me between a tram and a bus, and when I had a front tire replaced the firm put one of the washers in the wrong place which had the effect of locking the front brake the first time I used it and a spectacular flight over the handlebars. I did feel a little badly however because the fellow that I sold it to may have found it difficult to replace any nuts which came off because aircraft threads are finer than those in general civilian use.

When I was nearing the end of my National Service, I not only graduated to be the airframe mechanic for the Oxford but as the Storesman had been demobbed and the stores were found to be extremely depleted they felt that I could replenish the stocks of kerosene suits and socks and screwdrivers as they were used to prevent further deterioration. I went a little further than that because I found that a battered piece of handle on one occasion and a mangled blade on another could produce two new screwdrivers from Central Stores, similarly socks could breed impressively but kerosene suits proved to be more of a challenge. In any event when the time came for me to leave they were in a much healthier position.

There were some good memories, but many that were not so good as I told the Officer who interviewed me and suggested that I sign on to stay in the Air force. One night when we were playing soldiers and defending the camp they asked me to sit on top of a large mound outside the hangars and warn of the 'enemies' approach. There were whizz bangs and blanks being fired all over the place and I found out in the morning that I had ben sitting on the kerosene dump. The local T.A. set up gun pits with sandbags on the edge of the airfield and I was there when the weekend fliers strafed the site and seemed to lift over the sandbags they were so low but I was flat on the ground with everyone else.

# CHAPTER 3

## METROPOLITAN POLICE

Military Service had given me a good deal of personal confidence, the ability to mix with people from all walks of life and to recognise the value of a smart turn out and appearance. There was also the ability to accept the responsibility which was placed on your shoulders.

In any event I had decided that I would try to join the Metropolitan Police. There was a small snag and that was that you were not supposed to apply for or start another job during your demob leave and the interviews for the Metropolitan Police were held during this time. So that little quirk of character came to my aid and off I went to apply. The interviews were held at Beak Street in London, and there may have been some kind of written examination but having memories of Hornchurch it was the medical examination that concerned me. One interesting coincidence marked my visit to the recruitment centre and that was while going up some stairs a dark haired chap was coming down and sure enough it was David Hughes. We chatted for a while and when I joined the Metropolitan Police on the 23rd November, 1953, Hughes had a Warrant Number that was just two or three behind mine.

Our training was carried out at Peel House in Regency Street, quite close to the centre of London, and it was much older than Hendon where some new recruits went to train. We lived in cubicles with walls that ended a foot or two above the floor which did not afford much privacy, in any event we were kept busy studying the Instruction Book. Our ability to master that and the practical lessons during the next twelve weeks would determine whether we actually became policemen. There seemed to be two kinds of written questions during the Course, 'A' Reports which related to behaviour and the law and which had to be word perfect, because a small error in an 'if' or 'and' could cause a serious loss of marks, and 'knowledge and reasoning' or 'B' Reports which posed hypothetical situations and asked you to deal with them in priority order, applying powers of arrest or summons or some other kind of appropriate action. It was usually easy to select the most serious situation to deal with first and then go on in descending order. For instance you would be told that a jewelers front window was being broken up the street, two cars had bumped together at an intersection, and a dog was running across the road without a collar. What to do first? and woe betide you if you forgot to mention finally that you would try to identify the owner of the dog for some kind of process.

A very popular insert was a misdemeanour which ordinarily did not have a power of arrest ... but if the time was mentioned and it was after 9 p.m. the The Metropolitan Police Act conferred a power of arrest during evening hours. Another was to have the item being stolen fastened in some way so that you could not 'permanently deprive the owner thereof' a clear requisite for Larceny, however, if there was a clear intent to steal then Attempted Larceny could be charged.

Some lessons dealt with specific areas as in 'Dead bodies and Women' where we had an acknowledged expert, a trainee who could always be relied on to insert some humour. He had a gift for dialects and when a Welsh Sergeant was teaching descriptions and he was called on to describe the steps he would take he said that he would measure the distance between one 'year' and the other 'year' mimicking the Sergeant's Welsh accent. The Sergeant bless him allowed some levity on occasion. The same individual had

P.C. Hanson, 2nd from left, second row
P.C. Harris, extreme left, second row

a girl friend who was the District Midwife and who used to send him some kind of bread pudding which he distributed widely and which I think was the cause of more than one incident when the toilets blocked up.

We still had drill orchestrated by a Sergeant who looked very much like our Drill Instructors of old, but as most of us had come from the Services he did not have much cause for complaint.

Perhaps the one test that was the most important of all was 'practical arrests' and if you did not pass that then you did not go any further, even the two Women Police Officers in our intake had to take the same tests. There was an area inside Peel House marked out just like an outside street, and you were admitted one at a time through a door, and routed away afterwards so that you could not alert your fellow students to the nature of the test. Two Sergeants were pretending to fight and when I approached in the approved manner saying "What has happened here sir please" one of the Sergeants grabbed my helmet off and pretended to urinate in it. At that point more or less instinctively I grabbed his arm and bounced him down the street, and in obviously good humour he asked me "Have you arrested me Constable" and I said "Yes Sergeant" and then of course he asked me what I had arrested him for. My reply to that was "I don't know ..........but by the time I get to the Station I will have thought of something."

When the class results were critiqued the following day, the Sergeant asked if I would like to know the comments on mine..... Practical 100% ... Theory 0 . Ah well that was the purpose wasn't it.

Our uniforms comprised the No 1 or Ceremonial which buttoned right up the front with a high collar with your numerals on it and no side pockets, and the ordinary serge or barathea jacket with lapels and your numerals on the epaulette. The helmet was common to both as were the trousers and boots with a regulation teak truncheon which fitted in a special pocket inside the pocket of your trousers. I never discovered if the ladies carried one and if they did whether special provision was made for it.

Part of the course dealt with some simple ways to avoid bodily damage and to restrain a prisoner. This we practiced on each other with various levels of intensity, to the evident concern of the instructor when someone would execute a hip throw and not hold on to the hand as instructed, resulting in someone flying through the air and meeting the ground with a bone shaking crash. We were on much safer ground when his high voice would say "Hammer lock and bar ... Go!!!" That was a simple way of holding someone's arm up behind their back and gripping the shoulder, which if truth was known, had first been learned in most school yards, a new but effective hold however was one where you hold the wrist and the elbow, and in that position it is hard for the person that you are holding to take a swing at you.

There was also First Aid where the Instructor was always called Crepitus after the bony grating felt and sometimes heard at the seat of a fracture.

John Harris and I

We all waited for our posting at the end of our training, and could of course be sent to a Station anywhere in the Metropolitan Police District. I was posted to the West End to Marylebone Lane Police Station 'D' Division and Hughes and John Harris went to West End Central 'C' Division. That meant that I would live in single men's quarters at Elliot House and they would be at Trenchard.

As a probationary Constable you always started on nights where the shift was 10 p.m. to 6 a.m. and longer if you had an arrest and had to go to either Marylebone or Marlborough Street Magistrates Court at 9 a.m. The first week or two were spent learning beats as it was called but it was really an opportunity for the older Constables to repeat the doctrine "You know what they taught you at the School ..well forget all that and we will show you how to really do the job," and that of course they did. How to ring in from the Police Boxes scattered around the 'Ground', where the prostitutes plied their trade how the weekend van operated on a Friday and Saturday nights to tour around potential trouble spots and answer a flashing light on a Police Box to be directed to where drunks were being troublesome and perhaps most importantly how to time your arrival at the Station or the Section House to make the most of your time for 'Refreshments' or your meal on shift and where to find a sympathetic restaurant for a cup of tea on a cold or wet night.

Before describing my first nights walking a beat ... and very often more than one ... I should recount my first outing in my No 1 Uniform for it was memorable but perhaps for the wrong reasons. I cannot remember whether it was towards the end of Training School or a few weeks after I went to Marylebone Lane however it was a Royal Procession of some kind involving the Queen Mother I think with a very ornate carriage and outriders from the Guards or the Household Cavalry. The Number 1 does not have side pockets but these are set rather sneakily in the tails of the coat and instead of a macintosh you carry a cape over your shoulder ... rolled with a strap around it. So when we were issued with a box lunch of sandwiches and sent on our way, there was no place to put them but in the tails of the coat. All the way to the procession site I did not sit down and pirouetted now and then on the Underground Train to keep them out of harms way. We were positioned at a little cul de sac at the bottom of Lower Regent Street and held the crowd in the shape of a U around the perimeter. As the sound increased and the procession approached, the crowd became a little restless as they would not see much from the bottom of the steps and a Mounted Inspector rode up and waved imperiously to the crowd and said " Come forward ... Come forward" which of course they did, leaving us very much behind them! We fought our way through the crowd and had begun to link arms to hold the crowd back when the Inspector realising his mistake began to back his horse into the crowd. Those horses are trained to ignore any pushing and shoving and the rider keeps his eyes forward, so when I was presented with the backside of an extremely large horse which pushed me backwards until I was lying on the crowd at an angle of about 45% and could not move because its hoof was on the toe of my boot and I could not make much noise with my helmet over my face, it seemed to be a hopeless situation but when the horse moved forward and the rider rode off without looking back I was told that a woman had saved me by coming out of the crowd to the head of the horse and saying "Its one of yours." The dent in my toe cap did not go for days and needless to say my sandwiches did not get eaten!

Accommodation in the Section House was a good deal better than Peel House. The rooms were small , however it was a place to call home and there was a closet to store clothing, showers, and a 24 hour canteen. This served what I suppose is termed fast food, but to a young man its usually the food of choice.

We were not paid a great deal by any means, seven pounds four shillings per week.

We were required to be at the Station 15 minutes before your Relief started, and that meant an alarm was essential to get you out of bed, washed shaved, dressed, breakfast and out of the door by 5.30 a.m. for a fast walk down to the Station on early turn. Once there you paraded in a small dark room downstairs which was lit by electric light but there were still gas mantles on the walls to attest to the age of the Station. The Sergeant would stand at an upright desk and allocate the twelve or thirteen beats according to the number of beat Constables. It was not uncommon to be given beats one to six, which meant that you took Oxford Street from Oxford Circus up to Marble Arch. Sometimes an Inspector would be on hand and carry out an inspection. It was then you wished that you had taken more time to clean your boots. An imposing Irish Inspector once stopped at the man beside me and asked "When did you last clean your boots"...... "This morning Sir" then with his nose about three inches in front of his, and a delightful Irish lilt "don't stretch my credulity too far!"

On occasion there was a request to produce appointments, and then you had to hold everything up, truncheon, whistle, pocket book, and sometimes some clever so and so would ask for marking materials on night duty when you were supposed to have thread and similar items to see if anyone had entered premises.

After learning beats you started on night duty and mine was in very uncharitable weather. It did not take long for me to get a bad case of flu. I stuck it out and wore a black scarf around my neck which is not regulation and a Sergeant caught me. I explained that I did not want to fall out and it be thought that it was because I did not like night duty. He told me to go sick and see a doctor. In asking for some recommendations for local doctors I quickly learnt

Police Constable: Michael Hanson
Metropolitan Police 'D' Division

that the Divisional Surgeon was not held in high esteem but an East Indian doctor in Paddington would not give you a chit for sick leave unless you were really sick but was known to give effective treatment so that is where I went on the following morning. After insisting that I remove shirt and vest and much pushing and prodding, he went off to a cabinet and produced a hypodermic the size of an elephant gun. When I asked somewhat timidly what he proposed to do with it, he told me to drop my slacks and then injected something which hurt abominably. He told me that this was penicillin, something which I had not been treated with before. I went back to the Section House, had something to eat and was sitting on the bed untying my shoes and the next thing I woke up to was being on the floor half an hour later. When I visited the Doctor again to be confirmed fit for duty and described this he told me that the antibiotic enters the blood stream and gathers itself at the site of the infection and when it joins battle there can be a reaction like I had if the dosage used was high.

Uniform duty is a continuous cycle of shift work, and normally eight weeks of alternate early turn and late turn are followed by four weeks nights. The continual change in meal times particularly when these are sometimes delayed, takes its toll on the body and is probably the reason that older Policemen often have digestive problems.

Some kind of survey was taken which I seem to remember had Policemen living an average of one year to enjoy their pensions. That would include those who died before completing their service and some who enjoyed their pensions for a very long time, but it was still a startling statistic taken that most would expect to go to pension by their fifties.

Being an old Station, Marylebone Lane followed the pattern of older buildings and had the C.I.D. Offices upstairs together with offices for the Superintendent and other senior officers. The switchboard was a mass of cords with bayonet connections and when someone phoned the 1113 number which was issued to most Stations or called in from a Police Box, the Reserve would take a cord and plug it into the appropriate hole where the flap had fallen down to the accompaniment of a buzzer, and take the corresponding cord and connect it to the extension required. There were cells on the ground floor and a canteen downstairs as well as the Parade Room.

The West End by night was an entirely different place and much depended on the weather. If it was cold the manhole covers and drains would issue some form of steam or condensation and the lights were bright. Sound carried very well and you could hear a person's footsteps long before you saw them and the characteristic noise of the engine of a London cab ticking over was very easy to identify. A night of fog or rain however meant that all noise was muted and visibility reduced to your immediate area. Street lights were small halos and gave little help in fog. Your imagination had jewelers windows being smashed all over the place, so it helped the criminal elements. Rain was considered to be the best policeman because criminals did not like to be out in it like anyone else.

Days consisted of large numbers of people and traffic, particularly in the main thoroughfares like Oxford Street and Baker Street.

Depending also on the time of day was the emphasis of your police efforts. At night the protection of property was uppermost, and you were very much aware of Banks, Furriers and Jewelers which were prime targets.

Three Marylebone Lane
Constables

Early Turn as it was called saw you setting out at 6 am armed with pawn lists if you had any pawnbrokers on your beats.

These had to be delivered, usually by pushing them through a letter box, and contained recent details and sometimes pictures of stolen property. You kept your eyes open for any obvious break ins, but if you had several beats to cover you tended to look at any high risk properties before the crowds and traffic built up. Then there were sometimes pleasing diversions on a nice summer day, like standing on Oxford Street opposite Bond Street tube station early in the morning and watching the models come out on to the street to walk to work sometimes in last night's fashion outfit, although as an older Constable once remarked "They wouldn't be much use to you lad" being convinced that the principle of the person with a free run at a sweet store soon tiring of it and wanting different fare, applied to the love life of the modeling and film communities.

By night you walked close to shop fronts, using your eyes and ears and trying to be inconspicuous. By day you walked close to the road and let people see you, although this was sometimes difficult in the press of humanity that filled the main shopping areas on most days.

My first few days on early turn were not uneventful. A walk up the Marylebone High Street after a meal break saw me pointing out to a number of shopkeepers that the tables and stalls outside their shops were not only on the 'curtilage' which was part of their property, but were encroaching on the path or 'footway' and making people walk round them, which constituted obstruction. When there was more than one angry reaction I wrote it all up in the pocketbook and handed it in at the end of my shift. The following morning the Sergeant was not pleased and told me he did not like residents coming into the Station with complaints against officers on his relief, and that the Inspector wanted to see me. It was the large Irish Inspector who looked at me from beneath his eyebrows and asked "Are you on the same beats this morning?" and when I told him "Yes" he waved my pocket book at me and said "What are you going to do about this." So giving him his stare right back I said "If they haven't pulled their stalls and tables back I am going to issue a summons to each one." His forbidding look disappeared, a large smile appeared and he said "You do that and if you write them up tell the Sergeant to bring it to my attention!"

There were no encroachments that morning and I realised that the Inspector had given the complainants a 'flea in their ear.'

The Marylebone Road was a racetrack for newspaper vans first thing in the morning and some unscrupulous Constables were known to stand around the corner of Lisson Grove when the lights along Marylebone Road were all green and when a van had built up impressive speed, one would stand on the pressure pad in Lisson Grove while the other would step out of the corner as the lights turned to red and the driver brought his van to a shuddering stop probably grinding his teeth.

If you were posted to the beats which fronted onto Oxford Street you would probably be asked to do traffic point duty at Marble Arch, and without concentrating once you had put on the white gauntlets, you could foul up the traffic in a hurry. A traffic jam there was an intimidating sight with buses nose to tail down the Bayswater Road so that you could walk a very long way on their roofs. Nearly every bus route you could think of seemed to use Park Lane, Oxford Street, Bayswater Road or Edgeware Road, and they all came around Marble Arch sometimes two or three abreast. The smell of exhaust gave you a headache, and you quickly found out who your friends were if they came to give you a spell so that you could nip up to the small room in the Arch itself for a quick cigarette. We really appreciated the Green Line drivers of the single deckers who always seemed to have a supply of boiled sweets and who would toss you one as they passed. With the possible  exception of The Elephant and Castle, Marble Arch was the busiest traffic point in London.

Walking the beat on Oxford Street during business hours was a euphemism, because it was so crowded with pedestrians that it would be easier to walk in the road. Nevertheless there were individuals that we called 'footway merchants' who set their case down by a shop front and sold cheap jewellery. This formed a crowd and grounds for  a legitimate arrest for obstruction ............. if you could catch them. They had lookouts positioned to warn them of any approaching constabulary. This led to moves and counter moves if you were to grab them before they made their escape into a Store. Firstly you could remove your helmet and sometimes get close enough, until their lookouts countered and  brought boxes to stand on and spotted the uniform. The best tactic I found was to walk up on 'C ' Division's side of the street because they ignored police on that side, and cross the road through traffic at the right spot. If you managed  it right the salesman found himself looking at your boots and then in a resigned way up at the rest of you.

The barrow boys sometimes accompanied you to the Station because it was an offence to sell 'In a restricted street' and the ends of all the turnings into Oxford Street were restricted. From their point of view it was the only way that they could do business, however if they picked up the barrow and moved it to show respect it was generally overlooked. Besides as their stock was the cheapest in Covent Garden that morning because it was probably overripe, in the season you would sometimes at the end of their business day become the beneficiary of a punnet or two of strawberries to take up into the Arch.

There were always visitors from other countries, and as the London policeman had a justified reputation for being helpful, they did not hesitate to ask for advice or directions. For this reason it was useful to have an A to Z Guide to refer to if their question was about another area of London. Sometimes this was not much help against an odd sense of humour. I was standing outside Selfridges one day with a red haired Welshman whose own English was hard to understand, when a tourist from the Mediterranean I should think came up to us with his English 'help' book and said very slowly... "Canna ...you ..tella me ...de ... whay ... to Marable Art.?." and Ginger leaned forward with his thumbs in his breast pockets and said ... "Yes!" The tourist looking puzzled then said  "Willa ... you" and then I stepped in trying not to laugh and pointed him in the right direction to Marble Arch. Still having my school French fairly fresh in my mind I sometimes got flashed at a Police Box and asked to come into the Station to help with some French visitor.

Parking in London was always a big headache for the motorist, and it was hard for them to avoid leaving their car in a restricted area or longer than the permitted time elsewhere. That was when the form leading to a Summons came out of your pocket to be completed with the help of the indignant car driver. They always wanted to know if you ought to be catching thieves instead of dealing with them, but a smile and a refusal to get annoyed often deflected their criticism. There was however one rigid rule and that was no stopping, never mind parking, on Oxford Street. One early evening a car stopped and it's driver rushed in to the chemists at marble Arch. I was waiting to read him the riot act and issue a Summons when he waved a packet of female necessities and said "Emergency" .....and was off before I got my mouth closed.

There was another occasion when I came around a corner to find one of our smaller officers, a Police War Reserve about to arrest a large military looking individual who had parked his Rolls and had every intention of leaving it. Ted had told him that if he did not drive off, he would arrest him and have the car towed. It was then, as the fellow started to walk off, and Ted grabbed hold of his arm, that I arrived because I had visions of him going round and round on the end of his arm like a windmill. We walked him down to the Station and in court the following day, the Magistrate who was ex military and had the Victoria Cross gave him the kind of lecture that Ted and I would have liked to give.

Christmas time was a particular strain on traffic and pedestrian movement, and then of course there were the traditional sales at the big stores. There were frequent accidents involving vehicles and people and sometimes not enough time to write it all up. When it came to injury however I was generally lucky, and when a small Bond mini car collided with an Armstrong Siddeley in the middle of an intersection, the Bond driver told me that his wife could not get out ... and that she was pregnant! My loud question to the crowd which always gathers was "Is there a doctor or anyone with nursing experience?" and a young woman stepped forward and I was saved again.

At some of the busier side streets, you had to control the crowd more than anything else to allow the traffic to move on the green light because the pedestrians just ignored the red. I was holding people back with my arm when a woman ducked under, and I grabbed her just as she would have gone under a cab who stood on his brakes. When I came into the Station later in the morning I found that she had made a complaint that I had torn her raincoat .

There were always accidents and injuries when the big stores put on their Annual Sales. These were nearly always the result of passengers alighting from buses and trying to rush across to the other side without looking.

During the day, the quieter streets filled with parked vehicles providing many opportunities for thieves, either to take the vehicle for a joy ride, or more frequently to steal its contents. This meant that you always had an eye open for an individual walking close to the cars and eyeing their contents.

One afternoon I saw such an individual in army uniform walking along a line of cars in Bickenhall Mansions, a turning off Baker Street, and I managed to get fairly close to him before he started to run with me pounding along behind him in full uniform. I was not gaining and then an elderly man he was passing took after him and held him for me until I could get my hands on him and then went to phone for assistance. That arrest earned me a Commissioners Commendation because the individual was 'wanted' all over the Country and was using an army uniform to cover his activities. I was able to get the name and address of the man who had helped me, and when I visited to give him my thanks, found that he was in his eighties although he looked much younger and attributed his fitness to yoga which he had learned in India whilst serving in the Army.

There was another arrest one evening in James Street when I had slipped into a doorway for a quick cigarette before going off duty, and heard high heel shoes coming down the street and stopping almost opposite me in the doorway of a glass and china shop. The woman was doing something to the door and making some noise so I quietly walked over and asked her what she was doing. She said in quite matter of fact fashion "I saw this in a film and wondered if it was as easy as it looked." So in we went to the Station where a Detective Sergeant Forbes went around to verify the marks on the door and took her statement and dealt with the charging and fingerprinting.

Although rain was unpleasant for street work it did seem to reduce break ins, however fog was a different matter and you were acutely aware of this if you had Baker Street for instance with its furriers and jewellery shop fronts which were vulnerable to 'smash and grab.'The bottom section of Baker Street, Orchard Street, is one way and I was close one evening when an older constable stepped out into the middle of the road to stop a car which was coming north the wrong way. He managed to jump away at the last minute when the car did not slacken speed and I threw my truncheon which just bounced off the windscreen. As I helped him up he kept saying "He wasn't going to stop." The vehicle had been involved in a smash and grab on 'C' Division and was later found abandoned.

Bryanston and Montague Squares still had their fair share of elegant houses occupied by wealthy families, although many had been converted into apartments or business premises. There was one house taken  over for the sons and male relatives of very wealthy people from the Middle East, and they were given to racing the latest sports model cars against each other and just abandoning them if they were wrecked. Someone made a complaint that the Squares were being used by prostitutes who had been picked up elsewhere in cars and were leaving unmistakable traces of their activities in and around the pavements.

After taking refreshments at Elliott House. the walk back to your beats took you along the end of the Squares, and at night it was a matter of a few seconds to look along the parked cars and see if one had its windows steamed up. Imagine my surprise one evening when a car not only had its windows steamed but was literally bouncing up and down on its springs. It was a small utility Citroen and when I opened the door expecting to find a street lady and her customer, I found a very embarrassed young couple instead. They proved to be almost local residents, and when I gave my 'wait until you get married lecture' they told me that they were going to get married a few weeks later. Both were extremely concerned that their names would appear in my report, and this was one incident I decided to forget for reporting purposes. An amusing sidelight was that I would sometimes see them together on the street, and they would give me a cheerful "Hello Officer" without of course anyone having the slightest suspicion of how we came to know each other!

There are some commonsense rules which are supposed to be followed when you are patrolling alone and the principal one is that you never enter premises on your own or without someone knowing where you are. This is meant to prevent you lying somewhere out of sight with a broken leg or other injury and nobody knowing where to find you.

One night on George Street I found the door open to premises where there were obviously commercial tenants. The only previous time this had happened was in the Marylebone High Street when trying doors I had literally fallen inside one which had been left unlocked. It was an undertaker called Tookeys and I did not explore the inside while I waited for the keyholder to turn up. I walked into the George Street situation without much thought and climbed several flights of stairs finding all the company doors properly locked, however it was quite dark and my torch or 'beat lantern' either did not work or gave a feeble light at best.

Mid way up a flight of stairs I distinctly heard a door handle turn! That stopped me dead in my tracks and after lightning analysis I decided that if someone was still above me I had them trapped, and if they were below me they had probably gone.

I went up the remaining stairs with my stick in my hand and the hairs standing up on the back of my neck, but all I found was a door slightly ajar to what was obviously an apartment of some kind so I quietly beat a retreat down to the street locking the outside door after me. It was then I ran into another Constable from the station and foolishly told him what had happened, only to get some hard ribbing about feeling scared in the circumstances.

I got my revenge a few nights later when he and I were told off to search the ruins of a house in Portman Square where vagrants and perhaps someone on the run might be sleeping in the basement

When we arrived we couldn't hear anything and I suggested that he went down and searched while I waited to see if he flushed anyone out. I could follow his progress by his flashing torch and dropped some small stones in his general area. It only took a few minutes and he was looking up at me white faced saying "Come down here Mike there's someone following me" .... childish perhaps but very satisfying.

There were several examples of the truism, forget what they taught you, here's how you do the job!

One evening the night duty Sergeant read out a complaint about a club at the Oxford Street end of Marylebone Lane, so another Constable and I took station on the other side of the road about 11 pm. Sure enough there was a lot of Rock and Roll type music which had become very popular and crowd noise every time the door opened and after a few minutes two prostitutes came out with two huge coloured men who were obviously American Servicemen and started to cheek us. I asked my companion to nip back to the Station and call the American Service Police in Brook Street and ask them to give us a hand. Just after he returned a jeep came round the corner with two American Snowdrops, who walked up to the two Americans with their night sticks behind their backs. One of the huge Servicemen bent down to say some thing and there was a sound like chopping wood as the stick hit the man behind the ear and the Policeman shouldered him into the jeep. His companion did not need much persuading to get in beside him and the Snowdrop looked over and said "Want them?" we nodded no and off they went. Meanwhile the two women looked chastened and striking while the iron was hot I suggested that they go back into the Club and tell the patrons that further noise and misbehaviour would be seriously dealt with. It seemed to do the trick!

Another example was a complaint about a Pub and Public Convenience on James Street, where the Public Convenience was locked half an hour before the Pub closed. I stood in a doorway expecting to deal with a drunken male, instead a fairly large woman came out and went into a corner and lifted her skirts. She was well known locally and probably a prostitute however I had to deal with it so I walked over and with thumbs in breast pockets tried to deliver a warning that any repetition would mean an arrest for drunk and indecent, but that was received with mumbled curses. The following night a very large Constable who had reputedly served in the Coldstream Guards during the War, walked out of the Station with me and when I explained that I had to deal with a follow up to the previous night, he said that he had better come with me. We did not have long to wait and out came the same woman, and my companion who gave the universal signal for silence and who had the largest boots I have ever seen crept up behind her and I swear she lifted a couple of feet in the air before fleeing down the adjacent Mews.

The same Constable gave a very good demonstration of how to defuse a potentially dangerous situation. We were in the van one Friday night doing the usual tour around the trouble spots in and around Marble Arch which was routine on Friday, Saturday and sometimes Sunday nights, when he answered a flashing Police Box and told us that there were some Teddy Boys at the back of a cinema on the Edgeware Road and the Manager thought that there was going to be trouble.

In their Edwardian dress they had a nasty habit of slashing seats with open razors. We met the Manager in the foyer and Bob took over, learning that the ringleader a mouthy little devil was sitting in the middle of one of the rows. At his signal the film stopped and the lights went up. We watched and as the patrons eyes adjusted our ex guardsman pushed along the row, picked the alleged ringleader up by the scruff of his neck, made his way to the aisle and with the fellow dangling like a dead rabbit with his toes just touching the floor he looked at the rest of them and just said "Out." They filed out meekly and were obviously not going to try anything. Size coupled with decisive action can be both intimidating and very effective.

As a rule the rank and file Policeman did not want anything to do with firearms. The general public gave their support to the Police because they were unarmed, criminals did not give much support to those with guns and it is surprising how common sense and a sensible approach to many different situations would disappear if you depended upon a gun to assert your authority. Imagine my surprise then when as a result of incidents between the Greeks and the Turks we were required to mount a guard on important Turkish buildings We had one in Portland Place and we had to be armed.

The actual circumstances were nothing short of ludicrous. You reported to the Station Sergeant in the front office who removed a webbing belt and holster from the safe which held a very large .45 naval Webley. You strapped this on round your waist and underneath your tunic which was buttoned and then you buttoned your macintosh and received six bullets which you placed in your outside pocket. You signed for both.

If a Mediterranean looking individual got out of a vehicle with a smoking cylinder labeled 'bomb' you would have to tear open your macintosh, tear open your tunic, unfasten the holster and get the gun out, find the bullets and load them and then if you could find the safety catch, point it and say "halt or I fire." The general consensus was that if you ever did have to fire it you would be writing reports for ever more.

A few officers who were mobile and able to reach fights and disturbances quickly, generally managed to keep a lid on things however there was a pub at the end of Praed Street, on Paddington's ground which was a favourite of the Irish fraternity, and who used to drink Merrydown Cider. This seemed to inflame their inherent liking for a fight and the opening signal was usually the pub's large plate glass window being broken from the inside. It took a large number of the Paddington men with our help sometimes, to restore order and it was hot and heavy for a while. Sometimes the prisoners had to be split between the two Stations.

In the Section House there were two beautiful full size snooker tables and this helped to occupy some spare time if you had any. There was also football played between the Stations but our home ground was at Hendon and meant allowing time to get there and back. If you were down to play, you went on day duty and started at 9 am , trying to find some process to hand in before you sloped off at lunch time with the tacit consent of the Desk Sergeant. He relied on you to let him know if there was an injury however, to show you time off or sick depending on the nature of the injury.

Besides a cynical frame of mind, young police officers have a strong leaning towards practical jokes. As you were on probation for two years, it was necessary to pound away at the Instruction Book in the Section House from time to time, and you would sometimes hear the voice of a gifted mimic that you would swear was Winston Churchill.

A practical joke played on any new Woman Police Constable posted to Marylebone Lane usually occurred on late turn when she assumed the duties of Police Matron. A transvestite who was given a hard time when he tried to solicit among the street girls would appear on our side of Oxford Street and be brought in, and put in Matron's room for searching. I am sure that he played it up, but after about five minutes the W.P.C. came out with a very red face and said "Its a man!" to a cheering audience of uniforms.

Before any lady reader becomes indignant, remember any of her colleagues who had experienced the same 'initiation' could have warned her....but didn't.

In any Service or Organisation there are many stories of unusual or humourous events which may have gained a little in their passage over the years, and I have included some of these in the next chapter called 'Legends.' There is a good deal more than a grain of truth in all of them.

# CHAPTER 4

# LEGENDS

### Albert and the Lion

Our first legend really deserves to be titled 'Albert and the Lion' although Albert was not the name of the individual concerned.

During the war many policemen felt it was their duty to join the Armed Forces, which left a serious shortage of Metropolitan Police Officers, already stretched very thin because of the visits of German bombers nearly every night.

The answer proved to be Police War Reserves who were usually men who could not meet the strict requirements of height, eyesight etc., but many of whom performed yeoman service. That is perhaps the reason that many were retained after the war.

Although most of them were neat and tidy and equal in nearly every respect to the regular sample there were exceptions and the War Reserve Constable we will call 'Albert' was one of them.

He was definitely shorter than the requisite height and the only way to describe him in uniform was scruffy! He had not endeared himself to the Relief Sergeants because he had a habit of hauling in all kinds of rubbish that he found on patrol as property found in the street.

By way of self defence the Sergeants would assign him the beats around Marylebone Station at the top of the ground where it was hoped that he would be out of sight and relatively inconspicuous.

This made it all the more curious one day when either as a result of a complaint from Albert or someone's mistake, he was posted on Oxford Street process, which meant that he did day duty 9am to 5pm, and was expected to issue a Summons to those motorists who parked in the wrong place or overstayed their parking time and to arrest the odd barrow boy or suitcase vendor for causing obstruction.

After one or two days without a single thing to show for his efforts he received some caustic comments from the Sergeant and realised that something, anything, had to be produced.

There was an individual who sold balloons from a suitcase and as an advertising ploy he would blow up a long balloon which was about six foot high and which easily identified his whereabouts. When Albert homed in and told him that he was nicked, he must have sensed some uncertainty because he tried an old dodge and told Albert that he was responsible for his property. Any experienced P.C. would have told him that the suitcase would be upended in short order if he, the prisoner, did not want to carry it.

In any event the Sergeant and Duty Inspector who were walking down Oxford Street and who were curious about the amusement being shown by some pedestrians, came face to face with Albert and his prisoner. Albert had one hand on the prisoner's arm and the other clutching his case and large balloon.

The Inspector was completely speechless as the Sergeant restored the dignity of the Station with a few words hissed in the ear of the prisoner and sent them on their way to the Station where it was quickly arranged that Albert would return to the upper beats forthwith.

In addition to annoying the Sergeants, Albert also raised the ire of the Wireless Car crews on night duty because his beats ran alongside Regents Park which was policed by St. Johns Wood, and on night duty he used to nip into the Park and have a snooze in an old hut which sometimes meant that he missed his ring into the Station and the car would be asked to check on him to see that he was alright.

When the Wireless Car had been called to the Open Air Theatre in Regents Park because someone had broken into the structure that housed the actors stage effects and thrown them around, and when they saw a lions head which was made to fit over an actors head, there seemed to be a ready made answer to Albert's sleepiness.

The following night one of the night duty P.C.s on parade whispered in Albert's ear "Be sure to keep a lookout for the lion that's escaped from Regents Park Zoo." Albert said "I haven't heard anything about a lion." "Ah well" said our P.C. "they are keeping it quiet because they don't want to alarm the public."

True to form, shortly after midnight Albert was seen to cross the road and find his way to his usual sleeping quarters, and it only took a minute to unfasten the temporary fastener on the Theatre repository. Time having elapsed to put Albert in a relaxed state of mind, there came a very realistic roar, and as he burst out of the shed with his flashlight waving around, as luck would have it the lions head poking through the bushes was perfectly illuminated.

At this point it was expected that someone would explain the joke to Albert, but they had not reckoned with the speed of his reaction because he charged off into the bushes yelling and screaming, so the participants speedily returned the lions head and went about their normal duties with what they hoped would be an outward appearance of complete innocence.

The next scene in this drama took place when the Duty Sergeant answered the phone from someone calling from the Police Box at the top of Baker Street. He summoned the van driver and said "Alberts gone stark staring mad, he is running down Baker Street blowing his whistle and yelling run for your life its the lion."

Albert was examined by the Divisional Surgeon, and apart from being soaking wet, there was just the unshakable delusion that he had seen a lion which had escaped from the Zoo. The Zoo of course could account for all their lions.

For reasons of self preservation complete secrecy was observed by the pranksters, and Albert was eventually transferred to a more rural Division no doubt still unable to understand why nobody believed his story. There was a sequel however, and that is when a member of the public brought in a policeman's helmet which had been found floating in the boating lake or pond of some sort in the Park. At some stage of his frantic warning run, Albert must have blundered in and mercifully managed to blunder out again.

**Lecherous old .......**

There was a dance on alternate Saturday nights at Elliott house and Trenchard House, which were always well attended and there were always plenty of girls, many of them nurses.

This leads to a second tale because although visitors, particularly females, were strictly forbidden in the living quarters of the Section House, it was not unknown for the 'C' Division Constables to establish which of the 'D' Division residents had booked out for the weekend in the appropriate

Register, and to try to use the vacant room for very illicit behaviour. One hoped that they left the room how they found it to forestall any complaint.

There were one or two crusty old bachelors who lived in the Section House and viewed the antics of the younger P.C s with complete disdain and who disappeared for the weekend to avoid the frivolity. One of these individuals, we will call him 'Mac' was in the habit of visiting friends and dutifully booking out in the Register when he did so.

On this particular Saturday he found himself the worse for drink, and rather than inflict this condition on his friends he decided to return to the Section House to sleep it off. When he opened the door to his room it would be difficult to decide who was more surprised, the couple occupying his bed or Mac. Predictably the result was an extremely loud roar from Mac and the hasty departure of the couple.

Being extremely inebriated and therefore wondering if he had imagined this, Mac sat on the side of the bed for a while and then decided that a cold shower was definitely required, so he stripped off, wound a towel around his waist and went off to the showers and conveniences at the end of the corridor.

Female visitors created a problem in a building which was primarily designed for the male sex, and this necessitated some kind of guard when ladies ventured into the facilities, but having heard the commotion their not so gallant escort had left his post so that when Mac went in he found two rather scantily clad young ladies whose screams only seemed to increase his rage.

When they shot out and ran down the stairs he followed in hot pursuit with towel flapping precariously around his middle, racing past some of the night duty relief who had come out of the canteen where they had been having their meal, alerted by all the noise.

Mac was eventually coaxed back upstairs and to his credit made no formal complaint but he still used to redden and fly into a temper when standing in the meal queue and some anonymous voice would say "You lecherous old B........"

### Using your head

Another tale which can probably qualify for Legend status comes from earlier times and although Marble Arch Underground Station is on Marylebone Lane's ground the Constable concerned was stationed at Paddington Green.

A man had committed suicide by jumping in front of a train and although the Coroner and other people had done their work and departed they had been unable to find the unfortunates head which eventually turned up and the Stationmaster called Paddington which was a telephone number with which he was familiar.

As is sometimes the way with Sergeants, he grabbed the first P.C. that came through the door and said "Go down to Marble Arch Underground and see the Stationmaster."

There were trams in those days and the one boarded by the P.C. went on its way to Marble Arch which was a terminus and where it waited for a while before making a return journey. There was an unwritten courtesy to police shown by most public transport that meant you did not generally get asked for the fare, but this particular conductor was an awkward cuss and had his hand out under the Constable's nose as soon as he boarded the tram.

The P.C. was entirely unprepared for the task of transporting a head back to the Station, but in the best traditions of improvisation he commandeered a fire bucket and tipped out the sand contents to make a carrier for the head which was duly inserted and the Stationmasters newspaper appropriated to cover it.

Back at the terminus the tram was still waiting and nearly full so the P.C. had a minute or two to wait after it started off before the conductors hand was once again stuck under his nose. He reached down to the bucket between his legs, whipped off the newspaper and said "Do you want me to pay for him too?"

It is apparently the only known case where a conductor passed his astonished driver in full flight up the Edgeware Road.

As a side note on suicide, it did not take me long to realise that the only way to keep your sanity and sleep at nights, was to form a hard shell around your feelings and try to be dispassionate or disassociate yourself from what was going on. It didn't always work in tragic or trying situations and although you would get through it by realising that you had to do something even though everyone else was yelling or crying or otherwise unable to function, you found somewhere quiet afterwards to lose your lunch or supper and if it had been a gas suicide you could always blame it on the gas.

The verdict usually given in those cases was 'Suicide whilst the balance of the mind was disturbed,' however our view was that there was no insanity involved as they were mostly seniors who had lost their mate, had nothing to live for and nearly always left their affairs in perfect order.

# CHAPTER 5

## COURTSHIP AND MARRIAGE

In the foolishness of youth I told myself that I should not marry a Police Woman or a nurse because they also had to control their feelings and it would affect their femininity, not realising that fate or nature or both generally decided your future mate.

In my case it was a Police Ball held at the Carlton Rooms on the Edgeware Road on 25 th of January 1955. In a crowded ballroom where Victor Sylvester used to demonstrate his dance steps on T.V. I met Patricia Nunney my bride to be.

Pat and I

It was hardly a momentous occasion, there was no clashing of cymbals or blare of trumpets, in fact Pat was conspicuous because she seemed to decline to dance with anyone who asked her, so I walked over, took hold of her hand to help her up and did not take no for an answer, in fact I cannot remember whether she actually got the time to say no. We danced a few more times, I managed to get her telephone number at Monsanto where she worked, and one thing led to another and we were married at St. Johns, Greenhill Parish Church in the centre of Harrow at 3 pm on the 3rd day of the third month in1956.

There are, however, some incidents surrounding our courtship and eventual marriage which are worth recording. As Pat worked the usual business hours, we had to meet on weeknights and weekends most days except when I was late turn but early turn and night duty did not present much difficulty, except that on early turn I used to put Pat on the last train to Harrow at about 1 am, get back to the Section House and had to be up again before 5 am so by the end of the week I had slowed down a little. I did however have a secret weapon. When I got back to the Section House I would ask for a glass of hot milk and stir in a large spoon of sugar. If you sipped this slowly and went straight to bed you would go to sleep straight away.

The evenings spent with some of my friends at the dance halls were discontinued but not before I had witnessed the discomfiture of one individual who had taken a young lady home on a previous occasion and spotted her on the opposite side of the dance floor. He told us there was no need to worry as everyone knew that she was very short sighted, and was not wearing her glasses but after she had delivered a spectacular slap after confronting him, someone said "They should have told you she just got contacts."

On the one occasion when I suppose it could be said that I used poor judgment was when Ken, the friend who was to be our best man, invited several of us to a party arranged by his girl friend because he wanted some support. Her friends were from the City and mostly stockbrokers or lawyers and would be debutantes. It was a night at the end of early turn week and Pat had suggested that I should catch up on some sleep. In any event I allowed myself to be persuaded and in company with the lad who did the 'voices' and an ex marine among others, we made our way to Kensington I believe. The hostess correctly concluded that we were there as a counterpoint, and started to pay some attention to an old boy friend causing my friend to get hot under the collar. I counselled outward disinterest, however he became more and more agitated and as a result we were probably drinking far more than we should.

One incident that stays in my mind was the dramatic entry of an individual who must have been something in the City because he had grey pin stripe trousers, a nice black waistcoat and a bowler hat. He stood in the doorway and announced to all and sundry "Am I late?" Our mimic was on him like a flash and in beautiful news reader english he said "Not at all old chap, here let me take your hat." He took the bowler and went to a food table and said "I suppose you must be hungry," and up ended a plate of sausage rolls into the hat and offered it to the owner. Putting the sausage rolls back on a plate he said "I say, do you mind, I have always wanted to try one of these." He put the hat on his head where in view of the difference in sizes, head and hat, he looked like a silent movie actor, and his attempts to pull it down to the proper position produced seam stretching noises. Everything deteriorated after that and I found myself in a communal washroom, trying to be comprehensively sick, when the ex boyfriend stuck his head in and said something fatuous like "Don't you feel well." I gather that I must have thumped the boyfriend because the next thing I remember was being in the ex marine's open tourer with my head over the side and him imploring me not to be sick inside the car. I have no recollection of getting to bed at the Section House or even how I got undressed.

The following day when I spoke to Pat I told her quite truthfully that I did not feel well and that I had an upset stomach. When me met and we were getting on a bus on Baker Street, one of my previous evenings companions called out, "Are you sober yet Mike," and Pat said "You......." to the obvious discomfiture of the bus conductor and nearby passengers. She had brought me peaches for my upset stomach as well!

Having agreed early in the courtship that early marriage was not really possible because of our financial position, I exhibited some commonsense by proposing on my birthday, June 29th that year 1955 . We started our married life in an upstairs flat at the end of Western Avenue, after a honeymoon touring Devon and Cornwall in a rented Anglia.

The Big Day

The wedding itself was memorable, as it probably is for most principals, by a rush of people, and a beautiful Service at Greenhill Parish Church in the centre of Harrow. A Reception which you wish you could remember better and go over slowly to enjoy it even more. You are left with the anxiety of giving clear responses, trying to greet everyone that you should, above all the beauty of your bride, the solemnity of the service, and the foresight of a father in law who put some delicacies in a bag for us to eat on the way to our first hotel in Salisbury, having guessed that we would not have had much to eat and what champagne can do to an empty stomach.

My best man and I did not set off exactly on time for the Church and that was entirely my fault because I seemed to be all fingers and thumbs. As we were driving towards Sudbury Hill in our full wedding outfit it was obvious that we were well behind time and as I could see the traffic held up by several lights in front of us. I pulled out and drove up the wrong side of the road and as we passed lines of stationary cars, my best man solemnly raised his top hat to them.

Our difficulties were compounded when we arrived at the Church because all the parking had been taken by those people who had got there in time and we had a fair distance to cover before arriving somewhat hot and breathless ... and without my hat and gloves which I had left in the car. Pat's father never let me forget that bless him because he had to be threatened with all kinds of dire consequences to make him wear his.

It rained that day, and there is a country which considers it very lucky to have rain on your wedding day. It was certainly lucky for me. Pat had a sister Peggy and a brother David and both her mother and her father had brothers and sisters giving us many aunts and uncles. Her dad was a remarkable man who had to leave school at eleven to help support the family, and without any professional training could repair just about anything, from delicate watch mechanisms to large steam boiler systems. He was born on December 17th 1903, the day that the Wright Brothers managed to get the first engine powered plane to stagger into the air for a few minutes. He lived in Hammersmith at Banin Street and went to school in London with Dan Maskell the well known tennis commentator, and when his after school employment was in a Knightsbridge, London Hotel which did not pay very well, eight shillings and sixpence per week, he knew that something better paying was required if he was going to marry Pat's mum so off he went to find fame and fortune in Australia at the age of twenty six. He had known Pat's mum from an early age because she lived on the opposite side of the road. Her maiden name was Read.

The voyage on the Orsova a coal fired ship took thirty two days and he was able to recount all the ports of call. When he arrived in Perth the work that he found was at the end of the line as far as civilization was concerned at a place called Burakin where he had to build his own rustic accommodation on a very large piece of land amounting to six hundred acres which had been cleared and that was to be cultivated. The owner came out to visit him once a month to bring supplies, and he spent most of his time ploughing where it took him almost a day to do one circuit. Being on his own for most of the time carried its own dangers, for on one occasion he was bitten by a scorpion and had to treat himself. These circumstances may have been the reason that he was ready to tackle just about anything. He did not receive any wages and was promised these at a later date, so that when the owner finally could not pay his debts, Pat's dad was left with nothing and had to spend some time on the beach at Perth until he could find a ship that would let him work his passage back to England.

A relative on Pat's mothers side named Read lived in Norfolk and was a breeder of flowers. He produced the Esther Read daisy which is now found all over the world, also many other original varieties.

Our honeymoon was spent in the West Country and after we reached Salisbury on the first evening we stayed at our only pre-booked hotel, The Crown, and then on to Paignton and a memorable stay at The Jubilee Inn at Pelynt which is just inland of the two small seaside towns of Looe and Polperro, really quaint and unspoiled then with pretty harbours. The Inn had been recently acquired by people from London who had renovated it, leaving the downstairs much in its old style with a large copper hood over the fireplace and dark exposed beams, whilst the upstairs had been completely modernised. They were joined by a spiral staircase completely enclosed in glass looking over the surrounding countryside.

We stayed at The Unicorn in South Molton where the Licencee asked to see our Marriage Certificate and then when we found ourselves in the middle of Exmoor with darkness falling we knocked for quite a while on the door of the Exmoor Forest Hotel before a dear old lady holding a lamp told us that the Inn was closed. When we explained that we were unlikely to find anywhere else at that time of night she said that we could stay and led the way with her lamp up the stairs, but it was very eerie with moving shadows and the animal heads on the walls. The next morning however was bright and sunny, and the previous evening forgotten. We were driving a Ford Anglia which I had hired and in turning round on the Moor we got the back end stuck in a ditch. The engine would start but as soon as I tried to get some power it stalled. For some reason I felt that if we got back on the road we would be all right and when a young lad came along on his bike I got him to help and we got the car out of the ditch. I thanked him and he said "Happen if we get stuck with the tractor you can come and give us a push." The car did seem to have forgotten its stalling and I reasoned afterwards that somehow the exhaust pipe was blocked in the ditch. It was however unlikely that we could repay the lad's kindness.

At the end of the week we started the trip back to London and after a long days drive we got into Salisbury. Do you think that some things are pre-ordained? Without much optimism I went into The  Crown  to see if they had a room, and they had the same room, number seven, that we had stayed in on the way down. It was the only one left and as I went out to get the bags a man walked up to the desk to ask for a room.

Pat continued to work at Monsanto and for some time my duties had changed from general beat duties. The rule was that under two years you could not do more specialist duties. Not long after twelve months I found that I was being posted at first as Uniform Observer and then as the third member in plain clothes to the Wireless Car or Area Car, which was highly unusual.

This was an entirely different world to that of the individual limited to the few streets around him and what he learned from the Reserve when he made his rings from a Police Box or picked up at meal times. It was a continuous stream of messages directed to cars in all the Divisions, and sometimes laconic requests for an ambulance or assistance depending upon the circumstances found. There was not only excitement but the knowledge that there could be potentially dangerous situations as well, because "unusual noises" or "silent alarm operating" and similar messages like "disturbance" meant that you did not know what you were getting into. In those days the 'key' in Information Room at the Yard which is where all the messages were sent from, was left 'up' or 'down' whichever meant that cars could listen to the messages going back from the cars as well as the outgoing. You could hear cars from adjoining areas booking on over the air and a quick greeting could be squeezed in before I.R. told cars to use proper procedure. That all stopped when the public started getting radio sets which could listen to the Police Bands, and it was a shame because some of the humour was priceless.

Being young and keen and in plain clothes did not always endear you to the driver and observer who saw it all every day and many of whom were of a size and disposition which did not make for moving quickly, so it meant some pushing and prodding to get them to patrol areas that could produce crime arrests. Not all of them I should point out, but their views were sometimes presented in a pithy manor. For instance we were called to an address in Bayswater because the Paddington car did not answer, and being first up the stairs, I found a young mother and her baby who had been the subject of domestic violence. Our guidelines were clear in those days, and meant that the police did not become involved in domestic matters and left it to the Civil Courts and the parties to work out, but when you see a woman who is badly hurt and bruised and in this case a very young baby with large bumps on its head, that hardly seems acceptable. Going down the stairs with the driver, a young fellow passed us going up and I called out " Is your name X or whatever the name of the upstairs family was." He agreed it was, and I was upstairs two at a time and I picked him up by his shirt and told him he could pick on me next time. Just as we got to the door his head came around the corner of the staircase and he yelled "That's it then, I am going to throw myself under a train," and the driver remarked to me dryly as he was pulling on his gloves. " We get a train suicide tonight Hanson and you are cleaning it up!"

They did however sometimes get their own back as in the call to a Paddington Mews to a 'Suspect on premises' where I bounded up the stairs and eventually on to the roof where I could not find a thief but a very large dog found me. I had to wait for his handler to take him off and as I suspected my driver and observer had let them send the dog on to the roof without telling the handler that I was there. If they thought that it would dampen my enthusiasm they were mistaken!

A more humorous situation was when two young prostitutes wearing very little clothing, had a fellow cowering in a corner and the gist of their complaint was that he had received 'services' from one of them and was refusing to pay. As solemnly as I could I took names and addresses including the scantily clad females, exchanged them and suggested the Civil Court as a remedy.

It became second nature to keep an ear on the radio calls and turn it up when you heard your call sign or something interesting like a car chase.

Our call sign was One D although some car signs changed later when they adopted Nato letters like Delta, we were One D for David, or as some crews would say if they got a particularly long string of suicides, One D for death.

Car chases always kept you glued to the set and moving at speed if it was in your area. The car's bell would be ringing, but I never considered it loud enough to get traffic out of your way so it all came down to the skill of the drivers who were superb and had the car under control and always giving its best.   The Operator of the pursuing wireless car had to keep up a commentary and let other cars know where they were going and descriptions etc. Some were very good keeping up a dispassionate level voice and releasing the mike so that other cars could call in and say the positions that they were going to use to intercept, even though they were being thrown about in the car. Others were nearly hysterical and almost useless to the other cars. The drivers however were first class, weaving in and out of traffic with the car under control at all times, with only the hard to hear bell and high revving engine to tell traffic to get out of the way, and match their skill and heavier Wolseley 680 against the lighter Fords which were chosen by thieves for speed and agility. They were masters in their own domain, and when an operator came on duty the worse for drink the driver drove him round and round a roundabout at high speed until he was comprehensively sick. If Traffic at the garage tried to palm them off with an old car they would wind it up on a suitable stretch of road until it was belching blue smoke and then return it as unserviceable.

I referred to the humour sometimes heard over the radio, and to give an example, one Saturday night when the time of origin of messages coming out of Information Room was a good deal earlier than the time it was transmitted, showing that they were extremely busy, a call came in from, if I remember the correct call sign Thames One five, a Police Boat with a message. The dispatcher snapped "Thames One Five Wait." A couple of minutes later the call came again, "Hello M.P.  from Thames One Five message for you." This time a much sharper "Thames One Five wait!" Finally with a note of desperation "Thames One Five with urgent message," and after an exasperated delay the Dispatcher told him to go ahead. "Thames one Five is just south of Blackwall Tunnel and we are sinking,"  and then the anonymous calls came in  "The sea shall not have them" "You must have been asleep you dozy twerps" and others which were all unsympathetic until Information Room called a halt.

There were times when I felt embarrassment when for instance I got out off the car and stopped an individual carrying a large and heavy sack which proved to contain lead, obviously from the roofs or piping of some of the older buildings. When we were waiting in the Charge Room I asked him if he had 'Form' or a previous Criminal Record and he muttered something about carpet. So I said " How much did you get for nicking this carpet" and he looked at me with some condescension. I then learned that 'carpet' is thieves slang for a three month sentence.

Another incident involved a very large prostitute who was fond of drink, which sometimes caused her to overlook some important occupational safeguards, and as a result she had six children, all with foster parents, for she had refused to allow them to be adopted. When she got drunk and a little maudlin she would go to one of the addresses and try to reclaim a child, we would be called and on this particular evening we took her in to a particularly crowded Paddington Police Station Charge Room where there was a long queue of prisoners and police and lot of light hearted banter being exchanged . The Sergeant stood behind a desk with a hinged lid which looked almost Dickensian, coming up to middle chest height. The old way of writing out every charge on a charge sheet in ink with a nib pen was gradually giving way to a stamp for some of the most common charges like drunkenness and prostitution, with a space to be filled in for time, date etc.

As she came up to the desk, looking round to make sure that she was the centre of attention to the delight  of the crowd , she unshipped an extremely large bosom and laid it on the top of the desk and said to the Sergeant with the stamp in his hand "There you are luv, put it on there!" and as quick as a flash ... he did!. About a week later I saw her showing it to a prospective client in the Bayswater Road and that says a lot about some peoples hygiene.

We had an unusual passenger in the Area Car one night when a Film Producer rode along with us to get some  'atmosphere' for a film being made starring Jack Hawkins, but there was an understanding that we could bump him if anything came up, which we did at the first opportunity. The average policeman had a justified contempt for the way in which they were portrayed in books or on the Silver Screen.

Pat and I enjoyed dancing to Oscar Rabin and his Band at the Lyceum Ballroom in the Strand.  There was a small theatre, The Adelphi, which was starring the well known comic Al Reed and a young singer just starting out on what was to be  a famous career,  Shirley Bassey. That was the night that I proposed and Pat accepted.

Our flat on Western Avenue was the first house past a parade of shops. When I was night duty it meant that I would be coming home at just about the time that Pat was getting up to go to work, and we would see each other in the evening before I had to work again. Late turn meant even less time together. On night duty mornings when I came home to find an area car outside the shops, Pat would say that she had heard noises during the night and this would have been the thieves using our side entrance to get to the back of the shops, so I would not mention the shopbreaking. It was, however, a most sensual experience to climb into a warm bed when you had been out all night in the cold.

# CHAPTER 6

## PLAIN CLOTHES

As previously mentioned I had somehow managed to get onto the cars before my two years was up and as soon as I reached two years I worked on becoming an Aide to C.I.D.. This meant that I would be still patrolling the streets, but in plain clothes with a partner, nearly always evening or night duty and only looking for crime.

When Pat and I came back from Devon and Cornwall where we had spent our honeymoon, we attended the wedding of Ken my best man. He and I had talked about trying to join one of the specialist areas in the Police, and as we were not horsemen or keen drivers, Special Branch or the C.I.D. were the obvious choices. To get into Special Branch you needed languages so we started at the Polytechnic with shorthand and Russian. I had always thought that my success in French would mean that it would not be difficult to learn other languages but Russian defeated me although Ken breezed along, so I dropped out and tried for the C.I.D..

As Aides we spent our time mostly in the streets around Oxford Street where thefts from cars and break ins were most common, however, we were

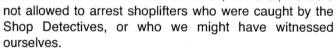

not allowed to arrest shoplifters who were caught by the Shop Detectives, or who we might have witnessed ourselves.

One afternoon when I found myself on my own in Selfridges, I saw the Scottish Store Detective and asked her how she managed to be so successful in catching them in the act as it were because I had only seen one incident when a young woman was stuffing briefs into her pocket in Marks and Spencers, and when she had met my eye I told her to put them back.

P.C.Martin and I

Instead of patrolling the Store to see someone doing some shoplifting, imagine my surprise when she took me to the front doors, told me to stand well off, because anyone would identify me as a policeman miles away, and she watched the shoppers coming in the store. After a few minutes she moved and walked by me saying " The woman in the red hat and gloves" and started to follow her through the store. When the woman eventually walked out of Selfridges she was right behind her and I stood by whilst she told her what she had taken without paying. The established Detectives at Marylebone Lane showed these arrests, but I asked her later on how she was able to pick out potential shoplifters by standing at the door, and her answer was "I don't really know, perhaps its their hands or their eyes, all I know is that I see them and know that they are a person that I should watch and follow and in most cases I am right!"

Her comment about anyone being able to identify a policeman in plain clothes was probably accurate, and that held true in many cases where you took trouble to try and wear clothing to disguise the fact, however by losing yourself in a crowd and not looking directly at someone you could sometimes get close enough to a suspect before they were aware of you. In some cases being spotted worked in your favour, and supported the Store Detective's theory If you stood in a fairly prominent position where passers by were bound to see you, and one of them dropped his eyes and shoulders when they saw you then that was the person you wanted to speak to, and its surprising how many times they would be known at the Criminal Record Office (or C.R.O) and sometimes 'Wanted.'

I had my share of arrests because despite denials, this was certainly one of the yardsticks if you wanted to get into the C.I.D.. proper. It was about this time that one of the observers on the area car was faced with an armed gunman when they answered an innocuous call to a Jewellers called Werhles on Lisson Grove. He was first down the steps to the basement when he ran into the man holding a gun who had shot the jeweller and fatally wounded his assistant. There was a struggle and the man pulled the trigger as it was held into his body and did not live to see a trial. The observer won the George Medal and  became a Detective soon afterwards.

In the late evening there was always a crowd at Marble Arch, and the people around the hot dog stand on the Hyde Park side were usually cinema and theatre goers with the odd tourist and prostitute thrown in. Sometimes one of the comics from the theatre on the Edgeware Road would entertain the crowd with the kind of jokes that he could not tell on the stage.

There was the driver of an S.L. Gull Wing Mercedes who would wait until the lights were all green up the Edgeware Road and would gun his engine and race away hoping to impress some of the young girls.

Earlier in the day some of the speakers in the park would draw a crowd and it was here that we found ourselves undetected behind a young Mystery from Birmingham. This term described a girl or woman who you were certain was practicing the oldest trade but had not yet been convicted. She was telling her companion about a dare or wager, where she had taken one of the regulars around the Arch, a fellow who wore a mac and gold wrist chains, and was always up and down the stairs to the Public Convenience, took him back to her apartment and tried to seduce him. There was a graphic description of the methods she had used but she finished up by saying that she had failed " He locked himself in the lavatory, and all I got out of it was a sick headache." The same girl was circulated in the Police Gazette some while later for acting as a maid for some homosexual couple and then taking off with any cash, valuables or easily transportable items. There is no substitute for practice I suppose.

My soccer playing had come to an end because it was expected that you gave all your time to police work. It also meant that there was no overtime for time spent working over eight hours or going to Court. You had to keep a daily diary, however if you worked nine hours or thereabouts you could charge for a meal and if you 'purchased refreshment for informant' that went in as well. Arrests were of course included.

Sometimes there was the unusual to spice up what became routine patrolling of the same areas night after night.

One evening when we came into the C.I.D. Office to start night duty, a Sergeant was waiting for us with a rather ominous smile, who said "The Detective Inspector is waiting for you in his office." At such times the mind races over the last few days and any transgressions, small or large, that you or your partner may have committed. When we filed in the D.I. was obviously not too happy, although this could be caused by having to stay so late in the evening. He just asked " Do you know about the Gloucester Place flasher?" and when we nodded he said "Well you will get him ... tonight!" It was not the time to argue that C.I.D.. did not normally deal with street indecency.

From the smiles and whispers from the uniform fellows it was obvious that they knew what was going on and we were the last to know.

This individual lived on Gloucester Place and was in the habit of coming out on to the street in the early hours of the morning when some woman was innocently walking along, and exposing himself. There was a power of arrest if you caught him doing this in a public place, but all the uniform attempts to do this had ended in failure, including the use of a nondescript car, because he could obviously watch the street from an upstairs window and see them wherever or however they were hidden. The silly part about it was that they could have easily got a Warrant and arrested him at home because they had plenty of complaints, but for some reason considered it a challenge to catch him in the act, and now the job had been passed to us.

On the face of it there did not seem anything different that we could do, so we retired to the snooker tables at Elliot House until the early hours when he could be expected to operate.

Waiting round the corner in a side street at about 1 am it seemed to take for ages until the door opened and he came dancing out in a bath robe, exposed himself  and quickly went back in again. We could not stop the woman as a potential witness in case he saw us but there was the glimmer of an idea, because there was a portico of sorts outside his door , and the only place he could not see was directly under it. He performed again a few minutes later, and as the door closed we crossed the street sprinting as quietly as we could and pressed ourselves against the door.

Then it really seemed ages before there was a click of the lock and the door started to open. We pushed it open to find him inside and tried to drag him on to the step, but he caught hold of some pipes and I had to hammer his hands to make him let go. The irony was that he was shouting " Police ... Police" at the top of his voice and we had already told him that we were police and arresting him. Finally in the street he asked if he could call a cab, to save riding to the station in the Van. I told him that as he was so fond of wandering about in his night attire, that we would walk to the station which really was not far away.

When we walked in to the Front Office it was a pleasure to see the surprised Station Sergeants face. He said "What have you got here" and we said "We've got your flasher Sergeant." There was of course  a good deal of curiosity from the uniform fellows who had been trying unsuccessfully to do the same thing. but we just told them that we had watched him come on to the street and arrested him for indecent exposure, stretching the truth somewhat, but they were not very pleased that we had succeeded where they had failed and did not believe our description.

It transpired later that the Uniform Superintendent had been having lunch with the Detective Superintendent and somehow the flasher had been brought up in conversation and the uniforms unsuccessful efforts. The Detective Superintendent had said "My boys will get him," and so the word had been passed down until it reached us and became " Get him tonight!."

We sometimes saw the 'A' Division officer on his bike locking up Hyde Park and rumour had it that the bulge under his coat was a pair of very good night glasses like the ones U-boat Commanders used to use. He had to climb a tree with his mates underneath and would home them in on the prostitutes who had stayed in the Park with their clients. I wonder if they ever realised how they were found so quickly.

In their wisdom the people who spelled out the rules to be followed by police on duty decreed that in addition to making sure that someone knew where you were going when you went in somewhere alone, you also did not deal with a female on your own. Watching the crowd whilst my partner was away for half an hour and at that time waiting to see a reaction from someone who saw me and thought "Oh oh Police" without realising really what I was doing, I saw a young individual drop his head and a few seconds later I had caught up and invited him up into the Arch where there was a telephone which could be used for a search.

To all outward appearances I had a young Irish lad and I was fairly sure that the name and other details that he provided were not genuine. To start work and perhaps apply for benefits they needed their Insurance Card and this was usually secreted somewhere generally tucked in the waistband of the trousers under the shirt. Imagine my surprise when in searching for this I found unmistakable evidence that I was dealing with a female. The use of a male name had been  suspicious and earned a lecture after the real name did not ring any bells at C.R.O.  however I was relieved to see him/her dive back into the crowd and made sure there were details in the pocket book.

One incident which did not go into the pocketbook saw another Aide and I walking in Regents Park on St. Johns Wood ground because one or the other of us was going on leave the following day and an arrest would have been an embarrassment. As usually happens in these circumstances, we saw an individual pressing himself up against girls and women in the crowd around some of the pens to their obvious annoyance. We had a hurried conference to decide what to do which finished with him saying " Don't worry I'll look after it." A few minutes later the head and shoulders of the pervert appeared above the crowd accompanied by a strangled scream, and when my companion returned a few minutes later and I asked the obvious question he held his hand out and quickly squeezed the fingers.  It does occur to me that practical justice of this kind is much more likely to prevent repetition.

There was not the problem with hard drugs in Britain, that was present in other countries. Most drug addicts were treated by doctors although some may have had a proportionately larger number as their clients because they knew how to treat them by weaning them off drugs by decreasing doses or using Methadone as a substitute. Drug addicts would not respect any confidence, so if the doctor suspected that they were getting more than he was giving them, their supplier would quickly become known.

We always saw the same short inoffensive man in a large coat who was a fixture most nights at Marble Arch on the corner of Bayswater Road so imagine our surprise when a large black car with four men in it pulled up alongside him and bundled him into the car. We looked at each other and said "Squad," because it was almost certainly the Flying Squad or C.O.C.8 who had many nicknames including " The heavy mob." They deposited him back there about half an hour later strutting up and down and patting himself down like a chicken which had its feathers ruffled. So just out of curiosity we grabbed him and took him up inside the Arch to search him and learned very quickly that he had no great regard for the police and could he please get back to business? His pockets were full of brown paper packets containing contraceptives which he sold to the prostitutes on the street.

That it transpired later was the reason for the interest. A doctor who had a drug addict as a client who was also a prostitute, was on the upper deck of a bus going round the Arch when he saw her approach this individual and hand over what looked like money for a package. Still you never know do you? so he called the Yard.

Another two incidents occurred about the same time which involved the racing community. A Tic Tac man who signaled the bets for a bookmaker at the racetrack was found stabbed on Bayswater Road and as the femoral artery had been cut he would be lucky to survive. His offence apparently was that he had placed some bets and that was something they were not supposed to do. Also Paddington had to deal with a very well known bookmaker, Jack Comer popularly known as Jack Spot, who had been razor slashed for the umpteenth time. As a side note Paddington C.I.D.. may have been considered a little old fashioned because they still insisted that their Detectives wore hats. A direct result of the second incident was that I had to take my turn on the front door of the bookmakers wife Rita, a bookmaker in her own right before she married, and vet her callers as she had apparently been threatened. It was a revelation to find how closely knit the racing community was, because owners, trainers and jockeys were all interrelated and connected to each other in some way. It occurred to me then and in my mind was confirmed later on, that these connections could influence a racing result and they would always know which horse or dog was going to win.

Towards the end of 1956, Pat and I found out that we were going to be parents, and that brought accommodation forward as a matter that had to be considered. Some time previously an Area Car driver had attended what proved to be a gas suicide, and had to kick the door in to gain entry. The theory afterwards was that the lady had taped up all possible air entry points and that there was an appliance with a pilot light that had ignited the mixture formed when the air rushed in to join the gas.

In any event the explosion blew the door back on to him and killed him, and a relatively short time later his wife and children were made to leave Police Quarters. This raised a storm of protest and eventually they looked after the family, but it raised questions about the advisability of relying upon your employer for accommodation, so Pat and I started looking for a house.

As for any young couple it was a daunting prospect, and most properties were completely out of our price range, but fate or good luck or a little of both saw us call an Estate Agent late one afternoon and he had a house that had just come back onto the market because a sale had fallen through and the people had already decided on another.

It was a semi-detached house on the side of Roxeth Hill in Harrow, an old Tudor but with a happy feeing about it, fortunately because we could not furnish most of it. We lived there for five years and our three children were born whilst we lived there.

We moved in three months before Mark was born at Bushey Hospital. I had transferred out to Harrow, and had returned to uniform duties as is usual in those circumstances, so when Pat went for her check up in May and they decided that she had to stay at the hospital, I was nearly always a little late getting there by bus for visiting time, however on the evening when I had managed to get there just before 7 pm, and was waiting for the bell that signalled the start of visiting, and charged into the Ward ahead of everyone else.......... there was another lady in Pat's bed!

When I said something which probably sounded a  little accusatory like "where is my wife" she started crying , so I beat a hasty retreat and found the Caretaker who is usually the most knowledgable individual, and he took me to the elevator, and up a couple of floors where we stood in the hall outside the delivery room and he yelled " Sister where is Mrs. Hanson?" and she called back , "In here, just wait a minute." He left and said " They will look after you now." A few minutes later a very tall nurse came out , dressed all in white, with white rubber boots and mask, and the look that all women seem to reserve for men in maternity wards, She took me in to the reception room which is as far as Pat had got before the baby arrived. They let me speak to her and look at our baby boy, because in times of great stress and pain Pat could not see and she needed me to confirm that there were ten fingers and toes etc.

We did not have a car and another Constable drove us back when Pat and the baby were cleared to come home, and very welcome that was because in those days a mother only saw her baby in hospital at feeding times.

Harrow was a much more rural setting than the West End, and patrolling in uniform much more pleasant depending upon the weather. On one of my first nights when I walked up the hill from the station and past the old houses that were home to many of the students at Harrow School including Winston Churchill at one time, I noticed that there was a window open over a portico and a boy trying to look inconspicuous beside it. The rules at Harrow were very strict, and a student could get thrown out for a breach of the rules, and this looked like being out after curfew. So I looked at him and said "You need to get from down here to up there?" and when he nodded I got him to put his foot in my hands, then the other on my shoulder until he could pull himself onto the small roof, and the last I saw of him was a big grin a wave and then his feet going through the window.

One day when I found a Rolls Royce parked outside Marks and Spencers in the main street, the chauffeur was apologetic when I told him that he had to move. He explained that one of the owners wives was in the store, and if she saw customers waiting to be served and no counter clerk, she would go behind the counter and serve them herself, furs and all.

I expect that it was that kind of effort which had been the reason for their success after their small beginnings in the Northeast

My first duty back in uniform on the Harrow Area Car 5 'X' was just before Pat went into Hospital to have the baby, and the only time in the whole of my service that I got injured. Someone had loaned me a brand new ' flat hat' to act as the operator, and we got a call to Rayners Lane to a building site where some labourers had a set to with the foreman. The foreman was bleeding from the ear and the driver promptly assessed this as Grievous Bodily Harm, something that would have been regarded as a minor assault anywhere else, and I took one of the Irishmen up a slope to the car in the wrist lock , as taught at the School. When I got to the car and took one hand away to open the door he swung round and with a fist like cement, caught me on the forehead and I saw the proverbial stars. The Acting Sergeant had seen this and rushed up, grabbed my truncheon and tapped my prisoner on the head with it. I was most concerned about the borrowed hat because it was rolling down the gutter in the muck and the wet. When we got to the Station and the Sergeant learned that a truncheon had been used, he said that the prisoner would have to go to hospital, and someone said "You had better go too." It was then that I realised that the blood on my tunic was not the prisoner's but mine and when I looked in the mirror there was a large cut over the eye.

At the hospital, a lady doctor stitched me up, and told me she would give me a pound for any stitch mark I could see after a few months, but her attitude changed when she saw the X Rays of the Irishman's head because there was apparently a groove clearly visible which could be attributed to the truncheon and it was no good me claiming that I had not used it.

Then came the tricky part when I got back to the Station and realised the effect that this could have on Pat, with the baby two or three weeks away. In the end I made sure that I had a lift home, because it was really only just around the corner, phoned Pat and said " I am on my way home and I got a bit of a bang," then hung up and was home in a couple of minutes. It was a little while before Pat would talk to me, but we did not have to cope with an early arrival.

The Wolseley 680 had been changed to a newer model which I think was the 690, and although the Area Cars still suffered from the weight disadvantage in short street chases it certainly had more power, and there was an unwritten competition among the Wireless car drivers as to who had the faster car. In the early hours of one morning we got a call to the Kingsbury area, where some of the upscale houses had sophisticated alarms, and the call was promising 'Silent alarm operating ... suspects on premises.' Our car wound up speed down Kenton Road and by my estimation we were doing close to 90 mph, when the driver looked in his mirror and said" Jesu.........." and a black shadow swept past us. As it came to the small humpback over the railway line it shot into the air and flew for several yards before smacking back on to the road. It was 3'X' the Wembley car, and all its passengers must have hit the roof.

When we got to the house, the Wembley crew were shaking their heads because the intruders had gone, but the dog handler was complaining to anyone who would listen to him that the human stomach naturally moves up and down, whereas the dog's goes from side to side, and the bridge incident had left his animal in a very sorry state.

Harrow had a wonderfully eccentric Sergeant who was the only Relief Sergeant I ever knew to go out of the Station after parade, and walk with a Constable for a few minutes. He was a Welshman and very interested in the welfare of his troops and the local Magistrates hung on his every word. This was shown when I saw four youths go behind the shops in South Harrow one evening and when I called for help and the Car arrived we had a good chase and caught three, but it was the dog who found the fourth hiding in a refuse bin. The Sergeant arrived in the van and inspected the damage to one of the shop back doors, and then told me to remind him when the case went to Court as he would give evidence, although I could not see what this would be. I had given my evidence when he was called and told the Lay Magistrates that he had attended after a request for assistance from P.C. Hanson (One of our bright young Officers your Worships) and had asked one of the youths what he had been doing, and he said " I was having a ...." ,so I asked him to show me, and he pointed to somewhere on the wall, and I said " It doesn't look very much like it!"

It was he, reputedly, who named the new Velocette Motor Bikes, which were as quiet as ghosts and Harrow was one of the first Station to get them. The Police Driving School did not relax any of their rules for police drivers, so several Constables had to go to Hendon and take the Course before they could use them for beat duty. At the end of Early Turn one day, no one was allowed to book off by phone and they were told to come into the station to end their shift. There was our Sergeant pacing up and down and obviously in a rare temper.

When the bike rider came in pulling off his gloves, the Sergeant said with icy politeness " Ah, there you are Constable." By this time we all knew that he was in trouble." Tell me Constable when you were riding down Station Road this morning did you see me ?" and when he said " Yes." The Sergeant went on " And who was I with," the driver said " The Duty Inspector" and when the Sergeant drew himself up and in even icier tones said " And what do you do when you see the Duty Officer Constable." You could see the driver's mind racing as he said " Well I would usually be expected to salute Sergeant" and then with the unforgivable sin revealed the Sergeant asked " Well why didn't you!" and then the driver thought he had the answer " At the School they told us to have both hands on the controls at all times." The Sergeant digested this for a few seconds and then shot his head forward and almost spat " Well you could have nodded couldn't you!"  Henceforth the bikes were christened Noddy Bikes.

It was not long before I was back in plain clothes again, and not only patrolling at Harrow but Wembley and other Stations as needed.

As there was now a baby in the house, and despite the fact that we moved in with only a bed and small kitchen table and chairs  in the way of furniture, because the Western Avenue apartment had been furnished, it started to become a tradition that Christmas would be celebrated at our house, and the relatives started to gather a day or two before. It was always amazing to me that so many people could find a way to sleep in one house but we managed by virtue of bed chairs, a couch, blow up mattresses, and children sharing the same bed. On the last working day before Christmas I used to go down to Smithfield Market in the afternoon when they sold off their remaining turkeys and was always lucky enough to get a large bird at a good price. I remember paying half a crown to have the tendons pulled in the legs. It was quite a weight to lug all the way across London and out to Harrow but well worth the effort. Christmas day was really for the youngsters and became more so as our family increased. There were games like musical chairs with the help of a gramophone and pass the parcel where some little gift was at the very centre wrapped in successive layers of discarded Christmas wrapping paper. When the music stopped ... always at one of the children ... they would tear off a layer of wrapping and sometimes find a sweet or a balloon or something similar with the excitement growing as the parcel got smaller.

Pat took the lions share of cooking the meal, which sometimes meant getting up early to light the oven for the turkey, and starting the saucepan boiling with the Christmas pudding in it, made to an old family recipe. The ladies helped where they could and brought their own specialties in the way of cakes and delicacies for later on.

I used to round up the men and organize the washing up after dinner, which always takes place at mid day in English households, after sitting Pat down with the ladies despite protests and making sure they all had a drink of their choice. When the men had finished and had their drinks it was time for reminiscing and even a song or two with somewhat questionable harmony, although Pat's uncle and cousin played the accordion and both had good voices.

In the evening with the children in bed there was plenty to eat and drink, and games of one sort or another including darts, table billiards and card games.

The only drawback was the requirement that a policeman works one of the holiday days, and it was nearly always my luck to work on Christmas Day so I did not see the children open their presents. It had not presented too much trouble in the West End because you could generally find a Scotsman who would swap and do your duty on Christmas Day in exchange for you doing his New Years Day or Hogmanay. I did this once and the Scot that I had changed with came into the Elliott House canteen with his bagpipes and full highland dress about 2 a.m. because he was always asked to play at one of their gatherings. He got up on one of the tables and started that awful wail which brought all the female staff out of the kitchen, but they fled when he finished because he twirled around, and we all know what a true Scotsman has under his kilt.

Neil and Mark

Harrow was not always a sleepy rural area when it came to crime however when you were paired with an established detective on night duty your horizons expanded to take in Pinner, Ruislip, Wealdstone and the other surrounding Stations. One night the Detective that I was with had been told by an informant that some thieves were going to try to get into the American Base at Ruislip and raid the P.X., so he phoned the Base to alert them and at about 1 am we drove out there. We were greeted by a sentry at the front gate carrying an automatic weapon and he called the Security Commander who came to the gate and invited us in to see the arrangements that he had made for any intruders. My companions eyes had widened when he saw the sentry's weapon and when he asked how anyone breaking in would be apprehended the Security Commander shrugged his shoulders and said that as the base was technically American Territory they would probably shoot them! We beat a hasty retreat and wondered what criticism could result from any shoot out.

At the top of the hill we lived on was the hospital and perhaps because I was close by I sometimes had to go up there for one thing or another. One night I started duty there on my own because it was to keep observation on an individual who had tried to murder his parents and then had taken an overdose of barbiturates. They told me that he would not wake up, so all I had to do was sit beside the bed until I was relieved in the morning. After about an hour he opened one eye and then asked "you are a policeman aren't you." I did not see any point in denying it so I said "Yes," and he started to get out of bed. I tried to keep him in the bed and it quickly turned into an all out wrestling match

There were some other officers in a ward upstairs watching some injured people who had crashed in a stolen car, and they just got there in time because this individual had two hands tightening my tie and trying to strangle me. We were all still wrestling on the bed when a Sister arrived with a hypodermic that looked like a large syringe and obviously intended to use it. I asked her how she was going to do this and she said, inject it into his backside. In view of the contortions taking place I asked her to be sure it was the right backside.

When this had taken place she assured me that he would be out like a light for the rest of the night. It turned out later that he had been taking large amounts of barbiturates and had built up a tolerance to them. When his eyes opened again at about 3 am, I moved my chair closer and pulled the curtains around, told him he had ruined a perfectly good tie, and what I intended to do if he attempted another try. That did the trick because he seemed to go back to sleep for the rest of the night.

On another occasion a fellow had been brought in with injuries from a fight which needed fairly urgent attention. He was still well under the influence and had refused treatment and by the time I got there he was on the roof and threatening to throw himself off. From an earlier incident which I remembered from the West End I got up on the roof and told him if he wanted to jump I would help him because I wasn't going to waste the time arguing with him, but if he came down I would see what we could do for his obvious pain. He came down but still refused treatment, so I took out my pocket book and started to write. He asked me what I was doing and I told him that I was writing out a statement that he would sign saying that he refused treatment. He asked what would happen then, and I told him that I would call the Van, take him back to the Station and put him in a cell.

I waited around for a while to make sure that he would not give the nurses trouble because he became a lot more docile at the thought of a cell for the night.

The large general store in Harrow was Sopers and its Store Detective, Arthur was a small individual, always smartly dressed with a hat. He seemed to have that ability given to all good Store Detectives, to get right up to suspected shoplifters without them recognising the danger. There are lights at different locations throughout the Store which are used for various purposes depending upon the colour lit up to contact different members of the staff. One day I saw an adult and small boy getting up close to shop counters, the man behind the boy, and could not tell if this was some kind of indecency, or theft, so I asked an assistant to "Put the lights up for Arthur." When he arrived I pointed them out and left him to it, taking station by the main doors through which they would have to exit. Not too long afterwards I saw them coming down the main walkway with Arthur dancing along behind them waving his hat. Outside the Store I said "I have reason to believe that you have taken things from the Store that you have not paid for," then I pulled the man's raincoat open and got a big shock because he had a gun in each hand!.

We found his car nearby filled with merchandise from other stores, and it was an agreement between the man and the boy that caused him to hold the guns because there was not room in his pockets. The boy was taking things from the counter and passing them back into the man's poacher pockets. The last items stolen were always something chosen by the boy!

Although we did not realise it at the time my partner and I were involved in rather an unusual case. Someone had noticed, probably as a result of analysis, that where vehicles which disappeared normally turned up some time afterwards, having just been used for joy riding or some criminal purpose, some never did turn up and these had been left at Stations around the Metropolitan Area. The cars did not seem the type to be broken up for parts, or disguised and sold so we settled on Harrow Station and watched the morning business people leave their cars in the car park and go in to board the trains. We had separated to be a little more inconspicuous, but both saw an individual go up to the car that an obvious business type had left a few minutes earlier and stare through the back window for a long time before he walked away.

On the following morning the same business man had hardly gone out of sight into the station when our friend arrived, opened the car door and got in. We both arrived at the car as it started to move off and there was quite an interesting couple of minutes being dragged along before the ignition got turned off and we got him out of the car.

We learned later that when he was searched, he had a powerful monocular with which he could read the key code through the cars back window, and then it was easy to go to a dealer and get another key cut.

He had some kind of reservation on an Air Freight from one of the airports South East of London   and by the time the business man was having lunch his car would be well into France. There were places like Andorra apparently where the absence of the car's Log Book would not prejudice its sale. Once this fellow was caught however his system rebounded on him because the Registration Numbers on the Freight Lists showed the vehicles that he had stolen.

I do not pretend to be any kind of psychologist, but Terry one of the chaps that I worked with, had a problem. He had married the daughter of a well to do businessman in Wealdstone, and although they had been trying hard, the union had not produced a child and the prospective grandparents were getting anxious. The couple had been to see Specialists in Harley Street, who could not find a medical reason and he was miserable as a result. When we had worked together, he was very jumpy and seemed nervous and I put this down to his Military Service, because he had been in some tight spots including fighting Malayan Terrorists in the jungle and before that in Korea I think, so in the middle of a night duty I gave him my theory that they were trying too hard to have a baby, and to forget it completely for a while and then go for a holiday somewhere sunny and different and then see what happened. I did not see him for a few months, until sitting in the canteen I felt a thump in the back and there he was smiling from ear to ear," It worked Mike!"

Wembley Police Station seemed to be more modern than some of the West End Stations. There was more space and it acted as a centre for Garage and Transport duties. In common with the usual layout the C.I.D.. Office was upstairs and on one of the first occasions I went to work a late turn there I saw what could only be described as an unusually dressed individual sitting in one of the chairs. He had a jacket with a large yellow check and a paisley around his neck with swirls and spots in different colours, so I asked innocently "Who is looking after the prisoner?" and then got a blast of very colourful language. It seems that this was the legendary "Flaps" Dawes from the Yard who had an encyclopaedic memory for pickpockets and would sometimes go out to the racetracks and dog tracks and if any were there he would spot them and bring them in. He obviously did not need to be inconspicuous to do so.

I had my first close contact with the so called "Sport of Kings" although this may not apply to dog racing which took place at Wembley Stadium. My partner on this occasion was widely known to be fairly successful in placing bets but when he asked me if I was going to put some money on any of the races I told him that as a family man I had to put my wages to better use. I was however curious as to how he managed to stay ahead of the game. It seemed fairly simple, he just backed the favourite and sometimes the second favourite to win or place.

There was really nothing for us to do as pickpockets or ne'r-do-wells would spot us as policemen miles away, and I suppose we were there in case the Stadium police wanted help.

After we had about five races the top dogs had come in second or first, and although the odds were not great he seemed to be doing well. Then on the next race they announced that one dog had dropped out and had been replaced by another. The big Totaliser clocks at the end of the Stadium had gone round on nearly all the dogs except the substitute, and I asked what odds there would be on this one, " Oh that thing has only got three legs, you would be daft to bet on it, but the odds will be high." So I dug in my pocket and came up with all my loose change and told him to put it on for me when he laid his bet. That substitute dog came in first by a very large margin. When he gave me my winnings, he said "You should give me your system" and I explained it as being very simple. If the Bookies have taken losses on the evening they have to find a way to get even, and where all the money is going on favourites, look for some unfancied dog or horse to win. I do remember going home and putting the money on the table asking Pat to take it because it did not make me feel comfortable.

Wembley Stadium frequently acted as the centre for all kinds of sporting activities, and these meant that local police had to be supported by uniformed Constables from surrounding stations. My first trip there had been in uniform for an England Scotland International and I was paired with an older Constable from Wembley. As we walked around the outside of the Ground there were a lot of Scots many in highland dress, sitting or lying around looking the worse for drink. I mentioned this to him and he said " Yes, just before the game starts we are going to stand well back because most of them have spent their ticket money on booze or have bought fake or expired tickets!"

He was right because we clearly heard the whistle go to start the game and all those 'bodies' were galvanized into activity. They went over the top of high metal railings, and although the turnstiles were locked into position they went over the top of them like peas from a peashooter with the attendant cowering against the back wall. He also told me that during the day, some of the Scotsmen would go down Wembley High Street and offer Scottish bank notes to the shopkeepers in payment, hoping to start a big argument if they questioned whether they were legal tender.

One memorable visit to Wembley came as an Aide to C.I.D.. assigned to an England versus Russia Football International. A Russian Referee had some personal effects stolen from the dressing room during a match some months earlier, so two of us had to watch the dressing rooms, something that was no hardship at all if you loved to play the game as I did.

The England strip was already hanging in their dressing room, and I think that they could have only brought their own boots. They arrived by bus and there was a lot of in and out so I had to keep my eyes about me. There had been a pile of caps on a table in the centre of the room and these must have been their England caps for playing. I wish I had looked more closely to

C.I.D. Pass

see if the individual player's name was on the cap or the package, because if they just picked one up as they felt like it, and the last one had a head size of seven and a quarter and the last cap was six and seven eighthsohe might look a little bit silly wearing it. Still I do not think it would have bothered me if I had won that kind of honour.

As it happened, we were able to watch the game from the end of the tunnel as the room was locked. but we had to be back there just before half time when they unlocked it. The teams lined up in the tunnel to go out to start the game with the Captains at the back, and I remember that it was Billy Wright's 98th International. He was standing last in line with the Russian Captain, holding his pennant that he was going to exchange with the Russian at the opening ceremonies. They were chattering away to each other in their respective languages but I don't know if they really knew what was being said.

At half time Nat Lofthouse had a cut on his forehead that they wanted to treat but he insisted he would like a cup of tea first. He was back on the field in the second half and still heading the ball. There were no impassioned speeches or back slapping. All the players with one exception seemed to know each other and were talking about everyday things or joking around just like any other team. It did seem however that a full back who was a new cap seemed to sit on his own in the bus.

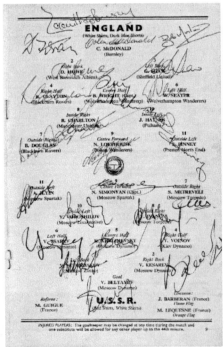

There was a large Industrial Estate at Wembley which acted as a target for thieves and some businesses were regularly broken into. It may have been then that someone started to realise that some better organised and sophisticated criminals were taking radios with them to listen into police calls and know when a car was on its way. In any event they were generally long gone before the Wireless Car arrived. Once, however, so the story goes, a large factory had been the subject of a silent alarm and had been well and truly searched by mobile and foot police including police dogs without any success. A motorcycle patrol passed a beat Constable and they discussed the call. Thinking that there might be a source of tea, and strictly against regulations which did not permit pillion passengers, they rode to the location where someone was just about to lock up. Sitting in the cafeteria area which was full of tablecloth covered tables, one of the officers saw one of them twitch. After a silent approach they whipped off the cloth and there were two ' villains' thinking that they had escaped detection.

The famous twenty four hour cafe on the North Circular Road, the Ace Cafe catered to a broad cross section of London life for in addition to late party goers there were individuals with more sinister reasons. Some of the motor cycle crowd used to bring their girl friends to boast and brag and inevitably there were speed competitions. One of these saw a bike on its kick stand with the engine ticking over, a coin dropped in the juke box, and the rider raced out and accelerated up the North Circular Road to a certain spot and turned round and tried to get back again before the record stopped. This gave rise to some spectacular crashes where the bikes were mostly in pieces. The tragedy of this kind of behaviour is when innocent people are involved with fatal results.

The cafe also served as a magnet for stolen cars or perhaps more accurately those which had been 'taken and driven away' which is the offence where no permanent theft was intended. Some of the Morris and Austin cars had a fuse box under the bonnet and by just simply taking one fuse and jamming it between two others the ignition was on. Then you just pulled the self starter and away you went. You stopped it by letting out the clutch in high gear. It was laziness however that was their undoing because if they did not restore the fuses to their proper position when they went into the Cafe, the ignition lights stayed on and if there were no keys in the ignition Voila!

It was just a matter of waiting for them to return to the vehicle and if they were 'mob handed' you hoped that you could grab more than one each.

There was always something going on at Wembley, but Harrow had its moments too. The railway line in Kenton was lined with house gardens on either side and someone was thought to be using the line to break into the back of houses and make off with cash and other easily disposed of articles, not the larger electrical items which were a popular thieves choice in those days.

Many of us were detailed to patrol the railway line area at night and some officers opted for dark clothing, leading my partner and I at the time to feel that if we crept up and down the line we stood more chance of being assaulted by some blunt instrument belonging to one of our own side than catching the real culprit, so we devised a plan of our own. When you carried out an authorised observation in plain clothes you could sometimes use one of the 'nondescript' vehicles belonging to police which you hoped would mean that you would not be recognised as policemen when one was in use. It was highly unlikely that we would get permission for something like that so we decided to use our own vehicles which could certainly qualify for the description 'nondescript' and sat at the end of one of the footbridges over the railway to see who used it at night.

We saw some movement on the other side of the fence beside the bridge about 3 a.m. and when we went to investigate someone ran away down the embankment and we found bundles of shirts tied up with neckties. We thought that someone must have broken into the Gent's Outfitters on Kenton Bridge and this was the result. My partner felt that we should call it in and take the property into the Station but I prevailed on him to wait and see if someone came back for the stolen goods. The first cleaning lady had gone across the bridge and it was just getting light when we saw some car headlights go out at the other end of the bridge and eventually a figure climbed over the fence on our side and walked past the car carrying a pile of shirts which covered his face. I got out quietly because I knew he couldn't have seen us but my partner got out having grabbed my truncheon and said "Gotcha". The results were unfortunate and of course predictable. All the shirts went up in the air and the suspect ran with me after him and my partner trailing behind. I had just about caught up to him when my partner made his second unhelpful comment and shouted "Let the dogs go." That produced an unwanted spurt from the individual who tried to get over a high wall and nearly made it. When I eventually did get him and we stood there winded and gasping for breath my partner walked up and said " Ah Teddy" and tapped him over the head with my truncheon which meant that he obviously recognised him but also that I had to support his weight as well as my own, and that we had to practically drag him all the way back to the car.

When we reached the Station there was my friend the Welsh Sergeant practically on his own, and when we told him that we would have to leave the prisoner in his care whilst we went back for the property he did not seem to mind. When we got back the prisoner was standing with his hands on his head in the corner of the Front Office because there was no Gaoler and the Sergeant was doing his paper work with a long heavy ruler in his hand. The prisoner was well known and had an associate known as 'Nutter' for his delightful habit of smashing his forehead into a person's face and causing a lot of damage besides breaking their nose.

# CHAPTER 7

## DETECTIVE CONSTABLE

There were two hurdles to overcome to become a substantive Detective in the Criminal Investigation Department. One of these was called an Area Board and was held in your own District and if you got through this which was practically unheard of at first try then you went to the ' Yard Board' where if you passed you were posted to a Station as a Detective Constable. As expected my first Area Board did not see me pass but gave me valuable experience of what to expect. The second time I got through and was slated for a Board at Scotland Yard on a given date. I should have realised that you were called in alphabetical order in view of my early afternoon time and as I was early the Sergeant I saw, who was probably filling in for someone called the ' Back Hall Inspector' in charge of the goings on at the Yard, sent me to an upstairs waiting room. When I opened the door I could just see the back of the top of someone's head sitting in a chair and it took me only a few seconds to realise and say " Is that you Taffy" and yes it was David Hughes and he was to sit the Yard Board the same as me. When I was called I said "David, we will either both get in or we will both fail," and we were both appointed Detective Constables in Police Orders on the same day, he going to a Station south of the River and I was posted to Harrow Road known for short as X.D.

My first day was quite memorable and perhaps a good example of what was to come. The First Class Sergeant showed me the actual C.I.D. Office which was upstairs as usual and quite large, as befitted the Divisional Headquarters, with a view on one side over the parade ground which had large stone paving, and Harrow Road itself on the other. Any interviews with Senior Officers must have been very short because I do not remember them, however I do recall that I was told that I would be on late turn and I could wander about a bit until about 6 pm when I was expected to be upstairs.

It seemed to be asking a lot for me to start doing regular Detective duties without any training because up to now I had brought in arrests and left that to the the Detective assigned to the case, although I had done some fingerprinting, but the next Detective Training Course at Hendon was not for some time. So a little before six I was at the spot assigned to me just inside the door, watching a D.C. in the corner on the phone taking the crime details or 'Grid' from the surrounding stations, because Harrow Road was the Divisional Station ... and we were the only ones there! He told me that the First Class Sergeant had rushed off to St. Charles Hospital because two West Indian  women had got into a fight and one had sunk the stiletto heel of her shoe into the other one's skull and he might have to take a 'Dying Declaration' The D.C. was gone a few minutes later because someone had backed a truck into the window of a T,V. shop further up the street, and I did not have too long to get nervous about being on my own because a call came in from the Area Car who had been called to a Bank Manager who was found tied up in the street with football laces and the keys to the bank safe were missing. That is how my life as a new Detective Constable started and my time there was not to prove very different. I understood that there were only two Stations in the Metropolitan Police at that time that had two Crime Books, one for odd numbers and one for even numbers, West End Central was one and Harrow Road the other. The Crime Books themselves were like large Ledgers, which I suppose in fact they actually were, and went across the two pages with details of the crime or allegation on the left, and the action taken on the right together with the classification and the name of the Detective assigned.

There was a good mix of Sergeants and D.C.'s , the former being a good deal older, certainly more cynical and not very tolerant of the high spirits which were sometimes shown by the latter.

It was quickly apparent that apart from reputedly having more C.R.O. men  (known at the Criminal Record Office) per square mile than any where else in London, there was a large resident contingent of Irish and West Indians who would cause trouble in their own communities but became an explosive mixture when they came together. This happened frequently on Saturday night when one faction would gather in the Prince of Wales and the other in the pub on the opposite side of the road. If they came out at the same time, one of the West Indians would suggest that the Pope should do something which was anatomically unlikely and the battle would be joined in the middle of the street. The Irish would fight with their fists, which became formidable clubs hardened and calloused by construction work. A West Indian tended to use anything available including his teeth, feet and often a knife. The uproar taking place almost outside the Station did not attract blue uniforms, however a quick call was usually made and the Catholic Priest would walk out into the road pulling on his vestments and saying... " Children ... children," and any weapons would fall and the crowd disperse and policemen would then appear in the vicinity.

With some relief in March 1960 I went to Hendon for my C.I.D.. Course and a few weeks before Easter for reasons which will appear later. I was very pleased to see that the Detective Sergeant who had taken my first crime arrest at Marylebone Lane was one of the Instructors, now Chief Inspector Ian Forbes.

The Instructors dealt with different aspects of the law as it related specifically to crime and most of it was not very inspiring stuff, although they tried to make it more interesting with reference to actual cases. The Course was not limited to Metropolitan Police, and we had police officers from other Countries, Government Departments the Services and City Forces throughout the United Kingdom.

METROPOLITAN POLICE DETECTIVE TRAINING SCHOOL. HENDON.

Front Row: D.C. Hanson, extreme right
C.I. Ian Forbes, third from right

Everyone sat up a little straighter when they showed slides of crime scenes and perhaps the most interesting presentations were by the pathologists, Drs. Simpson and Camps, who had been involved in some of the more sensational cases in recent times. The so called Acid Bath murderer, Haigh, who had sought the company of older women, induced them to make a will in his favour and then murdered them and disposed of the bodies by using concentrated acids. In that case most of the attention seemed to be paid to the evidence surrounding the very few remains of Mrs. Durand Deacon the unfortunate lady who had been his last victim, however there were some facets of the case which did not necessarily form part of the evidence. When the disposal method was first suspected, the pathologist was called upon to see if it actually worked, and he therefore needed some kind of 'body' to work with, so it was rumoured that he enlisted the help of some individuals who used to work in the basements of the large Department Stores at night and shoot rats as they scampered along the pipes. Imagine his surprise when concentrated acid did not destroy the rats, and it was not until he found that there was some necessary relationship between the size or specific gravity of the 'body ' and the volume of the acid which may have been revealed by the murderer himself before it would work, or that is how I seem to remember it. The other feature of that case involved a classical dilemma in which police find themselves from time to time. You strongly suspect that someone has committed murder(s) and find that the individual is stalking someone else and you just do not feel that you have enough evidence to arrest or convict, what do you do? If you make the arrest and do not get the conviction then he will be released among an unsuspecting public. Happily in that case they made the arrest and obtained the conviction.

Another case which underlined the skill of the pathologist was the murder of an Army Private in Germany named Watters which started when someone noticed that an apparent suicide by hanging showed lividity or post mortem staining in the wrong place. It should have been in the lower parts of the body but was along the back leading to the suspicion that the man had died earlier and then been 'hanged' later. The body was exhumed and the pathologist found that the hyoid bone in the throat had fractured in the wrong way, that is to say that if in hanging cases the bone normally fractured vertically then this was horizontal or vice versa so it was more likely caused by a blow to the throat which could be equally fatal. There was a conviction in that case too, but one of the questions that I asked myself was how the pathologist could say with complete certainty that a blow to the throat would cause that kind of fracture because I could not see him being asked to do many post mortems involving that kind of injury. As he was doing post mortems on a daily basis perhaps that is something about which we should draw our own conclusions.

The fact that your new career as a detective is not confirmed until you have actually been appointed as a Detective Constable, means that there is no prior training in criminal law except fundamental things like Judges Rules as they affect cautions and arrests that you may make as a Uniform Officer.

There is a great deal to learn in a short space of time about things like the use of photographs and identification parades to pick out a criminal and by following the correct procedures ensure that any subsequent prosecution results in a conviction, the different levels of crimes or offences and the Courts which will try them, and the fundamentals of evidence including the many different characteristics of fingerprints and the way that a fingerprint expert can bring a satisfying level of proof to a case with sometimes only a partial print to go on.

Some of the Statutes were 'old' in that they had been introduced many years before, however, in the case of the Metropolitan Police Act of 1839 which was uniquely relevant in London, the Vagrancy Act of 1824 and the Larceny Act of 1916, their age meant that there was a good deal of experience in applying their provisions and the way in which these were interpreted by the Courts.

One of the newer Statutes, the Criminal Justice Act of 1948 introduced Corrective Training and Preventive Detention, and produced a dangerous situation when the death penalty was removed. The areas of Fraud, Company Law, Forgery, Drugs and Counterfeiting for example became specialised areas to which detectives were assigned at the Yard in the same way that the 'Flying Squad' dealt with serious crime in the London area and there was a section that provided experienced senior detectives to other areas in the British Isles and throughout the world for serious crimes like murder.

The Duke of Edinburgh visited the class and shook hands here and there and gave a short speech. He then went out to the 'Skid Pan' which is a huge tar macadam dish which is oiled and greased and used by the advanced police drivers and I believe sometimes by London Transport for testing and training. To control any kind of vehicle on that surface seemed almost impossible, but the usual test had tires placed here and there which the driver had to negotiate being at all times in one kind of skid or another. The Duke took a turn and did not get very far before disturbing the tires, however, we learned that when he got out of the car his command of language was both descriptive and picturesque.

I was very fortunate to finish the Course because they fielded a football side and played some very good amateur teams. For the first few games I was fighting for wind and decidedly unfit after a long layoff, but just before Easter I was playing better, and on a very wet day on Hendon's sloping pitch I was taking a lot of throw ins. When I tried to get out of bed on the following morning the first of the Easter break I couldn't manage it. Pat tried to pull me up and I yelled. The doctor arrived and said that I had slipped a disc in the upper part of the back and I would have to stay on my back for six weeks. Although we had a few days off over Easter, I knew that if I missed more than a week of the class I would have to come back again. So it was a sheet of plywood under the mattress, and a few steps every day. I made it back to the Course but sitting on a hard chair all day was extremely painful and meant that I had to take the days outline home and look at it in bed. Still without getting an actual placing I gathered that I had done fairly well when the Course ended.

After I went back to Harrow Road I found that Hendon was still to play a part a few weeks later. because there was still the question of whether I could drive police Vehicles, not Area Cars of course but the Sunbeam or Hillman used by the C.I.D.

From what I could learn you took a one time test at the Driving School which was situated at Hendon, and most failed because the School was firmly of the opinion that no one could drive a vehicle properly unless they had been through the long Hendon course. So I quizzed everyone that I could to find why they had failed. Not using the mirror, not signaling properly, not increasing speed when leaving a restricted area etc. etc.

Off I went to Hendon on a very cold and icy day, and showed my Driving Licence to a Sergeant who was most unsympathetic when I told him that I had never driven a steering wheel gear shift which was on the huge Wolseley that was standing outside. He just said "First gears here, second there......" and so off we went slowly and after a short while I  said, more in hope than anything else, that I was matching my speed to the conditions. After about twenty minutes driving in different speed limits he had me stop just past a 'T' Junction and back around the corner and park. Then he told me to switch off and asked, "Please tell me without getting out, how far your front wheels and how far your back wheels are away from the kerb." I tried to appear confident and said the front about two feet and the back eighteen inches. He said "Get out and look." The front wheel was a couple of inches away and the back was touching. He said " Used to driving small cars aren't we Hanson" and I said "Yes." Then sarcastically "So that's why we have been missing things by that much," and he held up a thumb and forefinger about two inches apart. Not going to be intimidated I looked him in the eye and said "Well do I pass" and he said "Yes." That meant that I could drive the C.I.D.. car and although it was a convenience it also was an opportunity to give you any routine chores that included driving, and as you pretty well had to drive on night duty it brought that into consideration.

It was important to maintain the car's log book, particularly the mileage to show that you had not been off joy riding somewhere and it was always a good idea to inspect the car before you drove to ensure that you only took responsibility for your own dings and scratches.

There was a routine to a normal day at Harrow Road, and its start was generally governed by what had happened overnight. If you were not going to Court with an arrest that had occurred during the night then you were probably there with some previous case, so that meant that you started at 9 am or earlier every day, and if you were not attending Court then there were the crimes reported in the Crime Book since the previous day which needed visits.  So all the D.C.'s were generally there at 9 a.m.. Usually there was only one individual that could be spared to make calls and so you took all of them including those that were allocated to you for investigation. Certain things could only be done in the evening hours when people were likely to be at home, so it gave most of us a day which started at 9 am and finished at 10 pm or later with perhaps one evening when you could get away at about 7.30 pm. Overtime was unheard of in the C.I.D. and the only monetary benefit was an extra meal that you could charge if you remembered to put it in your diary. The daily diary was also the place to record 'incidentals' which generally took the form of buying a drink for an 'informant' and in most cases that was someone that you thought could give you useful information. Some detectives did actually have regular Informants and there was one phone in the corner of the office which you never answered with something to identify you as police but just gave the number.

It was only when I was away from the fairly relentless work load that all detectives had that I began to realise that we were fighting a losing battle. The arrests that we were dealing with were the ones that 'gave themselves up,' in other words the individual responsible was obvious at the start or very soon afterwards, because with one or two exceptions you did not have the time to give to any complex or lengthy investigation. That gave those criminals who had a few brains a chance to prosper undetected, for they used radios to scan police calls and in some cases made bogus calls to draw off the Area Cars. Their only chance of ending up in our hands was if they boasted too loudly or someone 'grassed.' Another troubling element was the growing tactic of making a complaint of some kind of impropriety against police and a Detective in particular, if he or she was causing a clever criminal too much grief. Even though the detective or uniformed man was usually found to be completely in the clear, it generally meant a transfer and achieved the criminal's object. If you added that to the fact that promotion seemed to come equally to those who never tried to use informants or get into areas frequented by criminals, it was increasingly a recipe for disaster and the death of old time effective policing.

We followed the principles which require police and any other authority to treat all people alike regardless of class, creed or colour but sometimes this is easier said than done.

The Hungarian Revolution which took place in 1956 was quickly crushed by Russian tanks, but not before patriots had taken to the streets and released those people in prison. The 'survivors' who managed to escape were greeted as heroes in Britain, but as a cynical detective would tell you, the patriots were the ones who died fighting in the streets whilst the erstwhile prisoners began to ply their trade in a new country.

The large number of West Indian Immigrants coming to the United Kingdom gravitated towards those areas which already had West Indian residents and that of course included Harrow Road. They packed themselves into roads and terraces where large old London houses had been divided internally to create what were ambitiously called flats or suites with shared cooking and bathroom facilities. Their living conditions and way of life was very difficult for the average English mind to absorb. The street vendors in the area had started to stock the tropical fruit and sweet potatoes that the new residents wanted but the fishmongers found that their new customers were not interested in traditional pieces of fish but wanted the fish heads and offal instead. I found that hard to believe until I saw a West Indian wife empty a tin of cat food into a frying pan for an evening meal.

There was trouble too when West Indian families moved into a house which still had permanent London residents many of them quite old. The West Indians would start a systematic terrorizing of the other tenants until they moved out, and let their friends in. There was always the cloying smell of 'Grass' or 'The weed' or Marijuana which they commonly used.

Aggressive and quick to claim that any police involvement was because of colour they always pleaded 'Not Guilty" even in the most blatant circumstances, they were childlike in others.

When you are the first person to be notified of a crime or hear a complaint there is no way to avoid any ongoing consequences. So when I found myself the only person in the office ... because everyone else had disappeared ... I received an excitable West Indian delegation alleging every conceivable crime in connection with 'The Club'. This it seemed was an arrangement whereby a fairly large number of individuals or families got together and formed a group which drew lots among themselves and after a given date they all contributed a certain amount, sometimes as much as one weeks wages a month, to each person or family as their number had been drawn. That individual then had a fairly large sum to buy a car or more commonly bring out more relatives to the United Kingdom. The fly in the ointment however was that once having received the money some of the early recipients disappeared and this is what brought the rest in alleging fraud and whatever else they could think of. It took a lot of explaining but they finally had to be satisfied with my explanation that this was a matter for the Civil and not the Criminal Court. Nevertheless I took the names of the absentees and by judicious inquiries found out who the area 'Elders' of the West Indian Community were. Shortly afterwards I went to see them and explained the situation and perhaps to be expected they shrugged their shoulders and said "Nothing to do with us." So I told them that the community would get a blackeye, there would be mistrust, and finally that they were the ones to sort it out. After some discussion between themselves they said "What can we do." Then I brought up the real reason for my visit, for there was always movement and contact between the West Indian Communities throughout the Country, a form of jungle telegraph if you like, so I told these elders that if they wanted to they could probably find the missing contributors and 'persuade' them to return, and if they did that I would like to see them at the Station.

I think it took three weeks before there were some obviously scared people at the Station to see me and although I gave them a lecture about honesty and letting their friends down, I knew that the reprisals from the elders was the reason for their fright, and the repayment which had already taken place.

It was probably about then that I learned the name that had been given to me by certain individuals ...the bastard with the black moustache!

Humour was certainly more unrestrained in terms of religion, race and gender in those days, which is why I had to apologize to one of my colleagues one morning. Despite the opinions of the insecure or argumentative I feel it is healthy to have people laugh at you and you laugh at them. and there is nothing wrong with ethnic humour. He had drawn the morning calls and wanted some company because at least one incident involved serious violence and he was going to get statements from witnesses. This was a home with an upstairs and he asked to see Miss so and so. An older black lady, probably the mother yelled up the stairs ... "Tulip ... Tulip!" When the young lady came downstairs, I had a great deal of difficulty in stifling laughter because the girl was probably one of the blackest Africans that I had seen, and so after reproachful glances I waited outside until he came out wanting to know what had got into me. So I told him he was obviously not a gardener, because they had been trying for years to breed a completely black tulip and today he had seen one!

It was sometimes difficult to carry on a satisfactory conversation with some West Indians and you became used to the uhmms and aaahs which punctuated their few words and tried to make some sense out of them. I was present at Marylebone Court one day when two West Indians had been involved in a fight . One of them had been stabbed, apparently surprised when he had jabbed a finger into the other ones eye and it had fallen out because it was artificial. A Detective Sergeant was trying to act as an unofficial interpreter for the Court and had said that the man in the witness box had an artificial eye. The witness leaned forward and in booming tones said "Yes your Honour, he done poked me in my ho..ficial eye," which reduced the whole Court to laughter.

As a startling change sometimes there were two very black individuals who we often came into contact with at Harrow Road. It would be charitable to say that they lived on their wits because like a lot of petty criminals they considered the coin fed gas meters in many homes, to be the white man's money box. What made them different was that they had been born and brought up in London and when they spoke to you it was an unexpected blast of pure cockney.

I was involved in some interesting cases, not all of them my own, but some are certainly worth remembering.

Many of these occurred when I was on the 'Q' car which was manned by a regular detective, an Aide to C.I.D. and the Traffic Branch provided a driver. We had our own call sign but rather than being asked to attend crime scenes we spent most of our time following up promising situations which seemed to point to more serious crime. One started out with a visit to houses around a chemists which had been broken into the night before, the safe removed and the break in not discovered until the morning. One of the residents was one of the witnesses that we always wish for but very seldom get. She had been woken up by the sound of something being dragged along the side of the house and when she had looked through the front curtains she was in time to see a car drive away from under a street light. Had she taken the number?.... Yes she had, and not only that but she had written it down.

This vehicle turned out to be owned by a young villain who we could not find immediately but was a recent companion of a well known criminal so we went through the proper hoops and got a search warrant for his address. At the time another young detective and I were both on the 'Q' Car on eight hour shifts 8 am to 4 pm and 4 pm to midnight, so we both went on at 8 am and stayed to midnight. When we executed the warrant we found a couple in the hallway just having left and the girl had a large radio that they could not account for. The apartment itself did not yield any property from the break in so we took the couple back to the station to check on the radio. The male kept on saying "Let the girl go!" so I took a chance with him and gave him three pennies for the phone and told him to find out where the property from the safe had gone and if he did I would release the girl. My partner felt that I had wasted three pennies but later in the evening he did call "There's not a lot Guv'nor, there's some dirty pictures under the television and two of the lighters on the mantel."

I told him that I would go and check and if it proved out then the girl would be sent home, but we would retain the radio because it was likely stolen but she could have it back if she proved ownership.

A warrant can be used more than once on a given day so we went back with different Aides and sure enough there were pornographic pictures under the T.V. and we took the two lighters and the individual protesting his innocence. When we got back I asked my colleague to go and get the chemist to identify the photographs and the lighter. "He wont identify those", he said pointing to the pictures. "I will bet you he does" and sure enough after adamantly denying that the photos had been in his safe, after I asked him to look more closely at one or two of them, he said "Do they have to be given in evidence" and I said "We can just put them down as a quantity of photographs" When he had gone, my mate asked how did you get him to agree to that, and I told him if he looked really closely and imagined the chemist to be a few years younger, he was in most of them!

The girl was pleased to leave the Station and she had never really been arrested, but she never came back to claim the radio. This would have been disposed of eventually by the Metropolitan Police Receiver as with any property believed to be the proceeds of crime without an owner.

The case was still missing the individual who owned the car and we eventually learned that he was in Devon. It required a little thought because we did not really have enough evidence against him because his partner would not implicate him, and the only way would be for him to admit the crime. For that we would have to interview him.

I was the one who always got to do the paperwork, so I put in a report setting out the details and asking if my partner and I could leave the Metropolitan Police District together if it became possible to interview this individual. At the time, no two substantive detectives could leave the district together without permission. So when we got an approval, I phoned the Exeter C.I.D.. and asked if they could bring this person in if he would volunteer, for us to talk to, and as soon as they did we would come down to interview him. There were a lot of questions as to what we wanted him for, but I would not let on, just asked them to be nice to him and we would carry out the interview. On the following day they phoned and we were on our way, But when we got there the suspect was in a cell and there was a very aggressive Detective Sergeant who would not let us talk to him unless he knew all the details, because he had apparently got a few unsolved crimes of his own that he fancied this fellow for. We looked at each other and decided to go out for lunch. It looked very much as if our suspect would be staying in Exeter, but we were lucky. When we got back to the station the Det. Sgt. had gone for his own lunch and my mate engaged the Desk Sergeant in conversation while I went down the cells until I found him. It became a straight choice, He could stay where he was and face the music if the locals really had anything or he could admit his part in the safe breaking and come with us.

I must have been persuasive because he admitted his involvement, so I got the uniform Sergeant to come down and listen to him admit our offence and then told him that we were taking him back to London to be charged. When he came back the Detective Sergeant was extremely annoyed and still asking us to see if he would 'Take some of his cases into consideration' if he admitted them.

That produced the kind of evening that I would not want to repeat. We were picked up at the Station and returned to Harrow Road, just about out on our feet, we took the statement under caution from our latest prisoner, and then as the abandoned safe was out in Denham in Buckinghamshire, my partner and I took the prisoner, handcuffed to a fresh Aide to C.I.D. and met a Buckinghamshire Area Car at their boundary and followed the prisoner's directions until we found the safe in the woods.

We piled this into the trunk of our car where it stuck out for all to see and in driving back in the early hours of the morning, I was very sleepy and having to concentrate when a van ahead of us gradually veered off the road and hit a tree in the median.

We ended up with police and ambulance called and us doing our best for the injured and getting dirty looks from everyone because we had a safe in the trunk and a handcuffed man hopping around with us. I suppose it did look strange!

One other case which was a result of 'Q' Car duty, and had some interesting moments started off with an anonymous call to say that there was a safe in the back garden at a certain address. It proved to be a three storied house in a row of houses and sure enough when we managed to make our way round the back there was a safe there but it looked as if it had been there for some time. What to do?. If we left to obtain a warrant there was a good likelihood that if we had been spotted everything would vanish, so I left the driver in the back garden and fortunately when someone arrived at the front door I just casually followed them in with the Aide to C.I.D.. There was a woman with a small baby in one of the rooms, and when she saw us she started to yell "Look out ... Look out," so I left the Aide with her and shot up the stairs where I found a man by the back window and when I looked out the driver was picking up clothing which we later found to have the shop's labels and price tags still attached.

There was also a case in the room which was full of keys called 'Twirls'. These were mortise lock keys which had been filed in a number of ways to act as skeleton keys, so I knew these probably were not ordinary small time criminals. When I had taken the male prisoner downstairs and left him in the care of the driver together with the clothing I went back for the Aide, and found him outside with the door closed. I had told him to stay with the woman, and apparently she had started to breast feed the baby and pushed him outside. After a few appropriate comments I took him back into the room and told him that we were going to find why she wanted him out. It took more than ten minutes emptying everything and going round and round under the accusing eye of the Aide before I finally opened the window and found a set of Oxy-Arc cutting equipment on a roof just outside the window.

When we got back to the Station I charged the male with Receiving the clothing, and found that he had previous convictions which could mean a fairly long sentence if convicted. He steadfastly protested his innocence, and although everyone can be fooled I prided myself that I knew when I was hearing a true account and so on the basis of a promise to let me know when the other villains who were truly responsible for the clothes and the safe, were going to do their next job, I did not oppose bail at the appearance in Magistrates Court.

To abbreviate a little I learned from him that these two were going to break into a television shop in a parade of shops on the edge of our 'ground' and their girl friends were bringing the implements which would be used to break in so they would not be caught with them. With the permission of the owner we parked the 'Q' Car which in this instance was a new Jaguar, in his driveway with a good view of the back of one side of the shops, and had asked the Area Car to park out of sight and watch the other side. We were in touch with them all the time until just before 10 pm when the women arrived and went round the back of the shops carrying fairly heavy bags, and then we could could not raise them by radio!.

Criminals seemingly know that Area Cars change crews at the station at 10 pm so their timing was not accidental, and I had a good deal of difficulty in keeping my crew from dashing around the back of the shops. We were very lucky because at about 10.15 pm a small Austin van drove up and they started loading T.V.s into it so I told the driver to 'Go....!', only the car would not go. Our continuous monitoring of the radio and frequent calls to the Area Car had run down the battery, and we had to push our car down a slope to start it as they were driving away. I began to try to contact Information Room to say that we were in a chase, but they told me that my calls were unreadable, probably from the state of the battery, so when we were passing the high wall of a cemetery I think and there was nowhere for them to turn I told the driver to pull alongside and sounded the bell and cut them off. Then there was a series of events that left me shaking afterwards, not just because of the danger involved, but the speed at which things happened and the need to make the right decisions in a hurry.

The passenger in the van got out and started to run back down the road, so I yelled at the Aide to go after him, and as I was getting out of the near side door, the van started up and drove right at me!. I just froze and it was our Scottish driver who saved me by pulling me backwards into the car as the van took the door off and thumped the outside of the engine compartment before driving off in front of us spreading bits and pieces all over the road. However, it was a third time lucky because we saw him take a turning right and my driver who knew the area said that it was a 'horseshoe' and came back to almost where we were standing. I sent him down to the other end of the turning and went into a house to make the kind of emergency call you don't make too often " Police require urgent assistance and the location". In just a couple of minutes the Aide turned up with his prisoner, who proved to have a nasty looking knife tucked down the front of his trousers, and the sky rained blue uniforms which I sent off into the turning and could even show them a photograph of the man they were looking for. They found him hiding under a vehicle in a tradesman's yard and the stolen van half way through somebody's front garden wall.

We had to leave the Jaguar where it was and our driver had to phone the Traffic Superintendent, and in hushed tones describe the damage. The prisoners insisted that a uniform Inspector who had turned up, should ride in the police van with them and me,  perhaps quite rightly anticipating that I had not taken kindly to the attempt to injure me. I gave the store owner very short shrift when he tried to claim that many more appliances were missing than those recovered in the van, I went over the circumstances, explaining that the van had only been out of our sight for a very short while, and asked if he thought that we had taken them? I suppose that I was a bit out of sorts!

That arrest cleared up a great many shopbreakings in the area, but it gave me a very difficult situation to deal with because the original prisoner had been committed to the Sessions for trial because of his previous record.

We were represented but he wasn't and in giving my evidence and answering his questions it soon became evident to the Judge that something was not quite right. So he looked at me and said "Officer can you tell me what is going on here?" There was nothing else for it, so I said" This man has been of great assistance to the police and as a result of arrests, a good many crimes have been cleared up involving large amounts of money and property ... and I now have very real doubts that this man committed the offence with which he is charged."The Judge thought for a moment and then looked at me and said "Why didn't you say this before" and then he turned to the prisoner and said " You have a great deal to thank this officer for ... case dismissed." When we were leaving Court, our Counsel said to me "Of course I know why you did it, but there will be a lot of people who will think it was for another reason." I suppose he was right but I had no regrets.

Night duty in the C.I.D. was, I suppose, a very big responsibility, because you were on your own except for an Aide to C.I.D. and something if you stopped to think about all the things which could happen at yours or any of the surrounding stations, a good cause for nervousness. In your twenties however you were brim full of confidence, and perhaps it was just as well because some of the more serious cases happened when I was on night duty, and where decisions had to be made without the ability to ask for advice. Paddington General Hospital featured prominently in some of these.  An Irish lad was found in the street rolling around and treated as a drunk to begin with until they found that he had been shot!. It seemed that together with others he had tried to gate crash a club owned and frequented by some Mediterranean types. When the Aide and I managed to get into the club later that night it was easy to spot the individual who had done the shooting. He was a bag of nerves because when the Irishmen had started pounding up the stairs, his companions had pushed him outside with the gun and locked the door behind him so he had just started blazing away. They would not tell us where the gun was but we found it when we pulled a table apart after we watched his eyes, and there it was in a compartment. Although any shooting is serious the real decision making came when I went to the hospital and saw the doctor who had operated on the Irishman. He gave me a fairly graphic description of how he had searched through the intestines which are piled on top of each other, and tried to find all the holes the bullets had made as they passed through. It reminded me of the way you examine a bicycle inner tube to find where the air is leaking, but in this case if he had missed one the results would probably be fatal.

So here I had a shooting victim in an oxygen tent, in very serious condition and if he died and I did not call out a senior officer, I was in trouble, however if I did call him out and the man did not die then I was in even worse trouble. I opted to place my faith in the skills of the doctor and the patient was still alive on the following day.

On another occasion I was still in the office and got called out to another Station when they transferred a call up to me from Paddington General Hospital and a Nursing Sister said "We think we have one of your young officers in here." That seemed odd and I asked why she wasn't certain, and then she told me about the injuries to his face which meant he could not really talk.

I got down there as quickly as I could and it was one of our Aides. It seemed that he and his partner were to have been keeping watch from his vehicle for a wanted man, but his partner had wanted to do something that evening so he had done this on his own. A crowd of youths had come along, dragged him out of the car and put the boot in whilst he was on the ground. They had damaged the car as well.

Because of the cuts and swelling to his face he really could not say much so I described some of the local tearaways and he nodded on two. I phoned the station and told them who I was looking for and why! In the meantime I was having to explain to a very hostile hospital staff why they could not treat his injuries properly until I had got a photographer from the Yard to take pictures, but he was on his way and realised the need for speed.

When I got back to the Station it did not take long, because everyone knew the circumstances, for a call to come in that three youths, two of which answered the description were in Kensal Town near to Portobello Road. The Aide and I rocketed off in the car and a few minutes later pulled alongside them in the street of houses with railings in front and steps down to their basements.

Getting out of the car I was alone on the pavement right in front of them and when a few seconds later the van and Area Car pulled alongside my car they were hemmed in. It was then one of them pulled out a loose vertical piece of railing and said "Come and get it" or words to that effect. I can still see that metal rod with a tip on it like a fleur de lis, but in a stand off like that the longer it took the worse it would get so I moved towards him and as he raised the iron, I kicked him hard in what I suppose I previously euphemistically called the lower abdomen.

As he went down everyone moved in and we put them in the back of the van none too gently. The iron came along as evidence.

When we got to the Station I found that the injured Aide was in the C.I.D.. Office and looking a lot better and just able to talk. I have always been surprised at the transformation that nursing staff are able to achieve when dealing with someone who is covered with dirt and blood. That is the reason that I may have mentioned earlier, that most police officers if they had to give a pound from their salary to any other profession, would give it to the nurses because we knew that they worked just as long and hard as we did and did not really get paid enough.

The Aide could hear the noises coming up the stairs because I had already told him that we had prisoners, and he looked at me in a worried way and I said, "Come down and identify them." If a man with over forty stitches in his face can smile, he did when he saw them and said "That's them!."

When the case was tried I cannot remember whether it was the Sessions or the Old Bailey because I think the most serious charge was 'grievous bodily harm with intent.' In any event, as was the vogue at the time, each prisoner was represented by a lady Barrister and they always tried to take liberties with the Court and did sometimes get away with a good deal. So after our Counsel had brought in the photographer and the Aide to substantiate the assault and the injuries, it was my turn to give evidence and I knew that it was going to be my arrest evidence that they would go after because of the rough time given the prisoners.

My fears were realised when she started on me in this fashion " I put it to you officer that on the night in question you saw my client in the street, you abused him, you kicked him viciously, you dragged him and his friends into a police van and continued to assault them all the way to the Station where they were also assaulted......." Whilst this was going on, my mind was racing because I was not being given a chance to rebut any of the things that she was saying so perhaps with that brilliant idea that sometimes turns up at the most opportune time, when she finally wound down I did not speak to her but looked up at the Judge and said "My Lord, I do not know if there is a question for me to answer." The Judge gave what seemed to me to be a wolfish look and said to the Jury "Members of the Jury you will disregard all that rhetoric which you have just heard and Mrs. ... will you please put questions to the officer that he can answer." She looked at the table for a minute and then came at me again." Officer when you did your police training did they not teach you how to restrain a prisoner without hurting him, and why was it necessary to kick my client so viciously." I said the first thing that came to me because it was true, "They did not give any training about how to deal with someone with a weapon who obviously intended to do you harm, so I kicked him to disable him and prevent him injuring me." Before she could say anything I heard the Judge saying "Quite so officer. Quite so". That was really the end of any attempt to sway the jury by discrediting the police and although in their final summary they tried to have you believe that these were just ordinary neighbourhood boys out for a good time the Jury wasn't having any and they found them guilty. I seem to remember that they got quite long sentences because the Courts, bless them, dealt very strongly with assaults on Police. They had previous convictions and one of them reputedly had a habit of carrying a sawn off shotgun down the arm of his overcoat, but I don't know if it featured in his convictions. That reminds me of another case involving a shotgun which will come later.

Another night duty case brought me back to the station well after midnight where a white teenager was huddled in the Interview Room with a blanket round her because she had precious little on. I managed to find a Woman Police Officer and we took her statement. It seemed that she had been to a party somewhere in the centre of London at which there was plenty to drink and 'grass' to smoke, and she had driven back into our area with a coloured man and when she reached his apartment she was under no illusions as to what they were going to do. It seems however that she changed her mind at the very last minute and she said he tried to throttle her and she managed to wriggle away and get out into the street where the Area Car eventually picked her up and brought her to the Station for me to sort out.

Her statement freely admitted that she had been a willing participant until the last minute and to me it seemed a Common Assault at the most which is not a crime, so while an Aide was going round to the apartment to try to rescue her clothes and she was being looked after by the Women Police, I wrote up the Crime Book putting in the classification 'Not recorded as a Crime.' When the Aide got back it was only with tattered clothing because the girl friend of the partygoer had got there first and tried to rip them to pieces, and the Divisional Surgeon had arrived and was examining the girl. When I suggested to the Station Sergeant that this was overkill he just shrugged his shoulders and I suppose it was his way of covering everything off. When the Divisional Surgeon came up to the office he seemed serious indeed. "She was nearly murdered you know Hanson," and when I asked how he arrived at that conclusion, he said it was because of the marks on her neck and invited me to go and look which I did. On either side of the adams apple was a livid thumbprint bruise! So when I went back to him I explained the circumstances and my conclusion that the only thing that could possibly be proved was some form of assault.

He got a bit sniffy then and said "All right how are we going to describe the result of my examination in the Divisional Surgeons report?" I said "How about marks conducive with a sucking of the skin!" I did not think 'Hickey' would be a term approved or understood in medical language.

I found a good informant in really unusual circumstances. The Aides were doing an observation for me in an industrial building not far from the Station, and I was on my own in a pub waiting to learn the results when a voice from another table said "All coppers are bastards." Now on a 'manor' as tough as Harrow Road you could not afford to let anything go, so I picked up my drink and went over to the table where a small tough looking woman was the one who had spoken. Her companions made themselves scarce and I said "You had better give me a good reason for saying that," and she came back .with "There's one law for the rich and one for the poor." She did not seem to be the worse for drink so I encouraged her to get it off her chest and found that she and other lesbians were being victimized by a large lump of muscle who was well known to be violent and who was breaking into their flats and apartments, taking whatever took his fancy, relying on the fact that they would not report it and for their part they did not think the police would do anything for them. We will call her Gerry.

I told her that when this happened again, to get the apartment owner to come to the Station and ask for me, and then the Aides came in and that was that.

A few days later the Desk Sergeant downstairs phoned up and said, "There's someone down here to see you," and it sounded as if he was laughing. When I got there he was still laughing and pointed to the Interview Room. Waiting for me was a girl who was probably 6 ft. 2 ins, very thin wearing cowboy boots and a western shirt. She just said "Gerry told me to come." I had a Woman P.C. help me take the statement ... she had left her apartment at such and such a time and locked up the premises, when she got home the door had been kicked in and so and so was missing. She had not given anyone permission to take anything.

When we got back to her apartment it had been turned upside down but among the clutter I found a bottle of spirits which she said had been in a cupboard and which was half empty, and obviously sampled by the thief. I took this down to the Yard myself and deposited it with the Fingerprint Branch, waited until I was sure they had some good prints and then gave them the individuals name and his C.R.O. Number to compare them with.

That was really that. I arrested him a short while later, and the Fingerprint Officer came to Court with his beautifully mounted photographs showing the ones on the bottle and the ones we had taken of the prisoner and the necessary number of matching characteristics, 16 I seem to remember. Criminal Records and Fingerprints provided exceptional service and it always amazed me how they were able to search the identities at Criminal Record Office overnight, verify fingerprints and come up with previous convictions before Court in the morning, and how Fingerprints were able to search so quickly and sometimes identify someone who had used a false Identity. They could sometimes work wonders with partial prints and it was said that a very small part of a fingerprint say that had been found at a murder scene would be in their personal memory bank should it ever appear in a set of prints somewhere years later

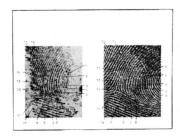

On the morning that the flat breaker came to Court it would have been worth having a photographer to take a picture of the Gallery. In addition to the lesbian contingent there were some peacocks who were their male counterparts and there seemed to be an air of satisfaction when he was sent up to the Sessions for sentence.

About two weeks later there was an envelope in my tray, no stamp and the name was spelled correctly with an 'o' instead of an 'e'. Inside was a short note. I owe you Guv'nor, come and see me... and there was an address. I thought long and hard about whether to go on my own, and one afternoon I took the plunge and found that it was a basement flat with a young fellow in pin stripes coming out of the gate as I went down. She answered the door and I asked "Who was that" and she laughed and said "That's our Legal Aid." I didn't realise what she meant until I went into the front room and found all kinds of skimpy underwear hung out to dry and a couple of young girls in and out. They were young prostitutes because after saying thanks she said "You can take your pick." It was then I realised what she meant about the visitor. He was obviously a lawyer and she believed in the barter system. I explained tactfully that I didn't do things like that and if we were going to discuss things she could get rid of the girls and off they went a few minutes later giggling up the steps.

I learned a lot more about Gerry, she had a number of convictions mostly for grievous bodily harm using a broken beer glass, and she was tattooed on just about every inch of her body. The young girls looked to her to keep them clear of pimps and the like. She gave me a big smile and said "A man for business, a woman for pleasure." I told her that she would have to find some other way to pay me back and when she realised what I meant she said indignantly "I'm not a grass."Then I reminded her that we had taken care of Mr. Muscle and there would be other situations affecting her community or the girls which involved crime and then she could get in touch ... but only by direct contact with me so that there could be no danger arising.

The arrangement worked very well and by meeting outside the Station and her apartment danger was avoided on both sides.

Some of the bright ideas that I had did not always work out well. There was some talk at the office about the possibility of there being a 'back street abortionist' at work on our 'ground' and that at least one girl had died after being admitted to hospital. So off I went to the hospital one morning and I asked one of the administrators if I could talk to some of the women that were being treated in the hope that they could give me some confirmation. After a few minutes a lady doctor arrived and said "Follow me," I could see that she was fuming and felt as if I was being led along by my ear.

We went up a couple of floors and arrived at the door into a ward which was full of women, all with their eyes turned towards us. With her hands on her hips the doctor said "Most of those women are over 40, they all had good reasons to want an abortion because they already have a family, they were all self induced or had some help, and no they are not prepared to talk to you!!" I left the hospital with my tail firmly between my legs.

We did not see the Detective Inspector in the office very often, in fact we did not see many senior officers at all, but one day there he was reading off a list of names that he wanted to be in the office at 9 pm that night. There were all kinds of theories and rumours but none near the mark because at 9 pm he showed us the photograph of an individual who had been terrorizing some of the local nightclubs and had been known to use a shotgun. Reliable information said that he would be at the Shepherds Bush Hotel that night with some other hard cases and we were to go in and help the D.I. to arrest him. The arrest was being co-ordinated with others elsewhere in London.

So we piled into cars and when we got near the pub we found that 'F' Division cars were going to be close by. Our D.I. always struck me as being rather small however he must have met the height standard to join in the first place, but he looked rather diminutive a few minutes later when the chairs and bottles were flying and although we got sundry bangs and bruises his agility meant that he wasn't touched.

We all went back to Harrow Road with the prisoner and one of our largest D.C.s  handcuffed to him. This produced a strong complaint at Magistrates Court the following morning when the solicitor who had turned up following the prisoner's phone call had not been able to interview his client alone. The magistrate asked for an explanation and the Detective Inspector said " We were unable to find the keys to the handcuffs Your Worship, but they were found this morning in the wireless car that transported the prisoner." That was probably as good a way as any to ensure that none of the other people were alerted before the arresting officers got there.

Despite the work load and the crusty behaviour of the older C.I.D.. officers we younger ones still seemed to find time for humour and there were many practical jokes. There was a very nice lady who sat next to my desk just inside the door and she was the typist, although she only really was supposed to type for the senior officers. We had to type as well as we could, mostly with two fingers which is how this is being composed. Legal Aid

Reports had to be completed for all serious crimes where we were going to need a lawyer at court and this meant six copies of the report and all the statements. It was not uncommon for some reports to come back for one reason or another, however I never did have this happen to me. I always made sure that it was neat and tidy, and learned the trick of cutting off the corner of an old envelope to keep the top corner square with a punched hole and a staple. When I sensed that the typist was not too busy I would ask if she could do a report for me, and would dictate it, for she could type as quickly as I talked. Sometimes she would tell me to leave the statements for her to do, however if there were any four letter words in these she would leave a note saying that at some places she could not read the writing. A gap always coincided with the four letter words and there was always exactly the right number of spaces for me to type it in!

Just before fireworks night there had been a break in at some kind of fireworks centre and they were flying around the office in quite dangerous fashion. If you were not observant the touch paper of a penny banger would be just protruding from under the files and papers in your box and a lighter used as someone was going by would see a spectacular eruption of paper. One of the older Sergeants used to sit at the back of the office in front of the coat cupboards, and someone had arranged a selection of fireworks which were pinned under the seat of his chair. As he sat there sensing that something was wrong and saying "What are you b.....s up to," a D.C.. hidden in the cupboard was putting a lighter to them and the results were very gratifying. He sat there in a cloud of smoke and profanity with continuing explosions as other fireworks ignited.

The whole thing came to an abrupt stop when a firework thrown across the office, probably at me, went off by the secretary typist and put a hole in her stocking.

Murder and sudden death are not pleasant events and always mean hard work for detectives. If this occurred at one of the surrounding stations then the Divisional Station is still fully involved.

I was called in the early hours of the morning after Guy Fawkes night because an explosive device had exploded on the windowsill of a caretaker's apartment and although he was sitting in a chair with his back to the window and only two or three inches of his head above the back of the chair, a piece of metal had hit this part of his head and killed him.

We were told to canvass the adjoining buildings and see who lived in the various apartments but not to ask questions at this stage. It was either the third or the fourth apartment that I called at and I was invited in to a small kitchen in which two girls were having breakfast, and I sat at the same table with my notebook while I talked to the mother. There was something in the way that the two girls were looking at each other and I finally said "Can you tell me anything," because the mother had already asked "This is about last night isn't it?" One of the girls said "Go on tell him" and they did. They had seen two local brothers with what they claimed was a bomb they were carrying in a holdall the night before.

I got the names of the boys and asked them not to talk about it, and that someone would probably be round to talk to them after school and thanked them of course.

I hot footed it back to the Station and I think I saw the Detective Inspector who raised his eyebrows but did not comment on the earlier instruction not to ask questions.

He and a First Class Sergeant went out to the boy's home and I followed on with another Sergeant and waited outside. The D.I. came out with the boys some time later and his Sergeant conferred with my Sergeant. Their car waited until the First Class Sergeant came out with a large jar which was full of some kind of powder. He gave it to me and said "Take the car and drive this back to the Station." I asked him what it was and he said "That's the explosive that they used in the bomb." So not very comfortable at the thought of taking this stuff, I said "I cant take the car Sergeant because its booked out to you." He gave a large smile and said "I've booked it back in over the phone and now its booked out to you!" Oh well that's why they make them Sergeants I suppose, but I drove back very gingerly and carried it upstairs like a box of eggs. They told me later that it was a mixture of easily obtained ingredients and the boys had stuffed a car starter motor with it and lit it with a model airplane fuse of some kind.

There was a certain irony I suppose when I saw these boys sitting at one of the C.I.D.. desks with paper and pencil playing a game where one player puts dashes to represent the letters in a word and the other guesses the letters. When he is right the letter is filled in and when he is wrong the pieces of a gallows are constructed. The game is called 'Hangman.'

That was not the only dangerous situation that I got myself into, for one night I was on my own in the office just before pub closing time when the special phone went in the corner. I did not even have time to read off the number ... a voice said "Prince of Wales come quick!" With thoughts of stolen property being sold in the bar or something similar, I put my coat on and rushed round and straight in. The Licencee was half ducked down behind the bar the lights were low because he had been ready to close and there were two groups jut about to come to grips ........and I was smack in the middle! It was a situation that could not be anticipated and where any hesitation would be disastrous so in the loudest voice I could manage I identified one or two on either side reasoning that they would know that I knew who to come for. There was a bit of shuffling of feet and then I said "You lot first, out you go and don't hang about outside." After some whispering, to my surprise they did but I could hear sundry thuds and other noises as they went. I gave it a couple of minutes and then said the other lot could go and then told the Licencee just what I thought of him for not giving any warning. The kinds of things we picked up off the floor would make anyone nervous, knuckledusters and pieces of chain seeming to be the weapon of choice. I was not about to take this lot back to the Station to be booked in and cause endless reports so I left the disposal to the Licencee, but I opened something wrapped in newspaper which proved to be a carving knife with a blade so sharp it would cut hair.

Harrow Road was no stranger to violence because the so called Notting Hill Riots where a coloured man was murdered took place in the Portobello Road area on Harrow Road's ground.

Shortly after I got to the Station some of us were told off to go to the cemetery where the victim was buried because they expected more trouble on the anniversary of his death, but there proved to be more policemen skulking about between the gravestones than mourners.

Another murder at Harrow Road attracted quite a lot of publicity at the time. An Admiralty Civil Servant had been reported as a missing person. Women Police are often asked to do these inquiries and the unfortunate W.P.C. was searching his apartment with the landlord when he fell out of a cupboard of some kind on top of her. He was completely naked.

The early inquiries showed that he led two kinds of lives. pin stripe suit and umbrella by day and leather at nights and weekends. Shortly afterwards an artists male model was murdered south of the River and a collective shiver went through the homosexual community at the thought that there might be a serial killer.

We found ourselves interviewing people from unlikely sources, names obtained from a photographic studio whose clients seemed to be into bondage, well muscled individuals from gymnasiums, and the whole cast of a stage show which had played in London and was about to go on the road. There were two actors I remember who were probably interested in making their current parts more believable.

I remember having to go to Chelsea and meet a Chelsea detective who knew a club owner who claimed to have information. It seemed to me that he was fishing for information from us rather than having anything which would help us but he had a habit which I hated of asking for a light and cupping your hands with his to draw the match or lighter to the cigarette. As we were leaving the bar the Chelsea man said "Did you like him." I thought he was referring to the club owner but he nodded at the brunette sitting on a bar stool showing a lot of stocking and high heeled shoes. Being just a country lad I suppose it was a bit hard for me to realise that this was a transvestite, because the Oxford Street fellow had been a lot more obvious. As we went out the Chelsea man said "Look at their hands, they are nearly always a giveaway."

As far as I know there was never an arrest in that murder, and when the insinuations and jibes about the moral character at the Admiralty and suspected espionage began then there were those that said we probably never would find our murderer.

I have mentioned earlier that there was some kind of system to determine whether you had Christmas day off or Boxing Day because you could not have both and I never did seem to be lucky enough to get Christmas Day and see the kids open their presents, but wonder of wonders I got Christmas Day at last. I threatened everyone with dire consequences if they brought in an arrest or anything which required my presence the following day. I had picked up a huge turkey fairly easily, all the family were gathering at our house and I set off for home earlier than usual in a very happy frame of mind. We had a few drinks, sang a few songs, and then on an opened out sofa, a bed chair and doubling up where necessary we managed the miracle of most English houses at holiday time and managed to sleep at least twelve people.

It seemed that I had only been asleep for a few minutes when Pat woke me and said "There's someone at the door." I said "Don't answer it," a few minutes later she said "He's in uniform and he's throwing stones at the window." So I went down and had to get dressed and go into Harleseden where an old man had been murdered in an alley ... and that was Christmas for that year!

The post mortem showed some mutilation in the groin area which eventually led one of our senior officers to advance elaborate theories about some Asian involvement. In any case when we had been chasing our own tails for a week or two, an old Detective Sergeant started phoning around the Institutions to see if any locals had been out on Christmas Eve. A Borstal south of London had such a youth who had been acting strangely since his return. He went down to interview him and came back with a confession. The mutilations were where the youth had kicked the old man in the course of the robbery to stop him yelling and screaming.

At some stage I had passed the exam for Detective Sergeant and eventually would have been posted away from Harrow Road.Perhaps it is difficult to convey the kind of sarcastic humour that was part and parcel of police work but one illustration would be the difficult situation that arises when someone comes into the station and says that someone is going to, or trying to murder them. There isn't any real action that you can take and you can hardly say "Well if it happens we will know who to look for." I was in the office when a West Indian lady was referred up to us and seen by one of the old Detective Sergeants who sat close to me. It was a familiar story where she had a man who previously had another girl friend and this other woman was threatening her and she said was trying to poison her. The Sergeant carefully explained that there was really nothing that he could do, but perhaps it would be helpful if she could find out how she was trying to poison her.

A few days later the same lady was back with some powder in a bottle and the Sergeant got up and as he passed me he picked up a clear plastic ruler that I was particularly fond of and said "I will just take this to our analyst and see what he says." A few minutes later he was back with a lower level of powder, I suspect just having used the bathroom and dropped the ruler back on my desk, telling the woman that he couldn't find anything. Shortly afterwards I noticed that the end of my nice ruler had become brown and bubbled. I took it to show him and said we should get the woman back. "Don't worry Hanson" he said "Some people have stomachs like horses."

There was another time when I admit that things were beginning to get to me, and I stood up and said to the office at large. "Here I am a Detective Constable, supposed to deal with small crime while the Sergeants and Inspectors are supposed to deal with serious crime. I've had safe breakings, grievous bodily harm something the Divisional Surgeon wanted to call attempted murder and other serious assaults and Its me that has had to deal with them." There was a kind of surprised silence for a minute and then one of the Sergeants said, "They shouldn't pay you Hanson, you should pay us. With the experience that you are getting you can go anywhere in the Met and nothing will faze you!"

# CHAPTER 8

## CORNISH FARM

My parents bought a farm in Cornwall after they returned from Africa where my father had organised and managed security for a man named Williamson, at his Diamond Mine. Doctor John Thorburn Williamson, was a bachelor, a very shy and reserved man who studied at McGill University in Canada and obtained a Doctorate in Geology. His family was thought to own logging concessions in Canada. He had joined an expedition from South Africa to Tanganyika to search for diamonds as Germans had discovered them in the past. When the expedition was unsuccessful, he stayed with two African helpers and although desperately short of money and suffering from malaria and a bout of blackwater fever he carried on prospecting with a pick and a shovel. The legend is that while trickling soil from a shovel he saw a diamond, and when he did it again he found another one. He found a businessman to grubstake him and help him stake a claim. This developed into a very successful diamond mine at Mwadui, and when security became an issue, father who had retired as Chief Inspector from the Sheffield City Police, became the Chief Security Officer. He visited the Oppenheimer Organisation in South Africa first to learn what he could about diamonds and security and then organised the security at Mwadui where they felt that he had reduced Illicit sales and theft by half during the first year.

Tanganyika had been a German possession and Britain started to administer it after one of the world wars. That created an unusual situation because it was apparently impossible to own land unless you could produce the old German title deeds and as a result most land was rented. Most of the mine labour was provided by local Africans who proved very skillful at hiding diamonds in the most unusual places and meeting the illicit diamond buyers outside the mine. It was possible to mount fairly stringent security inside the mine but hard to locate the transactions outside.

One day in returning to the mine father saw some tall, aloof tribesmen standing with their spears and was told that these were the Masai. They were hunters and did no menial tasks. He approached their leaders and promised flour and salt if they brought in the sellers and buyers to the mine. This arrangement worked very well for a while but he had overlooked the laziness they sometimes demonstrated, and when they started bringing the diamonds and the ears of the unfortunate miscreants it was time to call an immediate halt.

The farm in Cornwall was mixed and included milking cows,pigs,chickens etc and Pat and I and the children spent some happy holidays there. In 1962 an adjoining farm came up for sale and they suggested that we buy it and farm the two together.

Neil and Mark with farmhouse in background

Although I had a promising police career ahead of me, particularly as I would soon be moving to the next rank, there was no prospect of the hours I spent at work getting any less and any C.I.D. Office gave ample evidence of the broken marriages that resulted. The children looked at me a little strangely when I did manage a day off and that may have been the kind of inspiration for that famous picture 'when did you last see your father.' Pat and I talked it over and we put in an offer on Thurdon Farm near Kilkhampton in Cornwall, and when it was accepted I put in my resignation papers.

That seemed to cause some surprise as it seems I had obviously been fairly highly regarded. My old Detective Inspector came out to see me and asked me to reconsider. Apparently he was to be involved in some new kind of Intelligence Squad at the Yard and it was highly probably that was where I would go as Sergeant. I did not reconsider and we became the new owners of Thurdon Farm on Lady Day March 31st 1962.

Eventually I received my discharge letter which had the pleasing assessment......his conduct was exemplary....... and the date that I left March 25th,1962.

Our old Ford had been replaced by a six cylinder Vauxhall, which certainly had more space for a growing family. Like its predecessor it had a mind of its own. The steering wheel gear shift had a nasty habit of jamming and I carried a stick in the car, so that when this happened I could give it a swift jab in just the right place and we were all right again for a while.

It burned a lot of oil, and some claimed that if I slammed the door too hard, the cylinders could be heard to rattle. Certainly we left a blue haze.

I did not think that breakers yards, my old standby, would be easily found in the country, so I found a Vauxhall which was relatively new and with a body that had been mangled in an accident, found a local garage which would take out the old engine and pick up and replace it with the new one and its accessories like the air filter and carburetor. Of course I had failed to take into account the way in which a car breaker removes an engine. They just work their way round it with an oxyacetylene torch and all the accessories I had hoped to see in the car were fried beyond recognition.

This took place not long before we were due to travel down to Cornwall so I was anxious to hear how the new engine sounded and very apprehensive when I got a call to go up to the garage replacing it. On the phone they had sounded unenthusiastic, and when I got there the mechanic said "Listen to this." He started the engine and there were spits and bangs and it ran very rough until it suddenly started to run very nicely. He said "You lucky devil, the valves were probably stuck because it had been lying on its side." In the course of using it that engine ran very well if I used a little Redex with each fill up, and eventually the rest of the car seemed to rust around it but the engine never gave any trouble.

This garage had an extremely large vehicle which was said to have been Goering's staff car with some kind of aero engine and heavy plating with bullet proof glass. There were dents and stars caused by gunfire presumably by exuberant Allied Forces. In any event the owner apparently had a bet with a noble Lord who owned a museum of classic vehicles, that he would repair it and deliver it under its own steam. I gather that this was probably an ambitious claim because although he got it running the brakes were not safe enough to hold the very heavy weight of the car.

Our family had grown, and Neil arrived on December 9th, 1958. The first born usually arrives in hospital but thereafter, in the absence of complications babies are born at home. We had a good family doctor for our second child and the midwife came regularly, however it was fortunate that I was there in the evening when Pat started to get contractions and when we phoned the midwife who had always assured us that she would come when called started to ask questions about this and that and was obviously reluctant to come. Pats Mother was there bless her, and when Pat was obviously in distress I called the midwife again and said "If you don't get here in a few minutes I am going to have to help her with the delivery myself." She said she was on her way and I was waiting by the front door when she arrived and going up the stairs she was trying to unravel the gas equipment but there was no time for any of that because as she came into the bedroom the baby was born.

The arrival of our daughter on December 8th, 1961 was not straightforward either. The Doctor had visited late in the evening and had given Pat something to induce the birth because she had been in labour for over 24 hours. The midwife attended and promptly gave Pat something to make her sleep, presumably so that she could get some, and booted Pat's

Mum and I out of the bedroom. That left Pat virtually unconscious, with a baby arriving and unable to rouse a sleeping midwife!

To add insult to injury, the midwife's car would not start afterwards and I had to go out in freezing weather and push her down the hill early in the morning until it caught, when I got back Pat was wandering about the upstairs landing and did not know where she was.

Cheryl

That was the reason when she woke up the following day and said, "I will be very pleased when this baby has arrived," and was really surprised when I went round to the cot at the side of the bed and put a baby daughter in her arms.

The farm was probably a big adventure for the kids,and although I had a taste of farm work in my teens, it was certainly a different way of life. On the day that we arrived a mouse ran across the front parlour floor and I shied a poker at it. When we went up to the village I told the people at the garage that we needed a cat. Within an hour of getting home we were presented with two young cats and two more followed shortly after and then we had to start turning them away as more people kept bringing them.

We did not have too much machinery or equipment of our own, and the farm did not have a Milk Licence, but we did buy an old David Brown tractor, which was a little unique in its way because it was possible for two people to sit side by side. It had a starting crank with a big brass sleeve that was very shiny because of the number of times it had been used to start it. Like most tractors it ran on a less refined fuel called Tractor Vapourising Oil or T.V.O.. but there was a system which started it from from a small tank of petrol......but you had to remember to switch to it before you stopped the engine, and I never did. It meant shutting off the T.V.O.. and cranking it round until that was gone and then turning on the petrol and cranking it until it started.

The farm was described as mixed, and all that really meant was a little bit of everything. The chickens were kept in overnight but let out in the morning which meant that very few of them laid their eggs in the nest boxes provided and so it became an ongoing battle of wits to find the various places they found to lay. The hay shed was always a favourite but in summer the nest could be in long grass somewhere. Your ear became sharply attuned for the congratulatory cackle which sometimes took place after laying and that coupled with audio direction finding would sometimes turn up a new nest. As we ran a cockerel with the hens, it sometimes meant a pleasant surprise when a hen appeared leading some small chicks, but they had many natural predators including the owls that lived in the old cob buildings which used to be the old farmhouse. I had seen pictures but did not realise that young owls leave the nest in various sizes and we quite liked seeing them perched around the stack yard until the chicks started disappearing.

I saw a young owl on a stump in the pathway leading to the vegetable garden and decided to creep up on it to take a photo with the old box camera. I had to balance on a wall with a six foot drop into the adjoining field which was thick mud with obvious traces of the pigs which used it. In concentrating too much on the photo I overbalanced and finished up in the mud with the camera held high to save damage. When I went back covered in foul smelling mud expecting to find the young owl scared away it was still there and I found that I could walk right up to it and the only thing that it did was to shut its eyes! The pig field was next to the house and much used by Mark and Neil to play and sometimes round up the pigs. They had wellington boots but when they ran anywhere in the mud the boots stuck and got left behind and I had to find the boots and  very often socks as well.

In case I leave the impression that we spent time playing, farm work is very hard indeed and I had exchanged a long hours job for one that demanded just as many hours per day. It started early with the need to feed all the animals, pigs,calves and chickens, and to hunt for eggs. I had an army surplus jacket with many pockets which was very useful because it had a warm lining. Unfortunately however I formed a habit of putting eggs in my pocket as I found them and then forgetting with the result that the pockets became solid and unusable. The day ended with the loss of daylight particularly in hay or combine season and there was sometimes night duty when a pig was farrowing.

The pigs were Landrace pigs which were crossed to a Large White Boar, and the resultant cross breed was a good combination with a long back for bacon and a good ham. The locals however preferred the Wessex Saddleback sow crossed to the Large White which produced a so called 'blue pig' because it was usually white with blue spots, and they felt that it converted feed into meat very well. We took the litters to market at Holsworthy when they were eight weeks old and sold them but the first time I took some the locals obviously recognised a newcomer and the Auctioneer was going to knock them down for a very low price when I said "I will withdraw them." The Auctioneer gave me a sharp look and then renewed the bidding and I got a much better price.

Pig breeding is a fairly chancy business because you need to rear about eight pigs a litter to do any good and the gilt or pig with its first litter does not generally produce that many. The mortality rate is very high during the first few hours,because the mother pig has a habit of flopping down to feed them without any regard for the ones she traps underneath her. I installed farrowing rails in the old buildings we used for pigs. These are rails about a foot off the ground and a foot from the walls which can provide an avenue of escape for young pigs. The best way however is to stay with the pigs while she gives birth and for a few hours afterwards to try to improve the survival rate. A pull on the pigs teat would soon show if close attendance was necessary. If it was close to farrowing, milk was present. I never managed to understand why this always occurred in the evening, meaning a night in a cold pig pen by the light of a paraffin lamp with the top part of the stable door open for a dive over the top which was often necessary with a pig in birth pains and an uncertain temper.

It was amusing to watch the newly born piglets fighting to establish position in the feeding order, and it was no accident that the best pigs always finished up at the teats closest to the mother's head and so on down to the weediest at the other end.

There were some very real advantages to living in the country. The family were together nearly all the time, and Pat helped me in the fields and with the animals as well as keeping house. In the early morning with the dew still on the ground all the hedgerow flowers and grasses smell wonderful as does the honeysuckle. There is a lovely smell to a hay field both just after the grass is cut and when you are baling hay on a hot day.

We had a good butcher in Holsworthy and if we could not get in on Market Day he would come round and deliver on Friday, leaving the cuts of meat that we usually ordered and we would pay him the next time we saw him. If we were in the fields he would tuck it up in the gutter over the back door out of reach of any dogs.

My favourite meal was always breakfast because going out early and working for an hour or so always gives you an appetite and I usually had cereal or porridge, followed by bacon and eggs with fried bread and toast and marmalade to fill up any corners.

It was difficult to keep some things from spoiling in hot weather, however when father took a pig to the slaughter house they would butcher it and give you back half nicely cut into manageable pieces on muslin in the back of your vehicle and their half paid for the service.

Our eggs were picked up by the Egg Board once a week and you were paid in cash for the previous week. You had to make sure that they were clean and any little blemish meant it was classified as a 'second' for which you got very little. What made me steam was the way they classified the large double yolk eggs as seconds when I had scoured the dairies when Pat was pregnant and paid a premium price for this kind of egg. Needless to say we retained these eggs for our own use.

Because I lacked the experience I often found myself doing things the hard way although Pat could always see a quicker and better way if she was there. For instance when I tried to dig my pitchfork into a bale of hay and lift it onto the rickety old cart that we had it took a great deal of effort. Then I watched the smaller Cornishmen do it and saw the way they would hit the fork against their thigh and lift in one movement. A lot easier when you know how! We were extremely fortunate during the two years that we spent farming, because the difference between success and failure or if you will happiness and unhappiness is very small as Mr. Micawber well knew. It only needed bad weather at the wrong time or the sickness or loss of an animal or perhaps your own health, to tip the balance the wrong way.

The popular belief was that you waited for a good seed head on the grass before you cut hay, but that first year we had an extremely wet spring and there was plenty of grass so we cut an 8 acre field early, baled it and sold it on the field. The last lot went off just as it started to rain. The other farmers had cut that little bit later and lost most if not all of their crop. Because we had cut early we were able to make a second cut at the end of the summer and had people asking us for hay during the winter. Similarly the barley which we grew we had combined, and although the local farmers used to leave the sacks in the field to let the wind dry them and turned them every so often, we were only four miles from the Atlantic as the crow flies. When we saw the storm clouds building over the sea a few days later Pat and I went out with the tractor and heaved the sacks any old how overloading the old trailer time after time and just throwing the sacks under cover before the rain started. Once more it rained for a long time. The other crops were ruined and when the agent came to buy our crop he argued about water content which is always a way used to barter down the price, but I told him that the water content would be a lot higher elsewhere!

Our real luck however centered around the Milk Licence., for the price of the farm was reasonable because it did not have a Licence, and the Agriculture Ministry made it clear that they did not want to issue any Licences, finding a reason to fail nearly everything that came their way.

Nevertheless we asked them to send details of how to apply, and they sent diagrams and a description of how to build an acceptable milking parlour. We chose a site in the old stack yard which had a solid shale base. I started to pickaxe out the foundations which the Ministry wanted to be four or six inches deep. My neighbours came to watch and thought we were mad, but if the Ministry looked for reasons to turn it down it would not be the footings. As the structure grew we called in an Agricultural Field Officer from time to time to check our progress. They were all critical of the advice received from the previous officer and gave us new advice for the next week or two. I always asked them to confirm with a letter, which they did, including their criticism of the previous instructions. Their letters were always signed over the name of some senior man in the Ministry, a Director I think. from Plymouth.

The real hurdle we had to overcome was the water. The Ministry did not care about water for human consumption. but the water for Tuberculin Tested cattle had to be clean and pure. Our source of water was a well outside the back door of the house which had been hacked out of shale and rock and probably acted as a drainage hole for every vile thing imaginable. We regularly had stomach problems that could probably be blamed on the water. In the end however the Ministry solved our problem for us in the instructions of what to do before we had the test. You had to buy a proprietary bottle of some germ killer used in the washing of dairy implements, and when notified of the date of the test you put a couple of cap fulls of this stuff down the well and the test would determine what and how many organisms had returned in that time span. I put a whole bottle of the stuff down the well the night before the test and crossed my fingers.

The test result came back with a remark to the effect that our water was a bright spot in an area where most water supplies were sub-standard.

Then came the real test of the milking parlour now completed, and on the appointed day the Ministry gentleman arrived in a lovely suit and tie with a lady to take notes. He put on his wellingtons and walked down to the site and was back in a few minutes asking for a ladder.

When he came back he had composed his face into what he probably thought was a sympathetic look and told me that he could not pass the parlour. The reasons that he gave were I think that the window was too small and there was some feature of the drainage. In any event I asked his name and to my surprise it was the senior individual whose name was at the bottom of the letters I had received. I laid out the letters in sequence and invited him to read them while I watched because I knew all the things he mentioned had been approved by the Field Officers. He got a little redder with each one and then said, "I still cannot issue a Licence." So I shrugged my shoulders and said that if he would write me a letter setting out his reasons I would send the correspondence up to a large newspaper and see if they thought it would make a story. He glared at that and said that he would confer with his colleague. So he went outside and when he eventually came back he said the Licence would be approved. Capitalizing on that I asked him to confirm this quickly as we quite truthfully had a cow that was ready to calve.

We officially became dairy farmers on the 21st December 1963.

Murphy's Law operates on farms as it does everywhere else, and on the day the cow's behaviour suggested imminent calving I asked my neighbours what they thought as experienced farmers and  Roy and Evan pushed pulled and prodded and then said no it would be a few days so we let her go down to the field with the others. We all heard the bawling later in the morning and sure enough the calf had arrived and we had the ticklish job of getting the calf and the cow back to the farm buildings. With the help of our neighbours and Pat driving the tractor with the trailer, we managed to get the calf into it with Pat driving in circles around us as the cow kept charging. The cow followed us up the lane and then charged one of the lads who backed up a muckheap with cow in full pursuit. Perhaps not unexpectedly we had to have the vet see to the cow which had milk fever probably as a result of its exertions.

That was when I got the Asian flu and spent two days in bed, so Pat with no experience at all had to do the milking,  Murphy was still exerting his influence.

The farmer assumes all the risk when he provides or sells the things that he produces. For instance when we sold the hay 'off the field' it was at our risk until the buyer picked it up. If something had destroyed all or part of the crop he would not have paid. Similarly when they picked up the milk at the end of the lane, it was our risk until it reached the Processing Centre. If there was a thunderstorm which turned the milk or their truck was late, it is still the farmer that loses. The Centre tests the milk for butterfat content. The Friesians Holsteins or Ayrshires were the most popular breed for milk production as they gave a lot of milk but it was blue water as father called it and you had to have a Guernsey or Jersey in the herd to add the necessary fat content.  The neighbours being traditional Cornishmen had Devon cattle which were dual purpose, being good beef cattle as well as milk producers.

It was the Guernsey or Jersey cow that produced the clotted or Devon cream which is so popular. Most farms had a kitchen range let into the wall which included the fire to heat the room and also an oven to do the cooking. The Aga was fairly common and its flat metal surface was useful for warming and drying all sorts of things, and also to produce the cream. A shallow metal container was used which held the milk, and as it heated ... not boiled... the cream formed on the surface and was skimmed off.

When you move to a different area it takes time for you to get used to the people, their speech and customs. It follows that they will take time to know and accept you. In the West Country that can take generations. At the age that our children were however, Mark four, Neil three  and Cheryl three months it was only a matter of time before they had local accents.

Our oldest son Mark had been heir to all kinds of infections and illnesses which could probably be attributed to an infected throat and this showed in his lack of energy. The London medical approach to children's tonsils was to leave them in. As soon as the local Cornish doctor had cause to examine him he said, "out" and so we went to Bude hospital, and he had them out and a few weeks later was chasing the trailer for miles with energy to spare. The same luck did not hold for his brother Neil, for when he had his tonsils removed eventually they kept on growing back.

We were not the only 'strangers' in the area for there was a German farmer and his partner in an adjoining farm. He looked strange at milking time because he carried on a German custom of using a one legged milking stool which was strapped to him and all he had to do was to sit by each cow without having to look for or adjust his seat.

Down the road opposite my parent's Forda Farm was the farm of the man whose family had owned all the land in the area and gradually sold off all the farms leaving him with perhaps the best location. This had a natural hollow with very good soil which suited his needs because he was really a horticulturalist and not a farmer. He grew some kale but this was to provide shelter for pheasants and partridges which he fed in the same way as his chickens. He had a large greenhouse in which he grew begonias and their flowers were as big as dinner plates.

He used to travel to Plymouth to act as an expert on some television programme from time to time and rumour had it that an unscrupulous neighbour took his shotgun and a bowl of chicken feed one day when he was away and blew holes in the kale in an attempt to have pheasant or partridge for dinner.

We did visit from time to time and the main meal is of course served in most European homes about 1 pm. and consists of meat and potatoes with a dessert to follow. To our surprise the bowl of thick cream on the table which we expected to be used for the dessert was liberally applied to our host's potatoes.

Each farmer usually has to employ an accountant every year, however, few if any farmers seemed to have to pay tax. There can be some close calls however. One neighbour had failed to include details of the egg sales which provided a small amount of cash each week, but over several years this amounted to a considerable sum and the Egg Board of course keep very good records. He had a venerable old car which used to make its way back from the pub in Kilkhampton late some nights with frequent collisions with the banks in the narrow lane. In consequence the old vehicle was held together in places with wire and binder twine. When the tax people demanded payment and an accountant had the 'forgotten' income explained to him he told the farmer that, he would either have to pay tax, or perhaps buy something like a new car to offset the substantial tax amount. That is the reason that he was showing off one of those beautiful aerodynamic Citroens a few weeks later, but the new car was soon to look like its predecessor.

The early sixties in addition to the start of an unknown Liverpool Group which was going to be phenomenally successful, also saw the rising popularity of Ian Fleming's character James Bond and of course the popularity of television. Not knowing then that one day we would move to Canada Pat and I were very impressed by a performance at the Winter Olympics by a Canadian. He was not one of the favourites in the men's skating but when all the others seemed to have an attack of nerves or fall or not go for the big jumps, Donald Jackson came on to the music of Carmen and just threw himself into everything. As often happens in these situations the crowd warmed to him and clapped to the music, so in the end he thoroughly deserved his gold medal.

The year we moved down to the farm in 1962 we had the worst winter in living memory. The West Country normally escapes the ice and snow which are a feature of winter elsewhere in the British Isles, but this year was to prove the exception with lots of snow and extremely cold winds and temperatures.

Our trouble began on Christmas Eve, when the pipes which ran up the wall of the house from the old pump outside totally froze up, and my attempts to unfreeze them with a blow lamp only succeeded in splitting the pipes.

The old pump had a big fly wheel which you had to help on its way to start with and then there were leaks all over the place, but in this case it was completely redundant and I had to look for an alternative. I found it in a pipe in the kitchen which suggested that a hand pump had been used before the mechanical pump was installed outside. So we acquired a hand pump and found that the last thing we had to do after use was to store some water to prime it with the next time we wanted to use it.

Feeding the stock apart from the bruising cold was not too difficult with hay and so forth but when water was required I had to break the ice in the old well outside the old buildings and lower down a bucket on the end of a rope.

The car was virtually useless and it meant using the tractor to go to Kilkhampton for fuel and provisions and that coincided with another bout of flu for me, and a rather terrifying ride for Pat on her own. The tractor was not easy for her to handle as it had such a strong clutch, and she found it impossible to let it out slowly. Having such a big engine it did not stall but just took off with a very decided jerk. If I was loading hay bales on to the trailer and standing on top of the load I had better be at the back when she stopped because I would end up flying forward and similarly when she started I had to be at the front and hope I stopped before I went over the back.

Modern farm houses are made out of brick or quarried stone, and do not efficiently keep heat in or the cold out. The front door for example which was not used very often, had a distinct gap at the bottom of the door and when the wind blew we used to put a thick cocoanut matting door mat up against it. We frequently found this several feet away from the door! For a week or two we went to bed with as many clothes as we wore during the day and Pat was constantly worried that the children would be warm enough.

When the weather eased the local garage, Trewins, gave exceptional service by welding all the split water pipes for us. There was nothing I think that they could not do in the automotive or engineering fields because when a part was broken on our old farm equipment which had really been designed for horse traction and regularly failed with the tractors speed, spare parts were no longer made. or available . Vivian Trewin would look at the broken pieces and if he could not weld them he would fish around in an old box that he kept full of old parts, get out his micrometer and make what we needed on a lathe. They seemed to look after everyone's car needs as well, and their old farm equipment, without the difficulty of obtaining parts.

# CHAPTER 9

## BACK TO THE CITY

The realisation started to become evident in our second year that although farming was a healthy life and meant closer family ties it did not hold out a very secure future and so we decided to sell the farm and go back to London. The sale itself did not take a long time and was probably helped by the fact that there now was a Milk Licence and this allowed us to realise a sale price which was a good deal more than we bought the farm for two years previously. The biggest wrench came when we had to part with the animals that we had bred and looked after. The ducks which used to follow us everywhere because although we had bought them for the table we could not bring ourselves to eat them, and so they formed a procession behind us wherever we went. The Guernsey cow we had reared ourselves that was really a family pet, and that Cheryl used to love to ride on. She had just had her first calf.

With the knowledge that we were going back to the City and had a little money to spend we decided that it was time we had another car. The old Vauxhall had performed well and when it got stuck there was always the tractor to pull it out, however the first time I used the car to pull out the tractor I made the mistake of attaching the rope to the spare wheel assembly at the rear ......which just pulled off. When I put the rope around the back axle I had better results.

Trewins Garage were happy to look for a car for us and a couple of weeks after we had asked them they suggested a Morris Traveller which they had sold new to a 'dog and stick' farmer. By that they meant that he just had cattle that he raised for beef and took a short drive out to see them every day, so the car had not seen much use. It was just what we wanted and ideal for a family.

An amusing situation took place the first time I took the 'new' vehicle up to the garage for a fill up. There are three grades of petrol and I asked for the Supreme or whatever the best grade was called. Vivian said that they did not sell much of that in the winter and when I asked him why, he explained that only visitors used that grade. His local customers seeing only one large tanker pull up to fill the underground storage tanks were convinced that there was just one grade, and therefore the visitors were stupid to pay more than the cheapest price!

The question of where we would live was also solved because Pat's Uncle Sid was moving to New Zealand and his semi-detached house in Iver Heath in Buckinghamshire, was for sale so we bought the house.

Moving days stir the emotions but there is generally a lot of hard work to take your mind off things and the children's questions to answer. They did not always travel well and Neil was sometimes car sick but with a new car he would put his head over my shoulder when we approached a slower vehicle and say "take him over dad!"

Now that we had moved I needed employment and had no intention of rejoining the police, so I found work as a dispatcher for a local Security Firm. It was not a very big operation and I was expected to sit in the office at night monitoring the Patrol Driver's calls and sorting out any problems. You might think, what problems can arise when a driver is just monitoring locked premises? One night the driver called in to say that he could not open a door wide enough to get in and punch his clock at the clock station. When I got there we called in the proprietor and eventually the police because it was the safe which was preventing the door from opening. It was generally accepted that although patrols by Police and Security Firms may be a deterrent, you could not prevent break-ins, the cardinal sin was not to find them! Another driver had the attributes usually attributed to some milkmen because he had any number of willing ladies on his round and had to be monitored carefully to make sure he did the required inspections.

We were watching the papers all the time for a good employment opportunity and I went for interviews here and there until I finally landed a position at the Motor Agents Association in Great Portland Street in May 1964. I started at a wage of one thousand one hundred and seventy five pounds per annum.

I cannot remember what the position was called but it was to assist the man who ran The Fidelity Scheme for the Association. This was really a credit to the person who had thought of the idea and to the Association for setting it up. The Association consisted of all sectors of the Motor Trade including those people who sold parts, but the Fidelity Scheme was conceived to improve and maintain its reputation by dealing with the area that consistently gave it a black eye, and that was car sales and repairs.

The dealers who had signed up were committed to have unresolved complaints made against them dealt with by the Scheme and if a settlement could not be reached the case was referred to Arbitration with the result binding on the parties. I seem to remember that there was an understanding that if the case went against the motor dealer and he refused to pay an award, then the Association would. There was a certain amount of publicity given to it and its members had a nice sign that they could display.

The Motor Trade complained with some justification that because a vehicle was made up of so many parts there were bound to be failures both in cars which they sold and repaired and attention always seemed to be paid to these failures as against the very large numbers of sales and repairs which did not produce complaint.

Most of the complaints that we received were dealt with fairly easily by talking or writing to the dealer and the complainant, and in the case of the dealer talking to the right person. We generally managed to propose a way to resolve the complaint that was acceptable to both. There were however one or two where, either because of its seriousness or the personalities involved, the customer elected to go to binding arbitration.

The arbitration process was extremely fair and relatively simple. The Institute of Arbitrators was asked to nominate an Arbitrator. With the knowledge that the case involved the Motor Trade an Arbitrator with some experience in this field would be nominated and the details supplied to both parties together with a complete list of letters or documents which would be supplied to him. Any comments or suggestion from Fidelity Scheme staff were always left out of these submissions. The parties would be asked if there were any more details or comments for the Arbitrator and if so the other party would receive these and also allowed to comment. Finally after each side had presented their case on paper and had full knowledge of that presented by the other side an Arbitration was arranged, generally at the Association's Head Office in Great Portland Street and the Arbitrator would notify us if he wanted one or both of the parties present and/or have any of the parts involved, inspected.

The Institute supplied Arbitrators for all kinds of cases and there were sometimes staggering amounts of money involved particularly those which were International and sometimes going behind the Iron Curtain, however every case received the same kind of meticulous treatment because about the only way you could challenge an Arbitrator's decision was to show that he was somehow unbalanced or had made a big mistake in law, and that they never did.

The parties were very seldom called but observers were sometimes invited, both members of the trade with no connection with the trade member involved and press people or Consumer Organisations, with the understanding that the names of the parties be treated as confidential.

Their general reaction was one of surprise at the care taken to present all the facts and the fairness of the procedure.

A few things nearly always occurred to me as a result of these proceedings. To begin with it was a simple and comparatively easy way to solve disputes because lawyers were seldom involved and never allowed to attend the Arbitration. The result was final and did not give rise to continued appeal usually by the party with the most money.

Never ever allow yourself to be sentenced by your peers. In every case where observers from the trade were asked as a matter of interest for their suggested settlement they would always deal more harshly with the dealer than the eventual settlement. Finally it was always satisfying to learn that although all proposals by Fidelity Scheme staff were never seen by the Arbitrator, his ruling nearly always came down along the lines we had suggested.

My time there was a very valuable learning experience in how to deal with disputes and also the law surrounding the sale of goods, and responsibility of the buyer and seller. They were a good employer, one of our staff outings was to Ostend in Belgium.

If you discount the short time spent on night duty for the Security Firm, this was the first time for a number of years that I had not worked a lot longer than eight hours a day and five days a week. To get on the train at Uxbridge and do the Daily Telegraph crossword on the way to work and to leave at 5 pm with an evening paper to read on the way home was comparative luxury and to get home on Friday, the weekend ahead of you, with the knowledge that someone was not going to call you out in the middle of the night made me want to pinch myself.

There was also a very satisfying feeling when lying in a warm bed with the wind  howling and it  pouring down outside, that some poor devil was having to work in it and it wasn't me.

It was a whole new way of life, and one which meant that I started to put on weight. My sports activities consisted of a trip to the Thames at Windsor to enjoy float fishing and playing tennis for Iver heath against the Chalfonts and all the other local communities with the results faithfully reported in the local paper, none of these activities calculated to involve sufficient physical activity to keep my weight down. As usual Pat came to the rescue and after seeing me mow a postage size piece of lawn for the second time in a week she told me that it was time that I found some kind of interest and showed me an article in the local paper saying that the local Conservatives were having a meeting to organize for the forthcoming Parish Council Elections. Our politics as a family had never been something of deep conviction and like a good many voters I suppose we tended to vote against somebody or something rather than espouse a particular cause, however we were certainly a little right of centre in our outlook so I attended the meeting in a local hall.

Listening to the comments I gathered that there were Liberal people who were the sitting members which was surprising because the area could be taken to be Conservative in outlook but it seemed that there had been a scandal of some kind a few years before which had hurt their cause. In any event they had some titled person who had agreed to run with one or two others who had failed the last time. I had asked some questions because it seemed that they were relying on a free mail out to all the local residents which would identify the candidates, and I felt that they had to do some door to door canvassing. Perhaps inevitably when they could not fill their slate of six, someone said "What about the fellow who had so much to say," and that is how I came to be a candidate and a young fellow who had not said anything piped up and said that if I would run so would he.

For the next few weeks I tackled the local district sporting a nice big rosette in my buttonhole that Pat had made for me, and knocking on doors. I just said that my name was Hanson, that I was a Conservative candidate in the Parish Council Election, and if they had any questions about me I would try to answer them. Most people just smiled and said "Thank you" but sometimes I would encounter some hostility. The Parish Council contained two or three areas besides Iver Heath and it was not really practical to go into Iver and Richings Park, but the youngster and I were tackling our own local areas and mentioning our other candidate's names.

When 10th May 1966, the day of the election actually arrived I took a day off work and worked outside the Iver Heath Polling Station keeping track of those voters who were ostensibly our supporters and later sending volunteer car drivers out to those who had not voted. When the chap arrived that had run the meeting, I handed over the lists to him and told him that I had left my district to last and would he please send the cars there. I went home to change and brought Pat back with me to watch the count. When I came into the school where the counting took place I was given the lists back with a note to say that there had not been any cars available.

I showed this to Pat and she must have realised that this would not help my chances, but pointed out that their organisation so far meant that the lists would probably not be much help anyway.

As the piles started to grow in front of the volunteers doing the counting Pat said, "Walk around and see if you can learn anything, I just heard somebody say Hanson." So because my hearing had already started to deteriorate, I walked around and came back with the news that I seemed to have a pile of reasonable size before each counter.

When the results were announced I came in second to the lady who had been Chairman of the Council for the last few times   and the only other Conservative with a chance was my young friend who was locked in a recount which he eventually won. So we were in a minority but nevertheless had broken the lock which our rival party  had previously enjoyed.

I received a formal notice that I had been elected and a nice letter from the Clerk two years later after I told them that I was resigning to go to Canada.

The duties were not onerous but included a meeting most months with a Clerk with sufficient experience to keep us on the straight and narrow, and of course the local press to pass on any useful information to the area residents. A Parish Council's responsibilities do not extend very far up the government ladder in terms of decision making but they do look into local problems including street lighting and make their views known on zoning to try and maintain a green belt and building proposals. When it seemed prudent to do so I challenged some of the thinking of the Liberal 'old boys' and bless them the local paper always picked up on whatever I had to say.

One of my suggestions that I was rather proud of was the erection of notice boards in each area with the first priority going to the Parish Council notices but then anyone could use them.

A local event which we used to attend as a family was a fete or fair in Iver, and this was often attended by the Duke and Duchess of Kent whose country home Coppins is in the vicinity. Their children were very young but even at that age they were being taught how to give the 'royal wave' when the contestants for the title of Beauty Queen rode by. Another local resident Sid James, famous for his humour in Hancock's Half Hour and Carry On films also used to attend gymkhanas and other local gatherings.

Pinewood Film Studios was just up the road and one of the directors of the Bond films lived in a house that we passed on the way to Uxbridge. Pat's cousins, Alan and Leslie Tomkins  made their living in the film industry. Alan was an Art Director and created the sets for some high profile films, including The Empire Strikes Back and Robin Hood Prince of thieves. His brother Leslie did the same kind of work with films like Passage to India, Yentl and Terms of Endearment. While she was waiting to fly to Canada, Alan took Pat to Pinewood, where amongst other things she saw the Fort Knox set for the Bond film, Goldfinger.

# CHAPTER 10

## CONSUMER AFFAIRS

I parted company with the Motor Agents Association in October 1966 and I suppose that we had been keeping an eye on the newspaper to see if there was a better position and I did see an advertisement from one of the new London Boroughs which was an amalgamation of the Wembley and surrounding areas, and now called the Borough of Brent. It was for someone to deal with consumer matters primarily complaints and I think that the title was Consumer Advisory Officer. I cannot remember the interview but I must have done alright because I got the job. It was the first position of its kind in the London area and there were only one or two others in the country.

I did not realise it at the time, but this was the start of a growing wave of public dissatisfaction with practices and standards in the supply of goods and services which quickly became known as Consumerism.

Most of the complaints fell into a familiar pattern and involved goods or services, with cars and house complaints leading the way. Very often high pressure salesmanship was involved and older people the main complainants. The traditional construction with brick and plaster meant that houses were ill suited to one central source of heating, usually a coal fire where most of the heat went up the chimney. That meant that the people who were selling so called central heating systems for which people paid large sums of money started to knock holes in house walls to allow heated air to circulate on the principle that heat rises. It did not work and it left an unsightly mess behind.

The Citizens Advice Bureau had dealt with complaints prior to this appointment and were very helpful and co-operative both in sharing their experiences and referring complaints. All their people were volunteers.

They were probably pleased to see some Government involvement as it seemed to carry more weight, but there were some unusual situations that I am sure they were happy to get rid of. The person who purchased some "blue films' and complained that they were not blue enough for instance. There was also the situation where the fuel supplied by the Coal Board to a declared smokeless zone was definitely causing smoke. This approved fuel was of course more expensive than ordinary coal which had previously been used. Eventually I met a senior official who admitted that one of their treatment towers was allowing untreated fuel through however he felt that repairs could be done without shutting it down and had no suggestions about the fuel already distributed.

I had heard him out without saying much and he must have thought that he had successfully avoided the embarrassment that this could cause for the Board, but he was certainly not pleased when I set out what I felt should be done if some form of public examination was to be avoided. The treatment tower to be shut down forthwith and not reopened until the treated coal met the smokeless standards, and all the fuel that they had supplied from this tower to be replaced without charge to the householder. A lot of households got a bonus supply of fuel and did not know the reason why. I was to find that preserving confidence in relation to negotiations and the identity of the parties not only facilitated better settlements for the complainants but also encouraged the business side of the equation to be more forthcoming if they had made mistakes. There are those who demand disclosure and in the usual course of dealing with most complaints I would agree, however where there is little likelihood of repetition and it resolves the issue sometimes this is not necessary where the alternative would be lengthy court proceedings with an uncertain result for a disadvantaged consumer.

One feature that I found extremely useful in dealing with quality or endurance matters was the presence of small independent laboratories who could be used to examine textiles or mechanical things and who both parties and I could rely on for an impartial report. There was always the question of who would pay the fees and this generally became the responsibility of the complainant to be picked up by the business if they were adjudged to be in the wrong.

Two unusual complaints owe their resolution to the services supplied by one such laboratory. The first was a complaint from an older couple who had bought an expensive carpet from a large London store with a very good reputation, and shortly after it had been installed the lady started to get alarming symptoms, a burning chest and nose and difficulty in breathing until her doctor told her to move out, when the symptoms diminished. The husband had started to suffer in the same way by the time they came to me because the store who had examined the carpet, were unable to establish the cause. With everybody's permission we took carpet samples, one for the store and one for the test laboratory.

For over a week the laboratory tried different treatments and analyses and were about to admit failure until one afternoon I got an excited call to say that they had found the cause of the trouble. As a last resort they had heated a piece of the carpet and immediately there was some kind of pungent emission which they quickly identified as formaldehyde. It seemed that this was sometimes used in a variety of manufacturing processes, usually as a stiffening agent in women's clothing but it was sometimes incorporated in the treatment of carpet backing or covering. We quickly found that its effect was aggravated in this couple's case because they had underfloor heating. The store were almost as relieved as the complainants and were happy to replace the carpet with one which did not give this kind of trouble. A good illustration of how a responsible business was pleased to identify something which could cause more trouble and which could be prevented.

The next case involved a little detective work on my part because the fashion world had produced something called 'fun fur' which was synthetic and closely imitated mink, fox and other natural furs which of course were much more expensive. These coats were very much in demand by fashion conscious women and one day a young woman brought in one of these furs which had a brown and discoloured area around the collar. The retailer and manufacturer both claimed that it had been exposed to heat and it did have that 'bubbled' appearance which say wool has when it has been overheated.

Back to our faithful test laboratory who after a few days, once again found it difficult to come up with an answer except that heat did not seem to reproduce the same condition. I was on the way to break the news to the complainant , and when I called at her home her mother said that she was still working at the hairdressers down the street. On the way there the mind clicked into gear and when she could talk to me I asked her when she wore the coat, and of course she said " When I go out," so I asked "When do you do your hair." The answer "Just before I go" and then "You do not do anything more to your hair with your coat on?" Then I got the answer I was looking for "Yes I spray some lacquer on."

The following morning I was at the laboratory bright and early with a container of hair lacquer that the young woman used and I just said "Try this!" Lo and behold the synthetic fibre curled up and reproduced the same condition. Then it became a little bit tricky because the retailer did not seem convinced that he should warn his customers about the harmful effects of some common household products, but the manufacturer was much more alive to the danger and potential legal consequences. They looked after the complaint and I suspect only until they could modify the fibre I think they started to include warnings or disclaimers with the garments.

- 125 -

In the course of the wider ramifications of the position, I came into contact with members of the Consumer Council who were interested in improving the legal position of consumers and also people in Government, particularly those who were interested in the work of Weights and Measures Officers who in many parts of England were trying to do the same job that I did in addition to their other responsibilities.

There was going to be a consumer gathering of some kind at Manchester University, and the Borough agreed that I should go but with a strong caution about any expenses incurred. In some of the presentations there were one or two things that surprised me and as a result were easy to remember. The different steps in the process of putting a new product on the market for instance. The market research to see if the public would buy another 'widget' if there were already others available. The advertising and theme to be used, the timing and to my amusement the very last thing of all to be decided was the price ... and that was not determined by the value but by the sector of the market at which it was aimed. Price was something which came under scrutiny several times. The big retailers knew that if they put something on display, for we will say a pound each, sales may be slow. but if they put the same items on display and say 'Sale .......were five pounds each and are now two pounds each while quantities last,' they can probably clear them all in a very short space of time.

One individual gave details of a failed promotion where the advertising theme centered around a cigarette and said that you could not be lonely when you lit one up. The advertising experts had not taken into account that most of the people selling the cigarettes to male buyers would be women who could not resist the obvious "Are you lonely ducky." Scratch one new cigarette brand!

I found myself making some cynical conclusions about the underlying tactics used by business to make the consumer want to buy and specifically those things that a business wanted to sell. As we have seen their plans do not always work, and a quick glance at women's fashions will show that these change almost annually to make women discard the old style and buy the new. It is amusing however, with the arrival of the miniskirt, many women really embraced the new fashion and strongly resisted attempts to change it.

Another fascinating thing about encouraging people to buy came about as a result of what could be called 'The Coventry experience'. When the bombing produced such terrible damage to the City centre during the war, one of the only things which survived unscathed was the 'Rag and Tag Market' and when modern buildings went up around it, the city fathers looked upon it as an eyesore and perhaps dirty and unsanitary. They commissioned a clean up which included better lighting, newer stalls, wider walkways cleaner conditions, and it did not take many weeks after the opening ceremony before the stallholders were making their views very clear to the City that they had lost most of their customers.

Who thought of it? perhaps it was because the old stallholders were demanding their old Market back, I do not know, but it was to have a large effect on future sales strategies, for they started to restore the Market to its original condition a piece at a time and found that they could change everything except the one feature that was essential to make people buy ... the distance between the stalls. Nothing else mattered, but you had to confine the potential customers in a narrow space if you wanted to maintain sales.

This feature you can see every day in stores and markets. The boxes and displays which restrict your movement between the aisles and counters are not put there by accident as the authorities in most areas insist on a minimum distance or clearance between the shelves.

There was quite a formidable lady who headed the Consumer Council Dame Elizabeth Ackroyd I seem to remember. Sitting at lunch before we were both to form part of a panel afterwards, the conversation somehow got a round to education. In view of our backgrounds and schooling, she from girls Private Schools and me from Grammar School, it was perhaps amusing that she espoused the Comprehensive System which strove to provide everyone with the same level of education, and I liked the 'streaming' of the brighter pupils into the Universities and Colleges where they would get the better teachers and feed the cutting edge of research. In any event we became so wrapped up in the argument that they had to send someone for us and we agreed to differ.

Around this time we bought a family sized tent, and our first try at camping was to the south west corner of Wales, a place called Angle. We arrived as night was falling and had to pitch the tent in the centre of the field because all the sites along the hedges had been taken. The reason for this became apparent during the night when it began to rain and blow hard. I got up several times to check the tent pegs and ropes because it seemed likely that the tent would just blow away, but the children slept through it. In the morning there was a vacancy by the hedge and we moved with some relief. An earlier holiday had taken us down the Wye Valley where the river marks the boundary between England and Wales. There were a number of ruined castles which had been built I suppose to prevent the Welsh from raiding. When we looked at the stone walls which were still standing, I tried to make the boys examine the features which had made the old builders choose that spot to build a castle and make it easy to defend. It was nearly always on high ground to provide warning of any approaching enemy and sometimes a side would have a steep bank down to a river or some other natural obstacle. I also tried to make them imagine what life would have been like living between stone walls particularly in winter with straw on the floor, a fire that would produce more smoke than heat and water running down the walls. My own imagination had been stimulated when I saw a suit of armour which had allegedly belonged to Henry The V111 th and which he used to fight in. When someone remarked that he must have been a tremendously strong man the guide said that history characterised Henry as a womaniser and a glutton but that he had been the wrestling champion of all England "and if you don't think his opponents tried too hard, his favourite way to end a bout was to pick the man up and break his back over his knee!" I have never been able to verify those claims but it was very hard to imagine how a man could wear such heavy armour and move about never mind use a sword or some other kind of weapon.

Things were looking up for consumers as in 1966 the U.S. Truth in Packing Law went into effect to spell out the products ingredients on the package.

Local Government is no different from other levels of Government in that politics play a large part in policy and the careers of those in the administration. An election in Brent which was on the horizon promised to bring in a different party who had made their views clear that consumer protection was not necessary and my position therefore was vulnerable to say the least.

When I announced that I was leaving and emigrating to Canada I received a very nice letter from Mr R.S.Forster the Town Clerk who said that in all his Government service he had never received so many letters of appreciation.

# CHAPTER 11

# GO WEST YOUNG MAN

Pat and I had discussed the possibility of emigrating and we began to gather information on those countries which seemed to have the best prospects for a young family. Australia, New Zealand, South Africa were all liberal with details of their Immigration policy and conditions of climate and those factors affecting employment. The country which really was not too helpful and confined its assistance to providing copies of newspapers which had Situations Vacant sections was Canada, and for Canadian conditions you had to go to the offices of the various Provinces.

We only knew two people in Canada, and they were not in a position to help, and we had little contact with relatives in Australia and New Zealand, none at all in South Africa. Australia was aggressively looking for immigrants and for ten pounds you could take your family there, however despite their natural resources there was no getting away from the extreme heat, and the unrest in parts of Asia could mean that their young men might be sent to fight at some time in the future and we had two young sons.

Canada had the same potential resources and although it was extremely difficult to learn much about different areas, any extreme of temperature there would seem to be cold. There was not much likelihood of conscription either, so we started to apply ourselves more seriously, and applied to go. The interview we had was not very encouraging. The policy seemed to be 'find a job in Canada and we will then look at your application.' How did one find a job half way round the world? and how on earth did you start? The letter we got following the interview said much the same thing and triggered that old reflex. They said we couldn't go? so we would find a way to do it!

Our reply letter said that we had resources enough to mean that we would not be a burden to their services and we were prepared to go. Their reaction then was, "You can go but we will not lift a finger to help you!".Then came the nervous waiting for the results of our medicals which eventually were acceptable to them and as we had already decided that I would go ahead to find a job and some accommodation, I had a flight booked on June 1st 1968 to Vancouver and Pat and the family were booked on a flight on July 13th, so I had to find somewhere for them to live by then.

Although I had been out of the country a couple of times, Pat and the family had only really moved around in the south of England, and I suppose that we were all acutely aware that we were going to settle in a part of the world that we really knew nothing about and have to do it without any assistance. Our decision to go to Canada and to British Columbia in particular was influenced by a gentleman named Haydn Hornby who worked in Weights and Measures in Trowbridge, and who had won one of the first Churchill Scholarships. This had taken him on a trip across the United States from east to west and across Canada from west to east studying consumer protection. When I asked him in confidence where the best place in Canada was to live, he thought for a minute and then said "When I travelled across Canada I met two kinds of Canadians ... the ones that lived in British Columbia ... and the ones who wanted to!"

We were to find that although Americans and Canadians are similar in some respects there are significant differences. There had been race riots in the U.S. in the mid sixties. Martin Luther King who probably could be looked upon as the reincarnation of a prophet of old, had given an impassioned speech in 1963 when he declared "all men are created equal" and just before he was killed in 1968 "I have seen the promised Land."

The Air Canada flight was a Boeing 707 I think. It seemed to chase and stay in the sun all the way from Heathrow until we were descending into Vancouver where it was raining. I know I suffered badly with painful ears. It was hard to leave Pat at the airport and I promised that I would phone and get her out earlier if things worked out all right. The reception there seemed to confirm the Canadian attitude in London.  Canadian citizens?......over here. American and other citizens?.........over here. Any Landed Immigrants?......you wait till last! The Immigration Officer did have the grace to say "Sorry its raining on your first day in Canada," so I told him that it had rained on my wedding day and I had never regretted that and I certainly did not intend to regret this.

To begin with I stayed at the Y.M.C.A. in Vancouver and spent every minute trudging around to anywhere that had advertised any kind of a job or where I thought I had some experience to leave an application on their files. Although I did not have any luck, I did find that at most places I was shown in to see a Managing Director or other senior man, and in nearly every case they suggested other places that I could try.

The weather was beautiful and Colin Burgess an old police friend took me up the North Shore Mountains one day, Mount Seymour I think. I wrote to Pat on a daily basis and that day I told her that I had gone from a temperature of 70 degrees in Vancouver and less than half an hour later I was standing in snow.

There was another urgency added to the failure to find employment and that was the regulations applied to taking money out of England. I had to find a Canadian Bank and then apply to have the money transferred which all took time and in the meantime I had to subsist on the money I was allowed to bring which from memory was about fifty pounds. That meant economy which translated eventually into one meal a day on Robson Street at a Chinese restaurant and walking every where. One day I walked from the Y.M.C.A. to Okalla Prison in Burnaby and back again for an interview for prison guard.

Pat and the children were staying with her Mum and Dad in Watford, and it could not have been easy for them wondering if they were going to see each other again. Most of our relatives and friends thought that we were completely mad to move to a new country that we really did not know much about and could not understand why anyone would want to leave England.

Then our luck turned. The money came through from England and I was able to buy a Volkswagen from Cowell Motors in Richmond. I found a job with Dairyland on the Lougheed Highway loading milk trucks on the late shift, and a duplex to rent on Steveston Highway from July 1st. My money had not lasted out and I had moved into a bedroom in Colin and Anne's house in Richmond, bless them, and it was there that Pat and the children stayed for a couple of days, because I had kept my promise and phoned to say get the first flight that you can. I got a telegram on June 24th that said ' Arriving 29th June Flt 2857 E.T.A. 1850 Love Pat.' Their arrival was the best birthday present that a man ever had!

Our cat had been a question mark before I left and we had decided that we should bring her because she was part of the family and there were no real restrictions against it. The difficulty was that the container which Pat had been told was approved for air transport did not suit the airline and her brother David had to race off and get a wicker basket at the last minute. Pat was assured there and again in Toronto that the cat was on the plane, but when she arrived in Vancouver ... no cat. I took them to Colin's and I went back to find that Colin had them searching the manifests of aircraft coming in to see if they listed 'a fur bearing animal.' He had gone out with a baggage handler to an earlier flight with one listed, and the handler had reached down to see if it was a cat and quickly pulled back with a damaged hand because it was an ocelot, well equipped with claws and teeth. The cat finally arrived although she complained loudly all night, but eventually settled down when she recognised the family.

Our stay at Steveston Highway was short because we found a duplex on Odlin Crescent at the north end of Richmond which we liked better, the only drawback being that the planes taking off and landing at Vancouver Airport flew right over the house, making a lot of noise and so low they gave the impression that they were going to suck everything right out of the house. Our early impressions of Canada and British Columbia in particular confirmed Hornby's travellers opinion that it was a wonderful place to live. It was clean, bright and everyone was friendly. During the first few weeks we had picked our own fruit and vegetables in the fields and this led to our first major appliance purchase, a 21 cubic foot freezer which at the turn of the century was still giving yeoman service and still completely full. Some fruits like raspberries, blueberries and black currants came out of the freezer better than they went in and when you saw a good buy in meat it was useful to stock up and then use it as required.

There were open air pools where life guards could be trusted to keep an eye on children leaving you free to shop and come back for them later. They enforced strict rules and children could not go into the deep end or off the diving platform until they had shown the guard that they could swim a breadth.

Richmond had one of the fast food outlets that were beginning to open in some communities with a sign outside giving details of 'the number of people served.' This was McDonald's and in those days the numbers were in the thousands, and the children loved to visit there.

The stores had regular sales and specials and in building up the household anew we took full advantage of them. There were store opening specials which offered toothpaste or other necessities at very attractive prices but there was always a scrum and the limited quantity soon disappeared. Pat's strategy was to position one of us at the appropriate counter with clear instructions what to get and we would then meet at a central spot to examine our 'catch'. That word brings back the memory of the time that my assignment was at a counter which was going to have women's shells or some other iterm which meant a blouse or a jumper.

On the stroke of the hour as the announcement was being made over the P.A. system, a clerk came out of a back room carrying a large box. As he got near to the table and saw the pushing and jostling that was going on he panicked and threw the contents of the box over the heads of the crowd. I focussed on one blouse that was flying through the air and in the fashion of a good football receiver I went up to catch it, only to have a stocky oriental lady who must have started her run a good many yards away, bury her head in my back and deposit me face down on the table. I joined our family meeting in triumph after explaining what had happened. The garment was the right size ... but had a pulled thread so it was all for nothing.

It does serve to remind me that many North American businesses accept the return of goods for a full refund with little or no questions in contrast to the sales practices in Europe.

Loading trucks at Dairyland meant that I had to be there at 6 pm and finished at 2.30 am or 3 am I forget which. I had to get used to driving on the right hand side of the road and on the first night I made sure that I was there in good time however driving home through deserted streets, up the Lougheed Highway, down Boundary and along Marine Drive quite a considerable distance, I came to a stop intending to turn left to Richmond. A bus pulled up beside me and the driver looked down at me and said two words ... the second of which was limey! I had driven all that way on the wrong side of the road and someone must have been looking after me because if I had been involved in an accident it would have certainly been my fault.

The loads consisted mainly of milk cartons in crates, churns and butter in boxes. All of this came down a moving chain in the middle of the platform and you had a large metal hook with a handle to pull off the crates which were piled five or six high. They told me later that a tall man was bound to have difficulty with his back. It was not easy to pick up a 50 lb box of butter and carry it into the truck and throw it up into the upper rack but it was probably hooking underneath the bottom of five or six crates and pulling them across the metal platform, up a ramp and into the truck which caused my back to go.

At meal break I often talked to the man who put everything on the moving railway. He was built like a fireplug and obviously very strong. His interests were the Financial Market where he looked for the price of his stocks and shares every night and he was also a walking dictionary on roses.

The back got me eventually. When the others took a coffee break, I would have to stand somewhere out of sight until the pain eased and it was very difficult to drive the V.W. home because of the driving position. I was determined not to lose the job as it had been so difficult to find. It was Pat who saved me yet again. I used to drive into the carport and get straightened up by the time I got into the bedroom and took my clothes off as quietly as I could but she had watched me walk across from parking the car, and in the dark a quiet voice said "you are going to see the doctor in the morning." He said very simply that if I carried on working and using my back like that, I would be in hospital, so that was the end of that!

After a couple of days I was looking for work again and this time I managed to find it at the fish packing company which is on the Fraser River at Steveston. Canada Packers I think it was called. They used to can salmon and tuna, and process halibut and other ground fish. Although I was only called in where necessary to begin with I was getting a reasonable number of hours . I spent a lot of time standing at the end of a freezing tunnel with a long spatula on the end of a pole freeing fillets of sole or hake on the moving belt so that they fell off the end into a box. That was like standing in the Arctic with a strong wind blowing in your face. The hardest job however was at the end of the machinery which was actually canning the fish and which sent cans down a narrowing chute into a metal tray. With another worker you had to put a stick in the chute when the tray was full, pick up the tray with short metal bars which fitted into slots on the side of the tray and carry it across to a small bogey on wheels which was going to go into the oven, and do all this in time to get back and remove the stick before everything jammed up.

I used to go round the back onto the staging beside the river to smoke during a break and watch the two old gaffers who dealt with the fish coming up from the fishing boat on the river below. The salmon were loaded into a rope net in the hold and then winched up and the loaded net swung over the planking which had two or three hatches with slides underneath. A rope was pulled to open the net and the fish cascaded down at their feet.

They had long poles with a metal piece at the end and they used to catch the gill of the fish, some of them very big ones, and flip it down one of the different hatches open in the deck. All the while they were talking to each other but although all the different species of salmon looked alike to me, they must have been able to identify coho from chinook and so on and the older dog salmon which probably became cat meat.

The tuna came in Canadian Pacific rail cars which were lined with plastic and as the tuna were frozen hard they were not too difficult to handle. We had to get into the car and toss them out into a box on the end of a towmotor driven by a large Korean. This was not too arduous, but if you dropped one on your toe it was painful and if you pulled the wrong one out of the stack they all came down on top of you. Sometimes the ice on the plastic made you an involuntary skater. Pat used to say that she knew when I was three blocks from home because of the smell of my overalls

# CHAPTER 12

## PINKERTONS

I had been looking for a more permanent job and found it with Pinkertons the old Detective Agency but now more involved in providing security for business.

The Company began back in the days of Jesse James and the wild wild west, and as it grew it took some part in battling labour unrest and looking after the security of Government figures, but eventually became a well managed International Organisation that looked after every conceivable facet of private investigation and private and business security. This was reflected in their internal procedures and an insistence that everything was done properly.

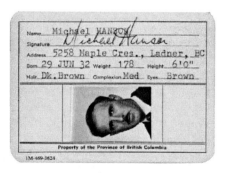

Their office was downtown in Vancouver, and perhaps as a new arrival ... and it showed, the first thing they gave me to do was undercover work. When you need employment you do what you are asked to do, but I confess that kind of work was not to my liking. It did not last for very long because there was an Oil Strike and Refineries were vulnerable targets if striking workers wanted to do some damage, and Pinkertons supplied their uniform security. They put me in charge of that and it meant finding extra guards from somewhere and kitting them out. There was generally a strong background check on new personnel and I maintained this but concentrated mostly on making sure that there had been no brushes with the law. Scheduling was one of the biggest problems and filling holes caused by sickness or what have you. One night I found that one of the guards was languishing in Okalla Prison because he had not paid maintenance arrears, so the following morning I had to get an advance on his wages and take it down there and then drive him to his post.

Some of the guards obviously did not expect to be inspected during the night, which to my mind was probably the most important shift, so I started to go out on night inspections without any prior warning to the Guard Lieutenants or the guards. As a result I found the gate locked at one Refinery which was being guarded by two of our men with dogs, so I climbed over the fence, patted the dogs on their heads and found the guards playing cards in one of the buildings. I fired them despite the shortages. The Oil Companies really look after their employee's welfare, and at one location there were free hot meals dispensed from a machine for night workers and free chocolate bars and cigarettes. I made the guards on night shift turn out their pockets and put their ill gotten gains back again. There were other locations besides Oil Refineries, and here I would ask one of the two Lieutenants to take me round, after giving some notice. It meant of course that everything would be just so but would reinforce the senior man's authority.

There were some interesting features not the least of which was the large snake which students at Simon Fraser University sometimes left out at the weekends and which coiled itself round some of the overhead pipes. The strike took me to Nanaimo where on the whole there were less problems in manpower, and that may have been because the guards were being housed in nice motels and obviously fed very well.

During the Summer of 1969. the Province of British Columbia advertised for a 'consumer position.' I cannot remember exactly how it was described but it fitted very well with my English experience, however there were sometimes restrictions placed on applicants and I was still a Landed Immigrant, not a Canadian Citizen. There had been no similar opportunities when I came to Canada except the Federal Government, and although I had tried through correspondence before and after coming to Canada it was an impossible nut to crack.

Long before I arrived there had been incidents where Canadian businesses openly stated when advertising a position that 'No Englishman need apply.' I could not lay my fingers on the reason although several theories were advanced. At that time the United Kingdom was falling under the power of the Unions particularly Nationalised Industry, and as a result the English workman did not work longer or harder than he had to. If you watched workers on a Canadian building site they were almost running, and sometimes stayed late to finish something without asking for extra pay. The real reason however I suspect was that Canadians are very outgoing, will speak to everyone and are very generous. The insular way that British people are brought up, discourages talking to strangers and makes them keep very much to themselves and this might be perceived as snobbishness by Canadians.

It meant travelling to Victoria in the Summer of 1969 for the interview, and although I had previously taken the ferry to Nanaimo, this has to be one of the nicest and most picturesque short sea trips in the world from Vancouver to Victoria. The Parliament Buildings where the interview was held were an imposing sight, right on the harbour.

There is always nervousness associated with an interview, particularly those that you know may have far reaching effects on your own and your family's future. In this case my old nemesis came to my rescue. A young fellow was being shown out of the room as I came in, and the first thing said to me by the panel of men sitting round the table was " why should you have this job, rather than the young lawyer we have just interviewed?" So I jumped in with both feet and told them that complaint resolution was not generally a matter of black and white, right and wrong. There was usually a bit of both on each side. That meant finding a fair settlement to fit the individual facts. It needed a good knowledge of laws which applied to seller and buyer, but lawyers by their training tended to view things as 'Guilty' or 'Not Guilty". Then I went into the way that lawyers expressed themselves when dealing with people, particularly in writing which was not calculated to encourage concessions but quite the opposite. All in all I had not been particularly full of praise for the legal profession and when I was shown out, the individual who I later learned was Ralph Baker the Personnel Officer, started laughing, something that nettled me I must admit so I asked what was funny? He said "every one in there is a lawyer except me!" So I said something to the effect that "there go my chances then," but he said I shouldn't worry about that. I went away knowing that it would be a little while before they made their decision.

In the meantime the Oil Strike had come to an end and there were two things of note which came up during what were to be my last days with Pinkertons. Apparently there was usually a visit or inspection paid to their guard locations in more remote parts of the Province which had not been done for some time and by deciding that I should do this I will be eternally grateful to them. It gave me a chance to see this beautiful Province and perhaps its early settlement character before some of its towns and cities expanded and at the best time of the year, in October, to see Autumn's impressive colours.

I flew to Prince George and had to walk a few blocks out of the City to the hire car location. Sitting on a corner on a pile of what looked like surveying equipment was a young man who had a promising beard and I suspect that he had just come back from some assignment away from civilization. Beyond there was just bush and trees, giving a foretaste of how cities and towns had developed in such a vast Province.. The car I hired was a Beaumont and I soon got the hang of the automatic. I drove west out of the City and remember turning off at Vanderhoof where the road quickly became gravel which does not seem fair to a new car. There is a trick to riding on these kinds of roads which are prone to 'washboarding' and that is to get the right speed otherwise the continuous bumping will loosen the teeth in your head.

There was a lumber camp near Takla Lake, and it was there I began to appreciate the remote nature of most of the mine and timber camps. The workers there mostly eat and sleep when they are not working because there is no alcohol allowed and they seem to go home very few times a year. The guards have to be on their toes however to defuse arguments and prevent fights which are always likely in that kind of closed environment.

At Fraser Lake there is a big mine producing molybdenum for Endako, and they introduced me to a local resident who took me out in his boat on Fraser Lake itself. It was a small boat with an outboard motor and we trolled with something called a 'willow leaf' but did not catch any trout although there were some bites. The lake is very large and capable of becoming rough when the weather changes quickly as it can on all Interior Lakes.

In traveling along this road from east to west across the northern part of the Province, there was frost most mornings and I noticed that local residents had block heaters on their cars which would be needed later in the winter, and they also had the habit of letting the car warm up in the morning before driving off. The scenery was really spectacular, the oranges and yellows in the trees close to the road with the darker green behind. For miles at one point the railway travels alongside the road and each train seems to be made up of dozens and dozens of cars with different names on including tank cars which would contain chemicals for the pulp mills. There would sometimes be a logging truck piled high with freshly cut logs, some of which had very large cross sections, and in the hills you could see evidence of the areas which had been cut and the lines that were the logging roads. In the rivers there were sometimes 'fish ladders' to ensure that the spawning salmon could get up the river around man made obstructions.

There was a very large lumber camp in the Bulkley Valley, and I slept in one of the accommodation trailers overnight. The Pinkerton Lieutenant there was a very large jolly individual and invited me to the bunkhouse for supper. I know that he had more than one steak and there seemed to be a huge amount of food, but I still heard some loggers arguing because there was only a choice of three kinds of fresh fruit.

The Lieutenant wanted a lift to Prince Rupert and I was happy to oblige him because he could tell me the history of the area as we travelled through. For instance there was a new road at Hazelton and he asked me if I had ever seen a beaver dam. I hadn't of course, so we took the old road and there where a stream crossed over the road at the low side we could see all the sticks piled up in a barrier and the water held behind it. There were some trees with their base two or three feet in water. The road ran through an Indian Reservation and there were dogs lying in the middle of the road which he told me to steer around because they would not move and we would be in serious trouble if we hit one. I was fascinated by the old structures of the farms and farm buildings most of which were made of raw logs which had been trimmed by hand. Many had what were called 'Mansard roofs' which not only gave more space in an upper floor for storage but helped to withstand the heavy snow load. I had been curious about the lack of roof gutters on buildings to begin with until I realised that snow would rip these off very easily

Their way of baling hay was to form a very big roll and in some cases this was left in the fields until needed. There were plenty of horses in evidence in the cleared areas when you broke out of the trees which sometimes lined the road and where you had to watch for wildlife that could wander into the road as an unusual traffic hazard. Deer and bears were quite common whilst the remains of rabbits and racoons testified to their lack of road sense. There is a scene near Hazelton which typifies that part of British Columbia which has been settled and still creates the beautiful scenery that is a feature of the Province and perhaps the rest of Canada. I took a picture of it and perhaps did not capture it as well as the people who create the covers for the B.C. Telephone Directory where it appeared for a year or two.

The coast at Prince Rupert has a more moderate climate than the Interior and as a result gets a lot more rain and snow. It is just a short drive to Kitimat where there was the last Pinkerton location that I inspected. I was due to fly to Alice Arm but when I phoned in my progress they told me to come straight back instead. I was a little relieved when I saw the aircraft that I would have flown in at Prince Rupert Airport because it was a very small plane a Goose or a Beaver which was equipped with floats and did not look as if it could carry more than two or three people.

The other incident that occurred before I left their employ resulted from the murder of a nurse as she was walking home from a late shift at St. Paul's Hospital in Vancouver. She had worked in the Emergency Department and was often late leaving. It caused a stir in the press, giving rise to the question ... were women safe walking alone at night? There had obviously been an approach made by the hospital to Pinkertons because they asked me if I would go to the hospital and talk to the staff about preventing danger from developing. I said that I could do this but the police would have to be asked first and I didn't think there should be any fees or charges. The police had been asked and were not going to supply a speaker and Pinkertons agreed to my going as a public service, so I started off with one of the hospital shifts coming off duty and then did the others as and when they wanted me.

It is a big hospital and there were quite a few people at each session, mostly female of course. I stressed the obvious, to go with company wherever possible and to have your wits about you and not get into elevators with a man on your own, or open the door to your building or car with someone nearby, and if faced with a bad situation... make a lot of noise. The questions that I got were interesting and centered around what some of the Martial Arts students felt was permissible defensive conduct in the circumstances. There was the older lady who from her uniform I took to be a Nursing Sister or some senior nurse, and her question was "can I use a cattle prod.?" I had no idea what that was but fortunately I underlined the doctrine that you can only use as much force as necessary to defend yourself. I later found that it could deliver enough of a shock to stop a charging bull!. When I talked to the trainee nurses at their living quarters I also warned of the dangers of hitchhiking because this was apparently very popular with them, and one girl said "I've hitched dozens of times  ... and nothings ever happened to me," delivered in a very wistful voice. One of the things I did with the older audiences was to ask them to raise their hands if they had been the subject of a street scare or some public indecency, and quite a few hands went up. Then I told them to leave their hands up if they had reported it! There were only one or two that remained raised if at all. I pointed out that in not reporting such incidents they might be condemning very young girls to similar treatment or worse, who did not know how to look after themselves. I always got a laugh when I told them that I did not want my talks to produce a rash of male patients in Emergency whose only mistake was to be on the street with a girl alone at night.

As a sequel, during one of my last visits, one of the Administrators asked to see me to thank me, and as a matter of interest I asked if the police had managed to interview all the men who came into Emergency that night because there had been another scare at the hospital a short while afterwards. He said as far as he knew they had not asked for the records.

# CHAPTER 13

# GOVERNMENT OF BRITISH COLUMBIA

The Government interview had taken place in the summer and as we got into October and November, Pat was trying to prepare me for the disappointment that a 'position filled' letter would mean. I cannot remember when exactly but she called me at work, something that did not happen except in emergency, and said that she had received a letter from Victoria and said 'Can you guess what it says?" and I said "Yes. I got the job," which was big headed I know and she told me so, but I had never given up hope. Ironically we had contracted to have a house built in Delta at a place called Maple Crescent by a firm who were German masons whose expertise was brickwork. I had to see them one day and found them starting a chimney in a nearby sub-division. One of the fellows went to the corner of the house which already had the roof on and said "Watch this!" He put his shoulder to the corner and pushed and you could see the house move. He told me that the chimney would be the main thing holding the house up when it was finished.

We had moved in to our new house and I had hung the last picture on the wall the night before we got the letter which meant a move to Vancouver Island. The Personnel Department had asked me to let them know when I could start and it resolved something which had been on my mind. I was on a kind of Management Programme at Pinkertons and this meant that you shared in the profitability of the office in some way by receiving a bonus at the end of the year. By telling the Government the 1st of December and also telling Pinkertons that I would be leaving, relieved my conscience a little because they had been good to me.

Management asked me to suggest my replacement, and there was another British lad Martin Parker who had not been with them long who could do it, and I said so. A little while later he came to see me to say that they had offered him the position and was quite worried for he felt that one or more of the Field Supervisors would resign because they would expect to get the job,

."What do I do?" I knew he was probably right so the advice that I gave him was that if this happened and he was threatened with a resignation, he should see the individual in his office, fetch a pad of paper and pen and tell him to write out his resignation and leave it on the desk and then get up and leave. My reasoning was that any discussion was superfluous if he had made up his mind to resign. By doing it this way you did not give in to some form of blackmail, if he really intended to stay. If there was no resignation he should make a point of going out with each Supervisor on inspection preferably at night and listen to their beefs and compliment them on the guards turnout. When I saw him a few weeks later he was full of smiles and it had transpired much as we had anticipated and the individual was still on the job.

Before we left the Mainland I started to give Pat driving lessons because although there are bus services, all the travel is by car. Putting our earlier English experiences behind us we found that the Volkswagen had a clutch that was much more forgiving and it was almost impossible to stall the engine. The test which I had taken shortly after arrival, required to turn my English Driving Licence into a British Columbia one had seen the examiner critical of lane changes and use of the mirror, so apart from general driving skills with a manual gear box, these were the things that I stressed. Pat went for her test and we remembered on the way there that we had not practiced parallel parking but it was too late to worry about it then. When she came back it took a little while to establish that she had passed because she was so indignant about something the tester had said. From then on she was on her way without any anxiety apart from one hair raising time when she drove us all from Steveston Highway onto the freeway connecting Canada and the U.S.A. into very fast moving traffic which flashed its lights and swerved with a lot of horn blowing.

Because there had not been a position or individual identified with Consumer Affairs in British Columbia before, I did not know what to expect, and I suspect the Government did not know either. There was a Press Release issued by the then Attorney General, Lesley Peterson.Q.C. in December announcing the appointment with a short biography which brought a certain amount of publicity in newspapers throughout the Province in January and February and Jim Ryan one of the well known photographers and a real character took my picture in one of the offices looking suitably solemn. This appeared in The Colonist of January 7th, 1970.

The salary that I received to begin with was $674 per month and to us this was eminently satisfactory in view of the cost of living at that time.

I could be forgiven for thinking that some of the Attorney General's people did not welcome the new appointment because my first 'office' was a desk in a corridor. I was to become the responsibility of Mel Smith who was there for any questions that I might have and who was a very good individual. He seemed to be the in house authority on the Consumer Protection Act, which had been introduced in 1968 about the only tool that I had to work with and which gave a three day cooling off period for itinerant sales but only those which took place at a persons home, specified the factors which had to appear in an advertisement which mentioned credit, including the cash price, and then or later tried to deal with referral selling.

There were highs and lows in those early days. I was commuting back and forwards between Victoria and the Mainland so it was almost like the police days when I did not see much of Pat and the family and there was the anxiety of selling the house without taking a loss. I did manage to get over there during the week sometimes because in those early days many people including the Consumer Association and media types wanted to speak to the new Consumer Affairs Officer. The weather at that time of the year is always uncertain and can give rise to strong winds around the coast, so sometimes the ferry would move about during the crossing and there were loud booms and a shudder through the boat when it hit big waves. On occasion Pat would be waiting for me at Tsawassen when shingle had been thrown over the causeway which leads to the ferry dock. There were bright calm days as well and then I used to really look forward to sitting up top at the front at the horseshoe bar and having breakfast while reading the paper and watching the really beautiful scenery that is one of the benefits of living in this wonderful part of the world.

One of the lows was the hotel that I lived in for a while behind the Legislature and which was mainly populated by very old people and reflected the fact. There was a Television Room downstairs which was always full and if I ventured to suggest a change of channel their combined heads would turn and they said 'Seen it!' Luckily Tom and Lilian took me in as a short term lodger until we could get settled and they were much more convivial surroundings.

One of the highs was bringing Pat and the family to the Island for the first time and their reaction to the scenery and surroundings. We found a new house in Colwood on Marlene Drive close to Royal Colwood Golf Course at about the same time that we sold the house in Delta and moved as a family to the Island on May 1st 1970.

The house was new and we rolled our sleeves up to tackle the brush in the back garden which consisted mainly of broom which is very tenacious and difficult to remove. After some weeks of this we contacted a man with a rototiller and he went all over it chopping up everything so easily. It did reveal however that there were lots of pebbles, some of them very large ones which had to be picked up and barrowed to the bottom of the garden where there was a disused railway line.

There was a car port at the side of the house, the upper part of which was a sun deck and we had really nice summer weather in the years that we were there. One of our first things to buy was a picnic table kit consisting mainly of two by four cedar lengths, which we put together with the help of a drawing and that table saw a lot of use. The children used to enjoy sleeping out there sometimes so that they could see shooting stars.

The only Legislation that could be said to confer any rights or protection on the British Columbia consumer, was the Consumer Protection Act mentioned earlier, which came into force in 1968. it gave a three day cooling off period for door to door sales, and if credit terms formed part of an advertisement then all the components had to be included with the cash price. This Statute also spelled out the right of a consumer to pay out a credit contract before full term. It eventually required the terms of any guarantee to be stated in contracts over the value of $50 and this dollar limit applied to most of the Act's provisions. To come were also provisions to discourage the supply of unsolicited goods or credit cards, redress against a third party Financing Agency for any defects in the sale by the retailer, an ability on the part of a Judge to find the cost of borrowing excessive or harsh and unconscionable and to re-open the transaction. The provisions which were the most useful to Consumers were set out in the Victoria Times of May 16th. 1973. This article also referred to some other Legislation which benefited the consumer although most but not all was not in force when I started work for the Provincial Government. There was for instance the Small Claims Court which was meant to deal with small civil disputes. Here it was one thing to win a Judgement and quite another to collect!

There was a Sale of Goods Act which when amended contained an implicit requirement that the seller had the right to sell the goods. It did not allow a Manufacturers warranty to be substituted for the old law that goods would perform as claimed and would be fit for the purpose to be used. It was modelled almost completely on the old English Law. The Statute which ultimately levelled the playing field for consumers was The Trade Practices Act similar to Legislation enacted in several Australian States and also in most of the American States.

There were some Statutes that I did not have very much to do with but which were amended to include provisions which specifically affected consumers. The Bill of Sales Act allowed someone to sue for the return of goods or the amount owing on the contract....but not both!. The Energy Act dealt with the cost of Oil Company promotions which they required the retailer and ultimately the consumer to pay. The Landlord and Tenant Act had important provisions for renters, the Debt Collection Act made it an offence to harass borrowers and the Conditional Sales Act sought to discourage sweetheart deals.

Some Legislation was introduced to deal with a very specific area. The Fair Sales Practices Act for instance was meant to stop pyramid sales, where you parted with a fairly hefty sum for the dubious privilege of recruiting others who would pay you and the person who recruited you. If you got in at the start then you could recover your outlay and more but after one or two levels the whole scheme foundered under its own weight of numbers and people lost their money. The Statute placed limits on recruitment until you had reached a certain volume of sales and included a buy back provision for stock.

The Hearing Aid Regulation Act was introduced to licence Hearing Aid Dealers and attach some supervision to the sale of hearing aids. I was to become intimately involved in this area as you will see later. So bearing in mind that a good deal of the 'protection' which I have listed was not in force, I had to try to resolve the consumer complaints which came in by phone and letter. I would not contact a retailer or supplier unless I had the written details and once again complaints about the sale and repair of vehicles were at the head of the queue. Although serious to the complainant and retailer they could promote humour in a third party.

In my first Annual Report I referred to a three page letter written by a disgruntled car purchaser. The new and expensive vehicle manifested strange symptoms after its new owner claimed that he saw a mechanic drop a large wrench in the engine compartment during a service. Some electrical components stopped working and when he selected a forward gear the backup lights came on., he filled three pages in itemising his problems Another dear lady who lived on one of the Islands, Salt Spring I think, was trying to come to see me but was delayed because "her pistons were loose." That first year I dealt with 650 complaints which resulted in cash refunds or account adjustments to the tune of $27,000. About one third of the complaints were not justified and I dispelled the popular belief that if you did not like a particular item you had the right to return it and get a refund. True some retailers made this part of their sales guarantee but in other cases there was no requirement on the part of the seller to accept a return if there was nothing wrong with an items quality or condition.

I was getting to know my new colleagues and they had a very practical habit of all coming together at one time in the morning for coffee which everyone took turns at making. The conversation not only centered around world and local news, but other topics involved cases that were being worked on and happenings within the Government. As the Deputy Attorney Genera,l Dr Gilbert Kennedy, sometimes came in and it was useful to sit back and use ones ears. There was a feature of the Department which gave an insight into policy and that was the extra copy of all correspondence which was put into a folder and circulated to everyone. You read it, signed the traffic slip and passed it on. It did provide some unwanted flare ups for me. A senior lawyer came up to me in quite a rage waving one of the copies, which was a letter that I had written to a complainant who wanted me to make a retailer sell him an item at the price that had appeared in an advertisement and where there had been a price error. I tried to explain that price displays or advertisements had always been regarded as 'an invitation to treat' and a contract did not arise until the buyer offered to buy at a certain price and the offer was accepted. I disengaged as tactfully as possible and went to find Mel Smith to explain the problem. He gave me a look, searched through the shelves of reported cases on the shelves and came back with one open at a page which supported my argument. I asked him what I should do, and he told me to leave it with him. I didn't hear any more about that particular matter but I did hear that one of the lawyers who had also been reading the copies, had been heard to remark "He's giving legal opinions and he isn't a lawyer ... besides the Department never gives legal opinions!"

The actual Government grade that applied to my position was Administrative Officer, and there was another A.O. in the Department, Arthur Knox, who handled a lot of the correspondence complaining about police or the courts. He had retired from the Royal Canadian Mounted Police and talked about times before they policed the Province when it had been the old British Columbia Police. He had the expected outward cynical and sarcastic attitude that you expected from an old policeman but when we had the Christmas Party he showed me some welcome consideration by quietly paying my share, realising that without a pay cheque it would have been difficult for me.... a heart of gold.

One of the early cases saw me benefit from some of my old Brent experiences, because it was an unusual story of an expensive boat with an aluminum hull which had ben taken into a Marina for routine maintenance and had subsequently developed pin hole leaks in the hull. The complainant had apparently seen the boat in the yard being painted with some anti fouling paint which the workman had rubbed off and began using one with a different colour, so in his eyes this was what had caused the leaks. By the time I became involved the two sides were firmly dug in and trading insults, so I got them to agree to allow a Marine Architect to examine the boat to see what his conclusions were.  The results were surprising, and expanded the little nautical knowledge that I had. It seems that sea water being slightly saline is a very good conductor of electricity, and as there is always stray electricity around, metal objects in sea water corrode and deteriorate very quickly. The way this is slowed or even prevented is by putting a lump of zinc on the boat generally on the motor. this acts as an anode and attracts the electricity to it so that the zinc is eaten away and not the surrounding metal. This was missing from the boat, should have been noticed during routine maintenance and could be taken to have caused the problem. Now came the potentially difficult task of finding a settlement and this eventually took the form of the Marina  sending the boat back to the Manufacturer for a new hull and the complainant would pay the cost of the transport. This is a common feature of warranties and this boat was well outside the warranty period. As a goodwill gesture the Marina also overhauled the engine as it had stood without use for a long time.

On the day that the boat with its new hull was going to be handed over I asked my secretary to draw up a simple statement to be signed by the complainant saying that this would mean a 'Full and final settlement of the matter.' At the dockside I met the complainant and his wife and the owner of the Marina, but if I thought it was going to end with smiles and handshakes I was mistaken. Before I had even produced my final settlement notice the complainant was heard to say loudly "But what if they put used parts in the engine?" I asked if I could use an office and I took the complainant and his wife in there and with my own feelings barely under control I explained that in my view they had been dealt with more than fairly, a hull replacement was very costly and if the case ever came to court I would say so!. I left the final settlement on the table, told them to come and see me when they had discussed it but I would not expect the Marina to give up possession of the boat until it was signed in view of the expense this had caused them. A few minutes later the complainants wife gave me the signed copies, thanked me I think sincerely   and after the engine started sweetly, off they went.

There were some marketing schemes and unscrupulous operators who took advantage of older people in particular, and some sales techniques which were distinctly misleading.

It was hard to resist the approach of a young teenager who claimed to be in some form of competition or other such plan which meant signing up a certain number of households in order to go to University, when  he or she was actually a member of a travelling sales crew brought into the Province to canvass a particular area for a company selling magazine subscriptions and they disappeared soon afterwards. There was little or no mention of magazines or the companies name in the sales pitch and the contract was almost immediately sold to a Finance Company.

Similarly the flyer which said that you had won a prize if you scratched a circle or lifted a tab and a certain number appeared. Of course the number always did appear and you looked at some really inviting prizes only to be given a very persuasive sales pitch for a vacuum cleaner and if you were able to withstand this the prize would eventually prove to be a set of barbecue tools or something similar.

A much more serious sales technique both in terms of the misery that it caused and its financial impact on the older population was the sale of aluminum siding. It was easy to persuade older people that their old house would need little maintenance once the siding was installed and to get them to sign a contract which was a virtual mortgage and meant that they would lose their home if they did not keep up the high payments, which was very often impossible on a fixed income.

Some so called builders travelled around claiming that the roof needed repair or that there were serious drainage problems developing and used similar contracts, however in their case the added insult was that as they did not have proper skills, more work needed to be done by a genuine tradesman and they either had paid or continued to pay for the first after they had disappeared.

A feature of all these schemes was the ability of the repairing company to sell the contract at a discount to a Finance Company who would aggressively pursue the homeowner to ensure payment.Very little sentiment entered into these cases on the part of the salesman or the method that was sometimes used to snare the victim. Bible salesmen would scan the obituaries and visit a widow or widower with a claim that the deceased had ordered or was about to order an expensive bible and hardly ever failed to make a sale using this technique.

The Managers of the Better Business Bureaux in Vancouver and Victoria, Vince Forbes and Bill Tindall respectively, were always on top of any new plan or scheme which was going to mislead consumers and had access to the media to alert people to the details and sometimes describe old ones as well This used to infuriate the companies concerned and Vince Forbes the Vancouver manager was always being sued as a result of this, but he was completely unrepentant and impossible to frighten or warn off. It became obvious early on that members of the A.G.'s Department did not enjoy publicity and confined their contact to the outside world to Press Releases prepared by professionals to ensure that there was not anything which could be considered actionable and as a result confined themselves rigidly to the subject. They did not seem to have any objection however to me making appearances as a speaker at Consumer Groups and trade gatherings, and as my speech making previously  had just been the school competition, the prospect of large and perhaps hostile audiences was the kind of thing that could keep you awake at night.

I found very quickly however that I performed better without a formal speech to read and just jotted down some old detective shorthand for the important points that I wanted to bring up and which suited that particular group. These were usually members of Consumer Groups or people who had an interest in Consumer Education or dispute resolution and there were a number of panels or meetings where I would sometimes be joined on the platform by the Better Business Bureau and the leading lights from Trade Associations to talk about complaint handling and how to avoid trouble. The University of British Columbia was a popular venue. These sessions had interesting Titles like 'Consumers in a changing Society' and 'Consumers Count'. The interesting part for me, as it had been when doing the hospital talks was the questions which followed the speakers, many of which described the individuals own horror story. There was one individual who complained about the Automotive Industry practice of advertising a new vehicle at what seemed to be an attractive low price and then many things which were called extras pushed up the price alarmingly. In the case he cited the wheels on a truck were classified as extras and he claimed with some justification that you expected a truck to have wheels on it. The tactic of attracting a potential buyer with a tempting low price and ensuring that he or she eventually paid a much higher price was very much in use in some trade areas. The buyer would be told that "The last one has just gone" and shown a more expensive model, or there would prove to be severe drawbacks to the advertised item but many advantages to the model at the higher price. This method was called quite appropriately 'bait and switch.' Public speaking did mean however that you had to be quick on your feet, not ashamed to say that you did not know the answer but would look into it, and careful with the ones who had their own political agenda for whom the legislation was not strong enough or alternately where consumer protection was an intrusion into seller buyer relationships .

In one sense the claims that stronger legislation was needed were right although it could not be admitted, for Australia and some of the American States had fairly new legislation which dealt with misleading and unconscionable trade practices  and gave suitable remedies, but the political climate was not right for that in British Columbia where the familiar words from lawyers even some in the Attorney Generals Office were " Why protect a fool from his own folly."

I had tried very hard to convince them and the Crown Prosecutors that I sometimes talked to, that some of the sales tactics bordered upon fraud, but they had grown up with the police approach, which conveniently labeled all complaints against businesses as 'bad business practices' and immediately forgot about them. It was clear however that both the Consumers Association nationally and particularly a very active group on the North Shore led by Ruth Lotzkar and Ada Brown were well aware of the Australian and U.S. developments and began to press for change here.

One of the first speaking invitations that was accepted on my behalf was to talk to this Consumer Group in North Vancouver and it promised to be a lively affair because the fair sex once they put their mind to something do not take no for an answer and these were two very determined ladies. It was a very useful meeting and well covered press wise before and after, and this is how I found a couple waiting to see me after I had dealt with a queue of people when I  stepped off the platform. The lady said "You don't remember me do you?" and of course I didn't. "Think back to 1953" which I did quickly and considered a cause for anxiety because it was the end of my R.A.F. Service and the beginning of my Police Service. I had not met Pat then and the gentleman with her was obviously her husband. She finally took mercy on my floundering and said that she was Mary Holder that was, and had been in my Metropolitan Police training class at Peel House, had seen the local write up with the name and Metropolitan Police mentioned and had come to see if it was me. I seem to remember that she had a family but I cannot remember what brought them to Canada. The irony of the situation however was that she said that she had written on the back of a class photo 'We'll meet again one day!.'Fate has some quite unexpected surprises sometimes.

The ultimate test of being able to think on my feet and perhaps to deal with some hostility was the first Radio Hot Line Show. I remember that I had to travel to Gas Town in Vancouver to the studio and I think the Station was C.K.W.X. In any event the morning host had been the celebrated Jack Webster and I was to go on with his side kick who at the time I think was a chap named Finlay. Coming out of the studio as I went in were the B.C. Lions football player Jimmy Young and the Sports Columnist who had just written a book about him, Jim Taylor. Webster was on his own and said with the growl that was meant to intimidate "You are Hanson are you..." and then went on to make a disparaging remark about Englishmen because as everyone knew Webster was a Scot. So I made an equally disparaging remark about Scotsmen and a fairly risqué joke to underline it and after that we seemed to get on fine.

Someone who worked with him on a daily basis told me that despite his gruff character projected in his programme, he was really a softie and would put his hand in his pocket for someone in genuine need. He was very astute and as a result of a previous career in journalism and some years of fielding unexpected questions on radio, he was seldom caught out. I saw this when I attended a meeting of North American Automotive Dealers and he was to be the feature speaker. After he had been introduced one of their members told the meeting that he had recorded Jack's programme for a number of weeks without his knowledge and had brought some choice clips which he played to the audience. They were comments about politicians or responses to irritating callers which were meant to be unflattering, and of course they gave him no warning in advance that they were going to do this. That was a very big mistake on their part! Jack started off by saying that the dealers thought that he considered them to be at the bottom of the social scale. He said "You are next to the bottom, anyone who knows me knows that I consider the lawyers to be the lowest!" From there he proceeded to tear into them and had them laughing whilst he did it.

It is hard to explain the feeling that you get sitting in a studio with no idea of the questions that will come in on the phone lines and knowing that any slip of the tongue will be heard by thousands, so you sweat a little and try not to show it. One of the early questions  did the trick however because a rather belligerent voice asked "why a good Canadian had not got the job rather than me?"

In those days I suppose my accent was more marked than it is now. So I just said "Probably because there was not one who had enough experience," to the amusement of the Talk Show host. A little later a caller asked "How much is the Province paying you?" and before I could reply he broke for a commercial but was still taking calls and the next caller said "Tell him that you will give your salary if he will give his." So I asked the host to leave the caller on and with real laughter he said as we started again "Mr. Hanson wants the next caller to put his question." So the caller made the suggestion and the host said he wouldn't disclose his own salary. "You are really not going to tell the listeners what you earn?" and I said "No if they want to know they can read it in the Public Accounts." However there were a number of good questions,which allowed me to preach a good deal of consumer common sense,....... read the contract  ... talk to friends or children before signing ... buy the car subject to a satisfactory inspection etc. You always remember the down side however and there was obviously still some resentment against people from the United Kingdom.

The radio shows that I did after that were mainly in the Interior and the callers there did not display the same resentment and all in all they were much more like the traditional Canadian, very generous and hospitable, willing to accept anybody and go out of their way to help them.Then came television and although this was mostly local television with a limited audience it was more scary than radio because you not only had to worry about a slip of the tongue but also any facial hesitation or mannerism that would be instantly broadcast and could not be recovered. In this though I was not the only guest as a rule for the Federal Government were invited because they had Statutes which could be said to confer consumer protection on a National basis. They used to show up with easels and graphs but to my  internal amusement would hardly ever answer a question and it fell to me with the one Provincial Statute to do this. In fairness the field did fall within Provincial Jurisdiction under the British North America Act, but I always wondered if the viewing audience noticed.

I somehow felt that Consumerism was not always welcomed by the Attorney Generals Department. I was supposed to share a secretary with another individual and had told her that I did not mind if she did his work provided she did mine first. This did not sit well with the Department but in view of the files and letters the work was producing Karen quickly became my secretary in fact, although nothing was said to confirm it. I was to say wholeheartedly later that behind any successful man there is a good woman whether it is his wife or secretary and he had better realise that he would not have got anywhere without them!

If I wanted confirmation of the way my appointment was being viewed the Deputy Attorney General once said that he considered Consumer Affairs a bottomless pit into which to pour money. Not exactly fair as there was only me. When the Regional Prosecution Counsels held their meeting in Vancouver the Criminal Law side of the Department set it up and generally everybody went. They flew or took the ferry. Because it was the last minute I was told if I wanted to go I would have to go in the R.C.M.P. plane. This turned out to be a Goose or a Beaver or similar small plane. In any event I sat shoulder to shoulder with an R.C.M.P. Constable and his handcuffed prisoner in the only small passenger space available. Crown Counsel were derisory about my arguments to treat some of the really bad consumer sales techniques as fraud, but at least I had an opportunity to put the argument and perhaps start some of them thinking. They still used to trot out the old 'Should not protect a fool from his own folly' but how this applied to old unsophisticated people I could never understand.

I began to think that the Department were practising the same theory as Canadian Immigration, make you climb over as many hurdles and barriers as they could to see if you could get there ... and stay! I had heard and seen some concern expressed by Government Ministers about the growth and spread of credit cards. Although the Banks claimed that these were only issued to credit worthy customers and upright citizens, a man in Toronto had sent up for one for his dog ....and had got it! Mel Smith who had always been supportive asked me to write something which could go into the Consumer Protection Act which would deal with the cards which were being sent whether you asked for them or not, in other words unsolicited cards... and that is what I called them. It is one thing to say you can't do something and quite another to make sure that you don't. There was some precedent for it so I wrote a simple section that said if you used an unsolicited card, that being one that you had not requested in writing you would not have to pay for the purchase ... and threw in a bonus of my own and applied it to unsolicited goods ... the Bible situation and others. I gave this to Mel and heard nothing more for a few weeks until it landed back on my desk covered in blue and red and totally different from the original. Mel was on holiday and when he got back I took this to him and he just smiled and said "This has been done by Caucus, you don't know who asked for this do you?" When the amendment was introduced it was just about exactly the way I had written it including unsolicited goods. Without anything to actually confirm it the rumours would seem to lend support to the theory that the Premier had wanted this and if that was so it didn't matter what anyone else said!

At some stage I moved to an office in the corridor behind the Legislative Chamber, which I think really belonged to the Speaker or the Master at Arms. At the same time I inherited a coat stand which was as twisted as the old Chesterfield Church spire and which was to stay with me through the moves which took place afterwards. It was relatively easy to slip into the House and sit up in the Public Gallery to watch the give and take of Provincial politics. The time to be there however is when your Department Estimates come up and may be debated and when the financial people and the Deputy Minister are sitting close to the Minister to hand him material if any particular item comes under attack. Barbs and insults are common and usually from the Opposition, but it was the Government Minister Without Portfolio from the Okanagan who raised some criticism and that had obviously got wind of the enquiries that I had been making about milk prices which fluctuated quite a bit depending on where you lived and could not always be explained by supply and demand. Fortunately her comments did not require an answer and could be construed as 'I hope that meddlesome Civil Servant does not encourage American producers to try to sell their milk in British Columbia.' Most agricultural products were controlled by Marketing Boards  and there had been a lot of debate by Consumer Groups about whether their  influence on prices was a good thing for consumers. The price of milk in the States was of course a lot cheaper.

Each manufacturing, retail, or service group had its own individual who maintained contact with Government at the Federal and Provincial level. Although the main reason for  these contacts was to find out if Government was up to anything which would affect their group's interests and to sometimes try to mitigate the effect of any criticism that might be directed at them, it was by no means a one way street for they were very useful if you had a question about general industry practices like warranties and to use as a sounding board. In some measure they acted like the postman who keeps you up to date with happenings in the district,........ who has got promotion and who is ill for instance throughout the whole of Canada.  It certainly helped me to learn quickly about some trade areas and the people that I met and talked to like Tom Caporale in the Finance Company sector and Ray Morris in Automobile manufacturing and retailing were always perfect gentlemen and never took any unfair advantages which might have resulted, to benefit their own company rather than the group they represented. Many of the complaints of the day seemed to have their origin in consumer credit and the ease with which prospective buyers or borrowers could get credit without understanding the full price that they were paying or their inability to make the payments. It may seem counter productive to advance credit knowing that there was a good possibility that the consumer would or could not repay, but remember the old house owners and the mortgage as security for payment of the siding installation?.

There were also situations where a new car would be security for its credit purchase and when the buyer defaulted the car would be seized and the buyer sued for the balance plus a host of fees and expenses.  If the car was resold at a suspiciously low price the balance was still high and a friend got a practically new car for next to nothing, known in the trade as a 'sweetheart deal.'

I confess that it was sometimes hard to keep my temper. A lady on the Island came in with a complaint about the collection tactics of a Finance Company. She did not have the ability to pay anything because of changed family or employment reasons, so the Company put her to work in their offices as a cleaner paying her an extremely low wage of $40 a month which she never completely received because $26 of it went towards the debt. Two men from their Office came to see me and confirmed the circumstances and were completely unapologetic until I asked them what the reaction would be if the case received some publicity. That changed things in a hurry but as they left the office one said "You realise Mr. Hanson that she will lose her job." It was tempting to speed them on their way a little.

In the early seventies Consumer Protection was becoming a household word and getting more media coverage and therefore more Government interest in the United States and Canada. Federal Provincial Conferences were held and as these moved from Province to Province it was a wonderful opportunity for me to see all the regions of Canada including the Capital. Each Province treated its visitors to some of its local history and tried to outdo everyone else with its own hospitality. I confess that I found that I enjoyed my visits to the Maritime Provinces the most, particularly Newfoundland and Prince Edward Island. There was a genuine down to earth quality about them that you had to respond to. Where the officials from the other Provinces would attend in suits and ties the Maritimers were more at home in open necked shirts and sweaters, and the drive in Prince Edward Island stopped at little townships during their Lobster Festival and you got a box with a freshly cooked lobster, a doorstep of bread with butter and a little cole slaw for a dollar. In one of those Provinces immediately before flying back we had a tour of a Lobster Processing Plant where they keep the lobsters in large tanks of sea water until they needed them. At the little shop I bought six containers of 'pieces' and when I got them back home Pat decreed that they would have to be eaten fairly quickly, not a hardship I can assure you, dipped in melted butter.

The Newfoundland representative Bob Barter was round, animated and we got on very well together. He had always asked me for a British Columbia lapel pin as he collected them and when we hosted the meeting I asked that a pin be put with the pencils, pads and other materials on every Province's place except Newfoundland. He arrived a little late and I saw his eyes looking frantically here and there. When I opened the meeting I said "Before we begin I have a very pleasant duty to perform," and walked around the table to his spot, asked him to stand up and pinned on a really nice B.C. Centennial pin which David Nicholls had found for me and Bob just radiated pleasure.

At the time that Toronto Airport put a second terminal into use it nearly always meant a big change there for passengers flying to the east coast and the luggage always got lost or delayed. Although we generally attended the meetings in suits and ties it was more comfortable to travel in more comfortable clothing. So when we all arrived in St. Johns without luggage it was not expected to present much of a problem provided it got there that evening, although one of the ladies was heard to ask "but what about my pills." It did not arrive and I remember us queuing for the only razor that a lawyer from Saskatchewan had brought or managed to acquire. As we sat around the table in our jeans and open neck shirts the locals did not miss the chance to have a little fun at our expense.

It is almost a National sport to tell Newfoundland jokes which characterize them as simpletons, however the best Newfoundland jokes I have ever heard have nearly always been told by Newfies themselves.

The Federal Government owed most of its presence in the field to the Combines Investigation Act and would have dearly loved to claim more credit for championing the consumer cause but the main powers were in Provincial hands if they chose to use them although these were limited to within the Province and vulnerable to marauding sales practices from other Provinces or outside the country.

On one occasion we prompted our Minister to ask the Federal Minister, Ron Basford about an Investigation that Combines had been carrying out for a long time into a National promotion. The Federal Minister replied with some agitation that he could not get the Director to tell him what was going on in that investigation or indeed any investigation!

One of the officials from Manitoba had made it a crusade to have a popular magazine acknowledge that a lady who ostensibly wrote to you to say your subscription was out of date or on similar subjects did not in fact exist. The twists and turns of this correspondence which were faithfully reported at each meeting, had us in stitches sometimes.

Cheryl with a tritribute to chicken manure

Our garden in Colwood was beginning to take shape and we were fortunate to visit a 'U pick' raspberry field where the owner said "Pick plenty because tomorrow the equipment is going to move in to clear the canes for housing." We asked if we could take some canes for our garden " As many as you like " was the answer.

These were Willamettes and very good raspberries so we edged the whole of one neighbour's back garden on our side with them. Raspberries and some of the other berries come out of a freezer almost as good as they go in. .A farmer named Volk had chickens in Metchosin and I would take the boys and clean out some of the chicken sheds in exchange for a truck full of chicken manure. The truck was much like a boat because you had to correct any steering movement quickly as it took some time to take effect. It produced an unforeseen difficulty when I drove it underneath the sundeck to offload the manure in the back garden and could'nt get back under the sundeck without letting air out of the tyres.

Another laugh at my expense was when we decided to remove a scrub oak tree, and I had some idea that the roots extended out to the ends of the branches. I dug three deep circles around the tree before finding that the roots were almost vertical underneath.

There were two other early speaking engagements which were noteworthy. I was asked to speak to a teachers group in Prince George in November or December I think because I went up there expecting cold weather. Imagine my surprise when I was greeted at the airport by a young woman in a short dress and high heels although she did have a warm coat on. Outside I followed her as she clambered over the snow drifts on either side of the road and we arrived at a sports car which had more than its share of dents and scrapes. As we were driving I must have made some unfortunate comment because she said indignantly "I race this car" and went on to describe how they put hay bales on a frozen lake and raced around them. She said, "There was a bit of excitement last week  ... the grader driver clearing the course went through the ice!"

An interesting piece of information I learned on that trip was that the teaching complement in Prince George changed about 50% of its members each year.

I also began to appreciate the way in which Interior communities dealt with isolation that the winter months could sometimes bring. They organised lots of communal gatherings like dances, plays and sporting events with the help of the schools and women's groups and one way or another maintained contact with everybody however isolated their house or farm. It produced a very strong community spirit.

The other invitation was right on the doorstep to talk to the Victoria Chamber of Commerce during 'Victorian Days.' This was another situation not prescribed for the faint hearted because it was at the Empress Hotel and all the leading lights were there including the Mayor Peter Pollen who was directing the proceedings .......and everyone seemed to be in Victorian dress which I suppose I should have anticipated. He introduced me which gave me time to recover a little, and said "Before we begin Mr. Hanson...." and he waved at a lass who was dressed as a maid including the mob cap and who had a tray of lovely red buttonhole roses one of which she pinned on my lapel. I started by saying "That was a very nice gesture Mr. Mayor ......but it is the wrong colour rose." There was a kind of stunned silence except for a hearty bellow of laughter from the back of the room and I later met the individual responsible, Peter Dixon who had the local Chrysler dealership and who was a fellow Yorkshireman.

In speaking engagements over the next few years I would talk about the sales and marketing practices which gave rise to the most concern including the common practice of seizing the goods and suing for the deficiency balance, substituting a manufacturers warranty for the usual warranty given by the seller and  on occasion the quality of items, for I remember stressing the inability of Mobile Home standards and construction to stand up to the conditions of the roads over which they were transported and the Interior locations that they were set up in. One unfortunate lady found that the chipboard floor affected by damp in the bathroom was not up to supporting a toilet in use.

It is also noteworthy that when I spoke to a Car Forum at Delbrook School on the 3rd May 1971, I criticised Car Insurance as being more punitive than reasonable and suggested there be some kind of reward system where three years of safe driving might mean a 40% reduction in premiums. Although private Insurance Companies that were providing Car Insurance had benchmarks to establish their premiums, such as age, sex, where the car was to be driven and its age, amongst others.,. there was never any specific allowance made for safe driving represented by a lack of claims that the consumer was told about. I am sure it was probably one of the factors taken into consideration.

The Insurance Company of British Columbia was formed in 1973, and there was some form of safe driving discount built into their premiums from 1977 onwards. This has grown to 43% for the best safe driving record. I am sure that this has the effect of reducing claims at the same time that it encourages the safe driver.

Perhaps someone was listening!.

I used to have lunch in the Belmont Building across the street from the Parliament Buildings, where there was a Government cafeteria which dispensed meals at reasonable prices and afforded a chance to meet people from different Departments. There was an election coming up and a gentleman called Woods who was the Administrative Assistant to the Opposition N.D.P. Leader Dave Barrett stopped me as I passed his table, and asked me who I thought was going to win. Without thinking I said that the other two parties would take each others votes and his party would come right up the middle, and eventually that is just what happened.

The early seventies were probably the peak of 'consumerism' if that is the word to use. The developments in technology which started to miniaturize and improve communications and the introduction of more 'improved' household products also brought complaints about quality and performance and the media interest began to grow as some of the more colourful leaders of the Consumer Movement began to make their voices heard.

Pyramid schemes claimed more and more victims as people were persuaded to put money in to get returns promised if more recruits signed up whereas the structure only saw the original promoters make money and they had long disappeared when the scheme collapsed as it inevitably must. Others were induced to invest money in chinchilla farming where there was such a large supply of furs that prices would not cover production costs. On one visit to an Association in the Lower Mainland that consisted of disillusioned chinchilla farmers I persuaded the Chief Veterinarian for the Province, Dr Abe Kidd, to talk to the group, but I had to accompany him on a whirlwind tour of Meat Packing Plants beforehand. They tend to smell rather strongly particularly where smoked meat products are produced. Mail Order so called was also responsible for a lot of customer dissatisfaction. Once the money had been sent to an address which was usually in Ontario or Montreal if anything arrived at all it was generally nothing like the picture or description and nearly always of poor quality. I once heard the figures that the "trade' relied upon to be able to continue their activities. A very small number of consumers, much less than ten percent, actually complained  or sent the goods back.

There was also a very frustrating practice by some of the larger Store Chains that issued Canada wide flyers with items at very attractive prices, only for the consumer who arrived immediately the sale opened, to find that the small number they had were all gone and no 'rain checks' were being issued. I suppose you could call this the 'bait' without the 'switch.'

# CHAPTER 14

# CHANGE OF GOVERNMENT

The incoming N.D.P. Government had given the impression that they were willing to listen to consumer concerns and do something, and so it proved when shortly after their election win they announced plans to form a separate Ministry of Consumer Affairs.

Consumer administration was still with the Attorney Generals Department although I had now moved to an office in the Law Courts with my secretary. We still felt however like a 'poor relation' because when we asked for benches for visitors to sit on, these were made by the prisons. The cushions did not fit the bases and we found that these had been made in separate places. So much for economy, and the filing cabinets also made by the inmates would not lock.

I was told to report to the Ministers Office one morning and Mel Smith was there, now the Director of Administrative Law, and Phyllis Young one of the new M.L.A. s. We were asked to wait because the Attorney General had a visitor. Things were very quiet in the outer office because changes were in the offing and there was no way of knowing how each of us would be affected. I considered it a situation where a very low profile was necessary. The Attorney General was Alex MacDonald and his visitor burst out of his office in an open necked shirt with the sleeves rolled up and hair flowing out behind him. He stopped at the outer door and then came back to stand in front of me and said "You are Hanson aren't you?" so I said "Yes." Then he said "Another Englishman got to show them how to do the job." I would have liked to vanish through the floor.

The move to the Law Courts gave  much needed space because in addition to providing a central point for consumer matters I had now assumed more responsibilities. Before the change of Government, the Deputy Minister of Health, Jim Sadler, had asked me to come to a meeting in his offices and that one of the lady Ministers Without Portfolio, Isobel Dawson would be there. They wanted to discuss hearing aids and the potential for abuse because these were high cost items and an elderly individual might not always benefit from the use of a hearing aid. At the time I answered their questions as best I could and thought that this was nothing more than information gathering but a few weeks later I got a phone call suggesting that I might want to be in the Legislative Assembly Public Gallery that afternoon because a Bill was going to be introduced regulating Hearing Aid Dealers and this would be administered by a Board of Hearing Aid Dealers and Consultants ... and I would be named its first Chairman.This meant that I had got to learn about this field very quickly, both as to the way in which the dealers interacted with the professionals in the medical area and all the factors surrounding hearing and testing and the sale of hearing aids.

It became apparent from the start that there were three fairly clear Interest Groups, each of which felt that their own members were the only people that could test an individual's hearing and decide if a hearing aid would be of any benefit; the Medical Specialists, the Audiologists and the Hearing Aid Dealers. Medicine and Audiology provided one representative each on the Board, there were two hearing aid dealers, one lady who worked with all ages affected by hearing loss, who understood signing and two mothers with children who had a severe hearing loss.

The Medical professional was an Otolaryngologist, and that mouthful can be translated to mean an Ear Nose and Throat Specialist and they felt with some justification that they were the only way that the cause of an individual's hearing loss could be correctly diagnosed. The representative on the board was Dr Irwin Stewart and he was highly regarded by everyone that I came in contact with.

The Audiologists were the people who tested hearing and understood the mechanics of the hearing components and felt that theirs was the only discipline that was relevant and they were represented by Dr John Gilbert who taught at the University of British Columbia.

The Hearing Aid Dealers themselves had a simple philosophy that said that they were capable of using the equipment to test peoples hearing and more importantly they sold the hearing aid and monitored whether it did really help the individual. They were represented by Gordon Stemson and Ken McLaren.

Three other members of the Board were Patience Towler who worked in Vancouver with people who had a severe hearing loss and who needed alternate assistance like sign language, and two mothers who had children with a hearing loss, Mary Margaret Moore and Mary Hutchinson.

Before any Regulatory Act can take effect it needs Regulations which set out the Licencing Procedures and any conditions which are part of the licence or which must be followed by the licencee. That was the first thing the Board had to do. It was quite a responsibility to look after a licenced area, prepare the regulations and even more daunting to set up the first licence issue, and learn the different checks and balances.

We wrote to dealers on the 22nd December 1971 outlining the fees and registration procedure.

The new secretary who looked after this area for me, Elizabeth, worked well with the other staff, however a potentially serious problem surfaced when we had our first audit. The Auditor came in to my office and said that we had a shortfall of several hundred dollars. After we examined our procedures surrounding our receipt of the licence fee and onward transmittal to Finance I noticed that the missing dollars were a multiple of the actual licence fee, so we went out to see Elizabeth and I asked her what happened when she made a mistake on the licence she returned to the dealer after we had received the fee, "Well I just tear it up and do another one!" As the numbered certificates which are issued are the confirmation of the monies received, this explained the discrepancy. Fortunately the Auditor accepted this and of course the seriousness of failing to keep and submit spoiled certificates was now clearly understood.

The Hearing Aid Manufacturers had a strong interest in the regulation of dealers but curiously did not make the same direct contacts that other trade representatives had in the general consumer field, leaving it to their dealers to do that for them. There was an underlying suspicion that some dealers were not very skilled in the use of audiometers which were used to measure the level of a persons hearing and which had to be used in a sound proof environment and that they would sell hearing aids to people that did not need them. There were however a majority of dealers who could and did accurately evaluate hearing loss and were highly respected by the other professionals in the field. That did not however diminish the initial animosity between the three main interest groups and I sometimes felt like a fight referee.

There was some justified criticism of the advertising and sales practices of the manufacturers, who played on peoples fears to encourage testing where sales could result and the vanity emphasis which, by stressing that the aid was small and hard to notice, built up the impression that it was somehow shameful to show that you needed a hearing aid.

My initial exposure to the dealers themselves was fairly memorable. It took place at an hotel on the Lower Mainland and Ken McLaren came with me. The room was packed and on a chair in the front row was a tape recorder with its lights glowing. After Ken had introduced me I said that if a full and frank discussion was what they wanted then the tape recorder would have to go. A chap got up and flicked a couple of switches which made the lights go out and made to sit down again. I said "Now pull the plug out of the wall." He went to do this but was obviously unhappy and on the way back to his seat he said "You don't trust anyone do you." I replied "No I don't and if we start on that understanding there will not be any surprises." Then the battle was on, and there were many comments and questions which showed the resentment of many dealers about Government's entry into their field and whether anyone looking over their shoulder was actually needed.

It really did not take very long for them to realise as time went on that the Board was more of a benefit than a drawback. The first real hurdle came when we set up a Course at the British Columbia Institute of Technology which involved audiometers and would be a good test of the rudiments of a hearing aid dealers craft. The biggest obstacle was convincing the powers that be to include a Regulation that allowed the Board not to renew a licence or issue a licence to someone who had not taken and passed the Course. It was a sensible way to weed out those dealers who received a licence originally but did not have the fundamental tools to operate the equipment and in the event some dealers quietly did not take the Course or renew their licence.

In talking to groups which included or represented seniors it was very obvious that many of them just did not have enough money to buy a hearing aid which cost several hundred dollars. I knew that the hearing aid supplied by the British National Health Service was relatively cheap although bulky and definitely not a 'vanity' item so I persuaded the dealers that if they could offer a very basic model at a low price to those who could not afford anything else it would certainly improve their image. They agreed to do this and with the caveat that it was an unsophisticated hearing aid which only offered sound amplification and would not help everyone, they offered this at fifty dollars.

Eventually the Government itself through the Department of Health got into the hearing aid business and both supplied these to those people referred to their Centres and serviced and tested the aids that they supplied. The dealers felt that this would drive them out of business, but they seemed to survive quite well as the main Government clients were children. It is extremely important to establish that those children with a hearing loss are diagnosed at the earliest possible age in order that their education does not suffer. With my deteriorating hearing largely contributed to by the tubes of the inner ear closing, I had managed with an ear popping technique taught to me by an E.N.T. man when I had to hear what was going on, but obviously needed a hearing aid and I privately felt that I could not get one from the regulated dealers because it would be seen as favouring a particular individual or manufacturer. So I was in an odd position of being perhaps the only person in the Province who definitely needed an aid but couldn't get one. The Governments entry into the field changed all that and I got a hearing aid.

A Vancouver radio station had perfected a system of 'test shopping' suspect businesses to see if they were supplying honest service to residents and publicizing any results which showed otherwise. The automotive repair field was a favourite target.

One of the Board members found out that this station had sent a young woman to many of the hearing aid dealers on the Lower Mainland, with the story that her husband felt that she was not hearing things properly and did she need a hearing aid? That would be quite a tempting situation for any unscrupulous dealer but apparently they had all told her that they did not find anything that indicated that a hearing aid would help her. That despite the fact that most if not all dealers were allowing people to try a hearing aid to see if it helped and taking it back if it didn't.

I spoke to the Manager of the radio station and he verified the details and said that it was not news if they did not catch a dishonest dealer. I pointed out that it would reassure their listening audience that they could confidently visit hearing aid dealers and they did broadcast a news item to this effect. All members of the Board must have felt that the hard work had paid off, and the dealers had something to be proud of too.

The amount of work was building and although David Nicholls had joined me to assist on the consumer side and a young lady to help with filing, there was still a need for some help to run the Hearing Aid Regulation side of things and the Department of Health were most resistant to supply anyone because they had always wanted to control it. I wrote to the Minister who at that time was Dennis Cocke and said that if help did not materialize I would have to resign. I received a fairly terse reply which said "I accept your resignation," so Health did get it back after all.

In the Consumer field the Federal Department still made a lot of noise and did very little. There was a case alleging price fixing by cement companies which had taken years to bring to court and which was torpedoed by the Judge. In a flagrant case where a big gasoline retailer was advertising its additive enhanced product in North America by showing a car which could be clearly seen in a plastic bubble as using its gas and one where the car could not be seen as using someone else's gas. The U.S. Authorities stopped the advertising as soon as they found that black plastic was being used for the 'other car.' I brought this to the attention of Ottawa but the same ad was still being shown in Canada weeks later.

The change of Government in British Columbia came at a time when 'consumerism' was reaching its peak and the incoming Government had been listening to the Consumers Association and Better Business Bureaux, so in addition to forming a Department of Consumer Affairs with its own Minister, work started on a new Trade Practices Act which would incorporate the best of Australian and U.S. Legislation.

The new Ministry of Consumer Affairs owed its existence to the Consumer Services Act, which was passed unanimously on October 12th, 1973 and Phyllis Young a Minister Without Portfolio was its first Minister.

The new Ministry was eventually housed in a building on Fort Street and we had a Deputy Minister from the Law Faculty at the University of Toronto, Bill Neilson who was well versed in this area of law and knew Jacob Zeigel who was probably the last word on developments world wide. The new Minister the Hon Phyllis Young wanted to hear from everyone and had arranged a Conference to which everyone interested in consumer advocacy was invited. She wanted a record of the proceedings and I suggested that staff from Hansard could do this for her with their experience of doing this in the House. This record was extremely useful as a catalogue of abuses described by the participants and I well remember an extract from a tape which Vince Forbes had made of a Debt Collector threatening a woman "When we have finished with you lady we will make the Nazis look like Nuns!" In compiling the new B.C.Trade Practices Act secrecy was maintained regarding its actual provisions but it was obvious that other people were at work along the same lines and specifically the Government in Ontario. Our young lawyers worked very quickly under the supervision of the Deputy Minister and many of the provisions were 'borrowed' from some of the earlier legislation in Australia and the U.S.

I saw the various drafts and was able to comment and much as I had done with the Consumer Protection Act, propose something of my own. I had never forgotten the way in which Credit Granters had been able to advance money to people in circumstances where they must have known that they could not repay and that they would eventually seize their assets and sue for the balance of the debt, so as a specific example of unconscionability I wrote a provision to cover that, making it unconscionable where the Credit Grantor knew or should have known that the individual could not repay. They all said that it would not get past the various levels of scrutiny, but it was there when the Act was introduced, and still there when the Act was unanimously approved.

There was an interesting and perhaps amusing situation when under strict control it was decided that Ontario and British Columbia would exchange drafts. It was almost like a meeting at the Berlin Wall for an exchange of prisoners, both held their own draft and did not release it until they were holding the others.

I had been appointed as the Director of Trade Practices and had a number of options to apply if a misleading or deceptive act had occurred or for that matter an unconscionable act or practice. The law had previously relied on 'caveat emptor' or the necessity for a consumer to beware when buying something and in many cases there had been a requirement clearly or implicitly that the seller had meant to cheat or otherwise take advantage of the buyer. The Act tried to change all that by making the test of misleading or deceptive its effect on the consumer and including a failure 'to disclose a material fact.' One of the first cases dealt with under the Act involved a Victoria car dealer. This sale took place on the dealers lot with a glowing description of the vehicle. The buyer had something wrong with a foot or leg for he asked one of the salesmen to drive it off the lot, which he did ......... over a large railway sleeper which was used as an edge, over the pavement and on to the road The vehicle later proved to be without a reverse gear. That resulted in something called an Assurance of Voluntary Compliance which is one of the Enforcement options under the Act,where the business signs an Undertaking which says that it does not necessarily agree that the criticized behaviour was an offence  against the Act but promises not to do it again  and agrees to some satisfactory form of redress. Any repetition would automatically become an offence. The proceedings under the Act were to be kept in a 'Public Record' and that meant open to the press and public which in this case proved costly for the business which sold the car without the reverse gear because some weeks later someone climbed over a wall into a storage area and damaged several vehicles. This case was described in The Victoria Times of November 8th, 1974.

There were other early cases which were targeted as long-standing abuses although as I had said just after the Act was introduced, I expected the worst offenders to head for the hills as soon as the Act became law, and I am certain that was  generally the case.

I had a meeting with the Sales Manager of the company which made a practice of recruiting young people and blanketing particular areas with the sales pitch that they were trying to earn points to go to University, whereas in fact they were salespeople for magazine subscriptions pure and simple, something which had been going on for years and had led the Better Business Bureaux to issue alerts whenever they identified the area affected. The Sales Manager knew that I had the evidence and obviously believed that I would apply the Act so he brought his principals and their lawyers from the east and they made a spirited defence of their tactics and said that their sales would fall off dramatically if they were forced to disclose the true purpose of the solicitation and the name of the company.

After their claims of potential disaster, their Sales Manager quietly said that after our earlier meeting he had issued Identity cards and told the youngsters to identify the company and what they were selling and sales had not gone down ... they had gone up!

Although I do not think that it had struck terror into the hearts of business, the Act had certainly been analyzed by the larger Trade Associations and its impact on their own policies in some areas had serious implications. I made myself available to them believing that it would be a good deal more satisfactory to clean up questionable practices voluntarily than fight about it. I had always believed in the old maxim that you walk quietly ........and in the case of the Legislation I had a very big stick!

A good example was the way in which new car warranties were being applied, and so called 'secret warranties.' Where a faulty component was identified in a new model, the company did not always issue a recall notice to the general public but sent what amounted to a confidential notice to its dealers saying that if the consumer complained they would cover the repair cost outside the warranty period.

Ray Morris, who worked for Nissan, headed up the Import Dealers Association at the time, and I always found him to be fair. He arranged a meeting at the Vancouver Hotel for me to talk to the representatives from those countries that sold in Canada, and I explained how the new Legislation could be applied and these so called 'secret warranties' were a case in point. They argued that any new car might have teething difficulties and they should not be penalized if they honoured the strict terms of their warranty. I pointed out that with the computerization of warranty claims and repairs and Parts Inventories they were quickly aware of common weaknesses and by failing to bring these to the notice of new car buyers it was a 'failure to disclose a material fact.' That they issued a warning to dealers was just a clear confirmation of this. They were obviously a very thoughtful group when the meeting broke up, and I said to Ray Morris as we stood in the corridor outside, "I think some of them must be worried" and he said "what makes you think that," because I said "the Mazda Representative has just gone into the Ladies Washroom.....". and he was out a few seconds later looking very sheepish.

We had four lawyers in our Legal Services Branch, and it became obvious from the start that we did not share the same view of how our two functions should interact.

When they were asked for a legal opinion on the Department's legislation in relation to a specific complaint, they nearly always liked to recommend an enforcement option. If it had stayed at that we probably would not have run into much difficulty, but in the case of the Trade Practices Act, I had a strong suspicion that the Courts would not readily set aside the old maxim of caveat emptor or 'consumer beware' and despite their insistence that the Act left no room for misinterpretation, I preferred to use the Assurance of Voluntary Compliance at least in the early days of the legislation, to halt many of the old abuses. They wanted to go to court and be able to refer to cases which had supported the Act and applied its provisions. Some situations led to fairly heated arguments and I remember when some traders were offering 'free' items to encourage consumers to buy from them, the argument was that something was not free if you had to buy something else to get it! From inquiries made by the Investigators it seemed that whatever was being sold, gasoline in most cases, the price was just the same as their competition who were not offering anything with it. In those circumstances we would only be denying consumers an extra benefit. The wording that they would like used 'at no extra charge' was something better taken up by our Trade Liaison Division, in my view.

The Deputy Minister had always encouraged a fairly aggressive approach to things by the lawyers and I soon found myself replying to vicarious complaints by them and requirements to consult and seek their advice. At the time there was an 'Affirmative action' programme which was being enthusiastically applied within the Government, and which I had difficulty with. It was designed to give preference in hiring to minority groups that were perceived to be disadvantaged and not well represented. The vacancy for an Investigator in the Vancouver Office saw a lady among the applicants from within the Department who knew the legislation but had no experience whatsoever of collecting evidence, taking statements and going to court. I fought off arguments within the Selection Panel and we chose an ex police officer as were most of the other Investigators, but it obviously did not sit well with the approach embraced by the Personnel Branches of the day. I had to point out that one of the first Investigators that I hired was a woman who all the attributes required and was a very good Investigator.

Eventually it reached the stage where we had to test the legislation in the courts, and the case which was chosen involved a common practice in the Credit field, where a retailer assigned a credit sale to a Finance Company, receiving a discounted amount for the contract. Perhaps because some consumers disliked Finance Companies, elaborate steps were taken to make the purchaser believe that they were still dealing with the retailer even though their payments were being made to the Finance Company which now held the contract. Household Finance engaged one of the best lawyers of the day, a Queens Counsel named Boyd Ferris and eventually I had to attend an Examination for Discovery which is often a part of Civil cases. One of the questions that he asked me was meant to be rhetorical because he said there is no detriment to consumers is there? I pointed out that the 'Holder in due course' doctrine which usually applied to contracts purchased by Financial Institutions had been modified to allow the purchaser to ask for assistance or relief from the third party for a failure to live up to the warranty by the seller. If they didn't know that there was a third party then they couldn't enlist their help.

When the case came to trial I was surprised that we did not bring this up as part of our submissions, as when they brought in the Examination for Discovery, Boyd Ferris did not include it. I was told that they alone had the option to introduce all, some or none. Our argument was to be based on the pure argument that it was misleading or deceptive not to tell the purchaser that credit would be assigned to the Finance Company.

The Court's decision fairly clearly required there to be some detriment to the consumer for the Act to be applied successfully and so we lost the case. The Judge highlighted the fact that there had been no complaints and "no consumer suffered" the emphasis is mine. I don't know what would have happened if we had included the part of the Examination for Discovery that they left out, but the court would have had to consider that in deciding whether there was detriment. It did however underline the predictable result if we had tried to apply the legislation to retailers who offered 'free' items without raising the price of what you had to buy to get them!

The next case that we took to court was more successful. It could be loosely called in the Credit field because it involved Tax Discounting and the offer to 'buy' your tax rebate for a discounted amount. Tax Discounters abounded shortly before the time when tax returns had to be submitted and some people, generally the ones who could least afford it, would give up a high percentage of their rebate for the instant cash offered by the Discounter. When I knew that the question of counsel was being considered I strongly suggested that they should try to get Boyd Ferris. This would not only deny his services to the credit field in this case but would also give us someone with experience in this area and I hoped very credible standing with the court. The case moved quickly because of its bearing on what was an annual practice, and I can remember Boyd Ferris anticipating the argument that would be used against us by telling me just before we went into the court that "This deals with Interest Hanson, and we will lose because that comes under Federal and not Provincial jurisdiction!" I shot back at him "This is not interest, it is a fee or a bonus applied by the Discounter." It was a little rewarding to hear our Counsel making that argument later in court and to hear the Judge support the criticism of the amount of the discount retained by the Discounter. Shortly afterwards someone threw a gasoline bomb through the door of the Discounter's premises but in that case it may not have been the revenge of a disgruntled consumer but more in anticipation of a visit from Revenue Canada.

In 1976 On January 31st we moved house again. We had been looking at new houses under construction in Gordon Head, and liked that area, but just before Christmas, for some reason we took a drive up the Saanich Peninsula and passed a house where there was some activity on Wallace Drive. We turned round and went back to find that it was 'open house.' As soon as I walked round behind Pat I knew she liked the house, so we talked to the agent who had some kind of guaranteed sale of your own house as part of the contract to buy this one. We put our house on the market with them at a certain price and the price fell in increments until 30 or 90 days I forget which and then we got the guaranteed price to buy the one on Wallace Drive. They had our first 'open house' slated in January when another agent from the same company brought an offer on ours which was exactly the lowest guaranteed price. They swore blind that there had been no collusion. Pat and I turned it down saying that we would wait out the prescribed period to see if something better came along. Within a few hours they were back with an offer which was only slightly lower than our asking price, so we had one of our quickest sales and moves because the builder tenant of the Wallace Drive house was either out or anxious to move. The new house had a lovely view over a hydro break, so we could see the Mill Bay ferry plying back and forth across the Saanich Inlet.

Pat was extremely sensitive to places! There were some houses that she would not enter, where she could not explain her reluctance, but I suspect that most premises have residual impressions of previous owners and events which make them a 'happy' or 'unhappy' house, in any event her instincts have been right throughout our married life.

Before we left Marlene Drive we had bought a boat. This was a Fiberform which we kept on a trailer and drove out to Pedder and Beecher Bays, trolling for salmon. One of the methods used caused some amusement when I took one or two visitors from the other Provinces out fishing. There was a plastic quick release mechanism near the end of the line to which you attached a disposable weight. There was no shortage of disposable weights in the form of the large pebbles which we kept removing from the garden and the best thing to put them in was a leg from some old pantyhose which was attached to the quick release. As I was seeing them off from Victoria Airport and they were on their way out to the plane, I yelled "Next time remember to bring your old pantyhose," and that got me a few funny looks from the Airline staff.

We had one memorable day when Pat and I caught two good fish at the same time, nice Coho and hers was slightly bigger than mine but otherwise we were not very lucky. We eventually gave way to Neil's urging to fish with bar rigs near the prison at William Head where there were promising reefs for cod and sure enough when we dropped lines over the side with the old anchovies which we had been using on the trolling lines we started pulling up rock cod and snapper. There was one bite that took off like an express train and broke the line and that was probably a big salmon.

Pat had a disconcerting habit of dividing the number of fish caught into the cost of the equipment .... including the boat ... to arrive at a price per pound and the inevitable conclusion that boats are an expensive (and unnecessary) thing to have ....depending on your point of view of course!

At work we were gathered as a Ministry in the Fort Street premises and I was still within easy reach of the Y.M.C.A. where I used to spend my lunch hour labouring round the track on the roof whilst  bright young things would lap me more than once without showing any sympathy.

There were a few of us who had our soup and sandwich fairly regularly in their small restaurant, one of whom was a Reverend who wrote regularly in the Time Colonist. The lady who managed the Y restaurant had a Finnish name which was long and difficult to pronounce so everyone called her 'Sam.' She handed round a questionnaire one day which asked for comments and suggestions to improve the service. One of these was filled out with bold letters saying 'strippers' and signed allegedly by the Reverend, who was quite surprised to find Sam standing at our table with hands on hips, reading him the riot act, and him arguing plaintively that it wasn't even his writing!

My secretary Karen had left to have her first child and there was talk of using a typing pool, an idea which surfaces from time to time in Government circles. The Investigation or Enforcement Section had taken shape with an Investigator in Victoria, Prince George and Kamloops and a number in Vancouver including two old New Westminster Detectives who in addition to everyday duties were a kind of fire brigade for emergency situations. With the exception of the Vancouver Office with its large Metropolitan population, the other Investigators had large areas to cover mostly sparsely populated and I encouraged a pride in knowing what went on in their own area, much like the old Town Policeman. They took this responsibility seriously and received little interference from me, knowing that I was there if they needed something and when reports of one kind or another were necessary. In one or two areas however I suspect they had some criticism of their Director. I was a firm believer that you did not return cases where a mistake had been made or something further was required and instead of highlighting the error, I would ask the Investigator to go through it until he or she identified the error or omission feeling that this left a more lasting impression. They also did not like to do radio or T.V. talks or interviews and draw attention to themselves and the Ministry was publicity conscious, so they retaliated by setting me up for these in their place whenever they could. There was one touchy area, because they came from a number of Police Forces, they all submitted their reports in a different way and would have of course strongly argued that theirs was the best if asked. My own U.K. Police history was well known and would be subject to united criticism if they felt I was introducing English methods.

My Deputy Director was an ex R.C.M.P. Officer who was well respected and who never hesitated to speak his mind if necessary, so one day having graphed out in headings my old C.I.D. Legal Aid way of reporting cases, I sent this to all the offices as being the new way that I wanted Investigation Reports submitted, and on the day that this went out I took their copy to the Investigators in Vancouver on a day that the Deputy Director and I were both going there. As expected without really looking at it the reaction was "This is no good!" I told them that constructive criticism was required and if they felt that they could make improvements I was willing to listen. I left them to it knowing that they would all go over it with a fine tooth comb to see if they could come up with valid criticism. Two or three days later my secretary asked me if I wasn't surprised that there had not been a fierce reaction. I had known that there would be immediate consultation between the various offices and when heated protest was contemplated someone would have suggested that if the Deputy and other Investigators had not been able to come up with improvements then discretion was probably the better part of valour.

The kind of fishing that I had done in the London area, either in gravel pits or the Thames resulted in small roach, bream or perch if you were lucky and ever since my spell at the Canneries, watching those beautiful silver salmon tipped out of the net onto the loading dock, I had wanted to fish for salmon, and that is why we got our own boat, however both Pat and I did not really like fresh cooked salmon and therefore anything we caught we canned in preserving jars.

When father visited us from Kenya where he, my  mother and brother were still living, the trips we took in the Saanich Inlet only produced small salmon or grilse and so we arranged for him to go out with a professional guide, Hughie, and took him down to the Inner Harbour in Victoria early one morning.

It was threatening to rain and blowing and we really wondered if he was going to enjoy fishing in a rough sea. We need not have worried! When we got back to the harbour about 11 am, the boat was coming in and we could see father up at the front sticking up his thumb. He disembarked with a plastic bag containing several large salmon and asked where we could have a cup of tea. The Empress Hotel just across the road was handy, but we

Dad and Hughie, with a good catch

weren't dressed for its august interior, and dad was not going to surrender his bag of salmon. When he heard our misgivings he just snorted and we marched into the Empress and had our cup of tea.

He was to go out a few more times with Hughie on subsequent visits. He never gave us advance warning of his visits, just called from the 'Airport' to say come and get me. On his last outing with Hughie, I went with him and realised that his depth sounder or some other equipment allowed him to find the salmon and then it was just a matter of talking on the radio to other guides in the area to see what coloured hootchie, a kind of plastic octopus, was catching the fish. There were always photos that Dad could take back to Africa to show what he had caught.

Sadly we lost Mother in February 1986, and Dad joined her in June 1995 due to prostate cancer. My brother Nicholas continues to live and farm in Africa.

The advent of the Trade Practices Act and increase of the pace in consumer protection made for interesting Provincial meetings and I was fortunate to be able to travel everywhere in Canada and meet local people, to see provincial industries and landmarks and appreciate its diversity. We had all become Canadian Citizens and although the Canadian Rockies are spectacular I did not see anything to rival the scenery in British Columbia, to confirm Hornby's earlier astute observation.

In addition to my other duties I was appointed to the Advisory Committee on Standards set up by The Canadian Standards Association and this was a worthwhile effort when dealing with things like the safety of bicycle helmets but it was tiring to fit this in and not to be away from my main duties for too long because the meetings were held in Ottawa. It meant catching an early plane about six thirty from Victoria to Vancouver to connect with the nine a.m 747 from Vancouver to Toronto and then a feeder flight at the other end to Ottawa arriving late in the day B.C. time with meal and sleep times thrown out of whack by the time difference. The Capital city did not have a covered walkway from the plane to the terminal so it was sometimes a frigid arrival.

The following morning I would attend the meeting with eyes barely open and leave in time to get a feeder flight back to Toronto and the 7 pm 747 back to Vancouver where I would catch one of the last flights back to Victoria.....and still manage to be back at my desk the following morning. Fortunately the meetings were not too frequent.

One meeting saw the Minister, the Deputy and I flying to Alberta, and driving to Lake Louise for a meeting at a large hotel which overlooks the lake. I started off driving but my pace was a little too sedate for the Deputy and he took over. As we were going through the National Park where there is a very low speed limit, an R.C.M.P. car pulled us over for speeding. They had had some kind of anniversary shortly before that and there were a lot of police momentos around. At the table when we started the meeting someone had put a little statue of an R.C.M.P. Officer in British Columbia's place!

Having started as Mister Consumer Affairs and doing everything, there were now Storefront Managers who handled complaints and a Trade Liaison Division which tried to establish business guidelines as well as Public Relations and Personnel Sections. My responsibilities centered around running the Investigation Branch and Enforcement. Sometimes there were a number of high profile cases going on at the same time, which did not give me the luxury of being able to concentrate on any particular one.

Time Share had arrived and was being aggressively sold as an inexpensive way of taking a holiday in spas and resorts or places with good all year round climate like Hawaii. The general concept was a good one. You paid several thousand dollars up front for a week or two each year in an apartment or unit in a large building. The developer was happy, because he got his construction money back straight away, and if he maintained the building in good order and resolved any disputes about who got which weeks in the peak periods then the Time Share 'owners' were happy too. However there was a strong incentive for developers to walk away from things once they had their money, or cut corners on insurance or maintenance and if you lived thousands of miles  away it was difficult to register your complaint. The Authorities which had Time Share developments in their jurisdictions were aware of these problems and working towards sensible safeguards but in the meantime slick sales presentations were being made in Vancouver hotels and somehow local buyers had to be made aware of the drawbacks as well as the benefits. The solution was the 'cooling off period' in the Consumer Protection Act which had to be included in contracts entered into away from the sellers usual place of business, and honoured if the consumer wanted to cancel and get their money back. This was not included in their contracts because they claimed that hotels were their usual place of business.  I contacted the principals in one of the larger active promotions and they were strongly opposed to including this, however they agreed to bring their lawyers to a meeting where I explained the Trade Practices Act and how  it could, and would, be applied if this change was not made. They agreed to an Assurance of Voluntary Compliance which served as a yardstick for any other promotions, and allowed cancellation. It may have no bearing  on the company's antecedents, but their lawyers came from Las Vegas.

There were misgivings about the Charter Flights which used aircraft capable of taking a very high number of passengers and little or no control over the "organizer' who was taking a considerable sum of money in advance and some anxiety expressed by the trade and consumers about these circumstances. Some Airlines had defaulted on scheduled returns from other countries and all this eventually led to regulation but in the meantime the Investigators and I had to do the best we could to prevent or limit questionable charters.

From time to time there were spectacular business failures where customers had paid in advance for goods or services that they did not receive, sometimes paying the day before the doors closed. Some individuals seemed to have perennial bankruptcies, and the consumer was on the end of a long chain of secured creditors which the Receiver had to look after first and so were out of luck. This was particularly so in the areas where some consumers were most vulnerable, Fitness Clubs or Weight Loss for those who wanted to improve their appearance and Dance Schools where you might find an answer to loneliness. In my early days in the Attorney Generals Department I had seen many of the 'boiler plate contracts' that were used to make sure you paid when the gloss wore off and led me to say in some exasperation "The only way that anyone gets out of these contracts is in a box, or by exhibiting some very anti-social behaviour."

Where there were more flagrant examples and any suggestion of fraud, I used David Hooper, someone that the R.C.M.P. would describe and had used as a Forensic Accountant.

I suggested to our Investigators that when they went with him to a business investigation they should watch him for the first little while as he went after the business records. It is perhaps unflattering but I compared this to a ferret being introduced into a rat or rabbit warren. If there was something wrong there he sensed it or knew about it almost straight away and if not it was probably not worth pursuing.

A good piece of work by one of the Investigators occurred when I held a meeting in Vancouver with some people who were going to circulate a magazine in which subscribers solicited companions for a fee. There was a strong suspicion that the Box Numbers in the magazine applied to fictitious individuals. During our meeting one of the principals asked one of the office staff to take his brief case down to the car. The Investigator followed him out..... looked in the case and found a copy of the magazine prepared for local printing and it had identical B.C. entries to the ones they were using in Alberta.

Another case showed how some promoters cynically target some potential customers. The Vancouver office was contacted by a printer who had been asked to print a flyer or small catalogue by some men he had met in the Vancouver Hotel. They had paid him a fairly substantial sum to do the printing and send it out to doctors and dentists and other professional people. His suspicions were aroused when he saw that it claimed that stock was held at a familiar address ... his own.

The contents were identical to a promotion which had circulated in Ontario some time previously and the individuals responsible had managed to leave one or two steps ahead of the posse, but with a very large amount of Ontario consumers money for which they had not received anything. The printers remorse came after he had sent the flyer out. There was a Post Office Box number in Vancouver to which orders would be sent together with payment and within hours I had a 'freeze order' made up and on its way to Vancouver to seal this box. Everyone felt that we would have trouble because Canada Post was federally operated, but they accepted the order and made sure that what was received stayed there.

Then began some fascinating correspondence with the lawyers representing two individuals in California who acknowledged that this was their promotion and wanted the 'orders' released so that they could supply the items. I said that I would be happy to do this if they would come up to British Columbia and explain things and also satisfy me that they had stock in the Province and would be honouring the orders.

A variety of excuses were offered to explain why they could not or would not come into our jurisdiction, including the last claim that one of their clients had suffered a gunshot wound the night before!

My last letter to them had said that in the absence of their appearance and a clear indication of their ability to satisfy these orders I was going to return the money to the people who had sent it in.

We went to Court as a precaution to ensure that my decision would not be challenged later and that is exactly what we did. In the meantime although they had sent in their cheques and not heard anything for months I think there were only a couple of letters asking where their order was and I do not think we got any thanks when they got their cheques back. It is a sad commentary on how easily some people can be relieved of their money without much complaint.

It was heartening to read an article in The Globe and Mail on March 25th, 1975 where the President of the B.C.Employers Council commenting on the Trade Practices Act said that 'there was a favourable reaction to the way it has been administered.'

After ten years of the Trade Practices Act it was interesting to examine the enforcement record. There were only two instances of a Receiver being appointed under Section 13A.The busiest years for the Assurance of Voluntary Compliance were 1975 when there were 23 and 1976 when there were 7. After that fairly frantic activity in the early years of the statute the use of Injunctions and Declarations and Substitute Actions and Defences under Section 18 and 24 increased, reaching a high in 1980 of 10 however these both might be a feature of the same case. The use of Prosecution under Section 25 certainly increased for in 1979 there were 11, in 1981 there were 10 and in 1983 12. When we reached the eighties the Criminal Code was sometimes applied and these cases often related to repairs where parts were charged for which had not actually been replaced.

To the best of my recollection our investigators did not lose a case as a result of evidentiary problems, and were only unsuccessful in the case I have already mentioned where the Court did not accept our legal argument.

Our boat was not used solely for fishing. With its fifty horsepower engine it was ideal for water skiing, and when the family camped beside Shuswap Lake in the Okanagan we all tried this out with varying degrees of success. The children could get up on the skis and did not want to get off, on the other hand I found it difficult to stay up, and when you hit the water at speed it is like hitting a brick wall.

The boat stayed on its trailer at the side of the car port, and sometimes became extra storage for something we did not have room for in the house, or similarly was used to haul things that we could not get into the car.

Came the day when after a foot or two of snow, which is not too common in the Victoria area, which was followed by rain which is, and a warming trend, Cheryl and I arrived home to see the sun deck bulging underneath with the added weight and in imminent danger of collapse. The cat we had brought from England was frightened by a dog on the driveway and was later found to have died. There was no time to mourn the loss however as we got to work shovelling snow over the side and when I looked over to where the boat was parked, I saw that the canopy had already collapsed inwards. That was the night I was joining Freemasonry and when Pat came home she bundled me into a shower and a change of clothes and got me out of the house on time.

Boats are made to deal with surplus water and I was able to carefully bend the aluminum canopy supports back in to shape so there was no real harm done.

The Wallace Drive house lent itself to entertaining and when we had a meeting in Victoria that was attended by all the investigators, I invited them up to the house for a drink.

It was interesting and also surprising to listen to some of the activities that never reached my ears at the office. Some of the Investigators had made use of their small tape recorders in interviews with businessmen in the course of investigations without informing them that they were being taped It was apparently legal to do this in Canada provided one of the parties in the taping consented. Shortly afterwards I sent out an Instruction that legal or not it had to stop. I felt that Government could be severely criticized if this came to light.

In one case I later heard a tape where the Investigator had interviewed an ex football player in his office and when he sat on a very expensive chair it collapsed. You could clearly hear his voice after the breaking noises saying "Who do I sue!" Full marks for presence of mind I suppose. There was also a description of a car chase before joining the Ministry where a small sports car was chased by a heavy police cruiser flashing its lights and sounding its horn for a long distance at high speed before the car pulled over. In some agitation the officer jumped out of his car to deal with the young speeder and was reading the riot act when he realised that the young fellows eyes were looking fearfully over his shoulder and turned just in time to see the cruiser which was rolling down an incline, crunch into the back of the sports car. He walked round to look at the damage, some to the sports car, none to the cruiser, put the books back in his pocket and said "Let that be a lesson to you," and drove off.

There was also a small safe which had been locked when an office was searched and the businessman claimed that he did not have the key. Being resourceful the two Investigators took the small safe back with them to the office, but the back door of the car came open in transit and they had to travel in one circular direction because it was half hanging out of the car. I thought of some remarks which were apparently attributed to Wellington when asked about his troops and he replied along the lines "I don't know if they scare the enemy ... but they certainly frighten me!"

These meetings provided a good opportunity for the Investigators in Kamloops and Prince George to share their views with the others who were closer at hand, but there was not enough time for them to spend with me so that I could hear about any potential problems in the large areas that they covered. I made a point of arranging a week each year, normally towards the end of the summer, when I would travel to their area and they could take me where they liked and talk about anything that they had on their minds. Besides being put down for the local T.V. and radio shows that they did not want to do, it was also a way of reminding me of the differences between the regions in the Province. One of the justified criticisms levelled at Government officials in Victoria who made decisions that affected residents in one area or another was that they never understood conditions in their area because they never took the time to travel there. A City dweller could not appreciate the distances involved in the Peace Country area for instance and the isolation which occurred in severe winters or the heat in the Okanagan during the summer and the importance of access to services which were not just down the street.

It was also a chance for them to show off their areas, something that I encouraged them to do. In Prince George there was what I suppose you would call a Hardware or General Store on 3rd Avenue, Northern Hardware and Furniture Company that had been around for many, many years, and where I asked the Investigator to drop me as he had to take care of family business for an hour or two, for when I was there we spent much more than eight hours a day working including the travelling. This store was probably among one of the first to open when the City of Prince George came into being and had just about everything you would need for wilderness living or homesteading. Things like waterproof matches, snow shoes, animal traps and the kind of adze they must have used to hollow out a canoe. There were old yellowed advertisements for things that were still household names and others long forgotten. A fascinating collection of Canadian history. When we went up into the Peace Country where there was still large scale ranching it did not seem unusual to see huge modern rotary bales of hay and the stooks of some kind of corn, probably oats, showing that an old fashioned binder was still in use, because there were horses everywhere.

Where forest came down to the roadside it was quite common to see wildlife, bears and different kinds of deer with the occasional moose. In spring they were apparently a road hazard and the males sometimes charged cars and trains. Although this was quite often fatal for the moose, it caused considerable damage to the car and sometimes its driver. There was an opportunity to travel to the West Coast at a more leisurely pace and meet the people in the rapidly growing communities of Smithers and Terrace.

Any visit to the south east part of the Province was a further reminder of the differences between the different areas, and even the areas within a region. The Okanagan with its beautiful lakes and fruit growing was a tourist destination as well as a magnet to those people retiring from the rest of Canada and even within British Columbia itself, while the Kootenays being more mountainous tended towards resource type industry like mines and forestry, and recreational skiing and other winter sports. Al Millhouse was our Investigator for the whole of this area.

When I spoke to a business audience in Kamloops there was a strong complaint about dishonoured cheques and what was I going to do about it. Fortunately before I could say anything there was an R.C.M.P. man in the audience and he said "If you would lay charges and follow it through in court it would soon put a stop to it!" At that meeting they presented me with a Kami pin and I never forgot to wear it when I visited the area, It was always recognised with some delight.

Al Millhouse made sure that I saw some of the historical things including the place where they drove the last spike in the Trans Canada Railway. That was in Eagle Pass at Craigellachie west of Revelstoke on the Trans Canada Highway between Sicamous and Revelstoke. There is a monument there to commemorate where the construction of the Canadian Pacific Railway from the west and the east finally linked up, and the last spike in the railroad was driven on November 7th 1885.

A road trip to the Kootenays, the mountainous area which marks the border with Alberta, took us through farming country with neat looking farm buildings and silos which would have made nice calendar pictures. These were nearly always religious communities with a Russian flavour because this is where most of the settlers originally came from, the Mennonites and Doukhubours, and they brought their European customs with them They were sometimes in trouble with the law and this was usually newsworthy because the women's favourite way of protesting was to take their clothes off! The Russian influence was to be seen in some of the hotels in places like Grand Forks where for breakfast in addition to traditional Canadian fare, you could get blintzes.

Once when we were on Highway 97, between Falkland and Vernon, we pulled in at a store which was not a General Store as you might have expected from its location but was full of old wood burning cooking stoves. Some of these, particularly those which had come from Quebec had some intricate enamel work and were really pieces of art. When I expressed some doubt that the owner could carry on a successful business from a relatively remote location, he told me that during the previous week they had taken a stove to Vancouver and used a crane to lift it twenty stories into an apartment. There was a sharp reminder of the kind of weather conditions experienced in the interior of the Province and that the Investigators had to cope with when we were caught in a blinding snow storm coming back from Revelstoke and on a trip to Trail in November when we climbed high up over the Nancy Greene pass and met first a little snow, then more until it was piled high on either side of the road. When we started to descend there was a little Honda ahead of us and Al had to brake continuously as it was sliding all over the road in front of us. When we got to the hotel in clear road conditions once more he remarked rather drily "I expect you will sleep tonight." I said "If you mean has my foot been driving itself through the floorboards for the last part of the trip then you are absolutely right!" There was a friendly session at the Radio Station, K.B.S. in Trail where the town is known for its hockey team and its smelter which has unfortunately left signs of its activity on the surrounding landscape. They probably take some consolation from an old Yorkshire expression, 'where there's muck there's brass.'

My relationship with the lawyers which had been deteriorating for some time began to cause trouble. I felt that their youth and relative inexperience was the reason for some of the posturing and even took one of them up to Prince George to hopefully let him see the field conditions we were trying to work in. As luck would have it a drunk scruffed another fellow over the hood of a car outside the office whilst we were there, as a useful demonstration.

They had the ear of the Deputy however, who began to lay down rules which were obviously meant to give the lawyers more involvement in the enforcement process. It threatened to break out into open warfare because I was still applying administrative solutions which were quicker, halted the act or practice and contained some redress, at the same time being something to use in market areas where somebody else looked like doing the same thing. They still wanted to go to court.

Eventually we finished up in the Minister's office where Rafe Mair listened to the argument which the lawyer they had chosen to represent them put forward and I kept my own counsel and waited to defend myself. That self control disappeared when he used a comment which had been used by them a number of times and went along the lines "lawyers will not continue to work for a client who continually ignores their advice." I said as dispassionately as I could "If I was in the position to do so I would have fired you months ago." We left after that and I suspected that I may not stay in my position for very long, even though I was very pleased with the enforcement results I had produced. Not too long afterwards I got a copy of a memorandum to the Deputy from the Minister which said roughly that as long as I still made decisions and carried out my work in a way that maintained confidence in the position then I would continue as Director of Trade Practices.

Very shortly afterwards three of the lawyers resigned and there was some publicity as a result. The Daily Colonist of 9th November 1976 speculated about their reasons and included a comment from the Minister that he had decided after some disagreement had arisen that it was the Director who made the enforcement decisions. It also referred to the earlier departure of the Deputy Minister. I refused comment however, and eventually it was suggested to me that they had probably harmed their careers more than helped them, that it would prove to be a storm in a teacup as far as publicity was concerned, and so it proved.

These were changing times however in a Government where, when I was hired, there would be a competition and the person with the most experience or credentials would generally get the job and that extended right up to Deputy Minister who often came from business or Academe without much emphasis on political persuasion. The Civil Service was there to provide counsel and excellent advice on matters that were the responsibility of the Department and therefore the Minister  He had an Administrative Assistant who would give him political advice, prepare his speeches and arrange his appointments. When those Assistants tried to interfere with what was considered policy or decisions in cases being dealt with by the Department they were politely or sometimes more firmly rebuffed.

The changes however saw first the Deputy Ministers and then Assistant Deputies and other senior positions appointed by Order In Council, which bypassed the competition aspects and allowed Government to fill these positions with whoever they liked. This would generally be someone, but not always, who supported their political thinking and could be removed very quickly if they fell out of favour. Those faithful servants who had occupied the positions were usually generously compensated and when they were gone there would be no trouble in replacing them with a Government selection.

One of the areas consistently complained about by the consumers who contacted the Ministry, was car sales and repairs. The Automotive industry always claimed with some justification that a vehicle had hundreds if not thousands of moving parts which could and did sometimes fail and that they tried to make sure that new and used vehicles provided good value and that repairs were honestly carried out when necessary.

Ray Morris showed me a facility on Annacis Island where any mishaps which affected the condition of new cars in transit were dealt with including a heat chamber to make sure that the paint finish equalled or bettered that produced at the factory. He also described some of the difficulties that the Manufacturer faced when a dealer charged them for new parts replaced under warranty and then used parts from some other source which were cheaper. This sometimes happened in the East when a train carrying new cars from the West coast on open wagons was used for target practice by some individual along the route and the bullet holes had to be repaired by the dealer. The customer would become very irate if some minor scrape showed a different coloured paint under the door surface for instance.

Another example of quality control was a delivery of cars for some Import Manufacturer which had experienced rough seas during the voyage. There are tie down points on the vehicles so that they do not move whilst in transit but if the movement of the ship is exaggerated by a storm and high waves, then damage can occur. On this occasion the new cars had cracked firewalls and with the permission of Canada Customs they were struck off the manifest of the freighter, transported to a crushing plant and turned into steel cubes.

It still could not be discounted that many of the complaints seemed to be justified, particularly about whether repairs were needed and the quality of repair. One of the things which may have contributed to this was the practice of some repair shops to pay a commission to mechanics on the parts which they installed. The large Franchises which specialized in transmission repair also attracted a lot of criticism because they always seemed to be able to demonstrate some feature of their old transmission to inexperienced customers which they claimed required replacement with an expensive reconditioned transmission.

# CHAPTER 15

## TEST SHOPPING

There was really only one way to determine if there was any dishonesty in Service areas and that was to use the tactics of the Vancouver radio station and set up a test of some kind. We found one or two vehicles which could not easily be identified as having official owners and a way of making a small change in an otherwise perfectly working vehicle which only required a small adjustment rather than repair. The initial tests were not only made at repairers that had been the source of complaints, but were broader in scope.

When two law students tabulated and analyzed the results it seemed to be about fifty fifty, honest and dishonest. This confirmed that there was a substantial amount of what really amounted to criminal behaviour. As there had been similar suspicions about television repair, another area where the consumer had no real way of knowing whether large repairs were necessary or had even been carried out. we tested this area as well and came up with just about the same proportional results.

What to do about this? The legal opinion was that there was a strong risk that the courts would consider these circumstances to constitute 'entrapment' where the accused was almost enticed to commit the offence, however there had to be a way of proceeding against dishonest repairers. I polled Prosecuting Counsel who were the ones who took the criminal cases before the courts and identified any weaknesses or deficiencies. Their advice was that the best scenario to rule out entrapment, for instance in the television area, would be to send in a newly arrived immigrant with poor English who only said "television not work." The parts inside the set would have to be marked in a way that could be subsequently identified. The same procedures could be used in the case of automatic transmissions.

To counter any allegations of underhand behaviour, the Minister issued a Press Release which described the testing which had been carried out and its results and that we would now be going after any repairers who continued to cheat the public, in other words a Fair Warning!

The Association which represented television repairers reacted strongly and I went to meet with them in North Vancouver in what could be best described as an unfriendly atmosphere. It was difficult to get my point across in the beginning because of interruptions but when I described how the set had been prepared, presented and examined afterwards and in some cases parts had been charged for which had not been replaced everything changed. By the end of the meeting their President said that rather than being critical they should be doing their best to identify these people. There seemed to be a sharp reduction in television complaints after that, and my own suspicion, which I did not voice too widely, was that the Industry itself knew who their black sheep were and that some contact would have been made along the lines, "any more of that and we will tell Consumer Affairs where to test!"

The transmission testing was carried out in most areas of the Province, and in one trip to the Kootenays the Investigator called in to say that he had dropped off the vehicle and received an initial analysis of unnecessary repairs, but the Individuals were real bruisers and he anticipated trouble when he went back to retrieve the vehicle and any parts which had been replaced. I suggested that he go to the nearest R.C.M.P. Detachment and explain the situation and that he anticipated that there might be a 'breach of the peace,' could one of the officers accompany him. The garage must have been well known because as he told me later everyone in the Detachment volunteered!

When Provincial Government employees go on strike, there are some services which are deemed essential and a skeleton staff has to be maintained, but management or people who are excluded from Union membership have to fill the gaps, and this is how I found myself at Tranquille Institution near Kamloops which housed young patients with severe disabilities. Along with others I worked in the laundry feeding large driers and the big ironing machines. Some had to work in an area where the soiled linen was processed and that wasn't particularly pleasant, and when the strike came to an end I was not unhappy to leave, but I did take up an invitation to tour some of the facility. All the doors were kept locked and some of the patients wore helmets to stop them hurting themselves. As we passed through one room a young lad took hold of my arm and was inspecting my watch, so I had to say as we were leaving that "you may be going out with one more than you came in with." That seemed to stay with me for a long time. During the second strike I worked at Riverview near Vancouver where the patients were mentally affected and here I cleaned toilets and had other general cleaning duties with the ever present 'sani', some form of antiseptic fluid which had to be used all the time. The patients here were elderly and for the most part their mental problems led to a lot of noise and sometimes violence or anti social behaviour. One of the things that upset my stomach however was the smell from the kitchen which reminded me of the tour around Meat Processing Plants some years previously.

There is a time when you start to think ahead to retirement and specifically what steps to take to have a secure income. I was impressed by the reasoning in a book that I read which spelled out the advantages of buying a second house as the best way of enforced saving when earnings were high to augment income after retirement. To do this you had to buy when the market prices were low. In November 1984 we took the plunge and became landlords This entailed working on a second house and garden but as house prices started to go up it eased the pain a little.

The worst abuses had been rapidly disappearing from the marketplace and I have described the changes which were starting to appear in Government. Some businessmen resented legislation which could be applied to business practices and by association the individuals who administered it. In the early days I had gone to Vancouver to our 'storefront office' at Kingsgate Mall to meet with one of the large automotive dealers to discuss an Assurance of Voluntary Compliance . The claim as I remember it was that the dealer had allowed a new car to be used by someone for a year and then sold it as a 'demonstrator' with all the expectations which would go with a vehicle which had been used for a short time by their senior people. I knew that they had arrived by the complete silence which occurred.

The reason for this was that staff had recognised their counsel as Lesley Peterson Q.C. the old Attorney General and my original boss. The meeting could not be described as cordial, and he had strong criticisms of the legislation. I formed the impression that he was going to advise them not to sign it, but they took it away with them and ultimately agreed to it. When Ministers changed so did the higher echelons of the Ministry. Sometimes people would arrive from the Federal Government, stay for a time and then go back.

Each time there would be a need for a briefing book which described the Ministry, its organization and the legislation together with the duties and responsibilities of the different sections.

There was always a certain amount of jockeying to try to impress the new Minister with the importance of each section and the amount of responsibility, much the same as activity at budget time when there was a need to support your budget allocation and sometimes ask to increase it.

When senior levels of bureaucracy become disenchanted with a particular Programme they find ways to show their displeasure.

There are a number of ways that this can be done in the Public Service. The use of that ubiquitous tactic 'reorganization' which Petronious is claimed to have so accurately described so many years ago as......... " When we were beginning to form up in teams we were reorganized. I was to learn later in life that we tend to meet any new situation by reorganizing, and a wonderful method it can be for creating the illusion of progress, while producing confusion, inefficiency, and demoralization........." There is some doubt now as to whether this was correctly attributed to Petronious in some year B.C, however it was definitely a tactic used by Ministry planners who saw it as a way of whittling away at duties and services which in turn impacted budget and staff numbers and the individual's classification which then came under review more frequently.

Most Governments recognise the wisdom of distancing themselves from enforcement decisions so that they cannot be accused of influencing this politically. When a new Assistant Deputy Minister was appointed, he arranged enforcement meetings where new investigations and the progress made in existing cases was discussed. He encouraged everyone to put their views forward and for the most part I kept as quiet as possible. Much to his annoyance I suspect after listening to all the comments including his own suggestions, I continued to make my own decisions and carried on as usual. This changed when a new Deputy Minister arrived. He had been a Deputy Commissioner in the R.C.M.P. and reputed to be very forthright.

He attended an enforcement meeting which followed its usual course At the end of it he said "Is somebody supposed to make a decision." There was complete silence and then I said as dispassionately as I could "Yes I am!" There were no more enforcement meetings and the A.D.M. left the Ministry.

We had sold the second house when the market was strong and we could realise a very acceptable increase in its value. The mortgage on the Wallace Drive house had been one of the last genuine 25 year ones with a fixed rate of interest and prepayment privileges every six months. The first one of these privilege payments that we made took us five years down the mortgage ladder.

We were able to retire this mortgage fairly quickly by means of these privilege payments although it was not always easy to find the money but it certainly saved us a great deal in terms of interest. We were also fortunate that the second house sold in the last year that there was a Capital Gains exemption.

# CHAPTER 16

## BUILDING A HOUSE

In 1986 we started thinking seriously about where we wanted to live in retirement. We both enjoyed our golf and it made sense to move nearer to the Glen Meadows Golf and Country Club that we had joined in 1977.

All the houses that we looked at did not appeal to us for one reason or another. We wanted a nice size garden, a view if possible. The Real Estate Agent that we dealt with persuaded us that if we sold our house first we would have no difficulty in finding another one and be in a strong position to buy at a good price having already sold. We put the house on the market expecting it to give us a fairly long time to look around but it sold very quickly. That saw us moving our furniture into the second house and a really difficult year spent searching the real estate market.

It gradually became obvious to us that we were not going to find all the things that we wanted in an existing house and in order to include all the

things we would like to have, we realised that we would have to build ourselves.

We discovered the last undeveloped lot on Jura Road, which was a short walking distance to the golf club and found that the owner would sell to us. The area relied on wells for drinking water and there were very strict rules which applied to septic fields, but we ploughed ahead and purchased the property which was a mass of blackthorn bushes and brambles.

To decide where to drill the well we brought in a 'witch' or Water Diviner who did not use a hazel stick but had a metal coat hanger, and sure

Unusual tree
on nearby Indian Reservation

enough after he had walked slowly over the lot, at one place it was pulled down in a spectacular way so we marked the spot for the driller.

I was at work when drilling started and regular phone calls kept me in touch with the progress, or lack of it, because they kept going deeper and deeper with no appreciable flow of water, so it became a decision of whether to pull out and drill somewhere else or carry on. We carried on and eventually the hole was over six hundred feet deep and the water flow was small but adequate. The depth would give us a respectable reserve, we hoped.

Starting a garden

There are hundreds of building plans and designs to choose from but here again we did not find exactly what we wanted and ended up modifying a plan to increase the size in those areas that are lived in most, the kitchen, the family room and the master bedroom.

We had a builder to find the trades that we wanted and to oversee the construction but first of all we had to get septic field approval from the Capital Regional District and that meant a percolation test carried out by an Engineer, an anxious time until he gave the O.K. and the C.R.D. accepted it.They imposed strict requirements on the preparation of the septic field and materials to be used. The site chosen next to the road had most of the blackthorn bushes and we were told that wheeled equipment could not go on it so the blackthorn had to be removed by hand. That was a strenuous and painful project for Pat and I and when they were ready to start building there were still a few left. The contractor just drove a back hoe up to them and in just a couple of minutes they were gone before the trucks with the field material arrived.

We left one or two 'wild' trees to see if they would bear fruit and one pear at the front bears lots of small sweet pears, and is probably the result of the core of a cultivated tree thrown away by someone long ago.

# CHAPTER 17

# GOODBYE CONSUMER AFFAIRS
# ................HELLO LIQUOR

When the frame of the house was about halfway done we went on a trip to Reno with friends, and flew over the house site as we left on the weekend. It was an anxious time because on the Friday I had been handed a letter which said that my position was 'surplus to requirements.' In other words I was out of a job!

When we came back we looked at the letter more closely and it said that as I had been a good servant of the Province they would look for another job for me if desired. My letter back said something to the effect that if my contribution was well regarded there should be no difficulty in finding one. I suspect that they already had something lined up because when I went back to work I was working for or with the Enforcement Director in Liquor Control and Licencing.

This was not a job that I liked but one for which I was profoundly grateful, because I kept my old classification and salary although it was 'redlined' and would not be subject to increases.

From the reports submitted by police and liquor inspectors I picked out the main features of reported offences, and it was fairly easy to identify the licenced premises giving rise to the most trouble from drunkenness or under age drinking and in some cases inappropriate behaviour by exotic dancers. Then I attended Hearings called by the Enforcement Director and presented the facts set out in the reports after which the Licencee or his representative had a chance to respond.

Some of the cases provided light relief. For instance when a small Chinese restaurant proprietor described what had happened during

Sandcastle Days at White Rock when police were having a lot of trouble with celebrants who were the worse for drink. He said "R.C.M.P. come in and say too much drink, half an hour later two of them come back, one grab my shirt and tie and lift me up and tell me ....You're closed!" When the Hearing was over and everyone had left, I said "There speaks the voice of truth!"

The Director had a number of enforcement options and it was only in serious cases or after a number of warnings or hearings that the Licence was restricted or suspended.

An additional duty proved to be a turn at night inspections mostly on a Friday or Saturday night when the Neighbourhood Pubs were visited early in the evenings to discourage their tendency to overcrowding and the Cabarets later as they were open to the early hours.

For my partner on 'learning beats' I had Peter Jones who had been transferred into an investigators position when the Rentalsman functions had been reduced. His wry sense of humour may have come from a stint with the C.B.C. before he joined Government, however he certainly knew the Victoria area drinking establishments and where trouble was likely. He also treated me to a heated and concentrated enforcement tour after we had stopped on Government Street and a Victoria Police motorcyclist who had put his head into our car noticed that Peter was not wearing his seat belt and gave him a ticket. Peter explained that we were making 'frequent stops' which should have been enough to excuse belt wearing, but he got a ticket anyway. He eventually convinced the Court with his argument.

There followed a whirlwind tour of pubs and clubs. Staff drinking after hours in one well known restaurant never knew what hit them and a Cabaret doorman was told to reduce numbers forthwith otherwise he would be closed down. Our last call was at the Police Social Club on Discovery Street.

I don't know how long I could or would have continued in Liquor. Fortunately the Government of the day wanted to decrease the size of its Civil Service and provided incentives for those who qualified to take early retirement. I just came within the guidelines that were based on age and service and would provide a lump sum payment based on years of service and waive the penalty normally applied to pensions taken before 60 years. It was still not an easy decision for Pat and I to make as 55 years of age is a little early to give up a well paying job and manage on a pension. We had however cleared off most liabilities like the mortgage and had updated the cars and appliances. Besides hadn't we said that we might look for a small business?

We had mentioned this to Neil, and he had been looking to see if there were any businesses for sale.

When we had decided to make the jump into early retirement I still worked for the last few weeks, but after many years there was a sense of not belonging any more. At an Inspectors meeting  when weekend inspections were being discussed, Peter Jones said "I see Hanson hasn't been down to Rumors for a long time." That of course meant that on just about my last inspections I had to visit this Club which was a meeting place for the gay community in Victoria.

A large Native Indian girl was acting as door person. She had a number of obvious tattoos and was holding a chain. The inside of the Club was darker than most but the music just as loud as I made my way to the back through a crowd that was so thick it confirmed overcrowding. The manager or proprietor was standing by a bar talking to a male 'peacock' who had some kind of light coloured suit, silk shirt, paisley and a colourful handkerchief hanging out of his top pocket. No one seemed anxious to clear a space on the bar for my report book, or to listen to my comments about the crowd.

There was a tall glass of some kind of drink on the bar and this somehow got knocked over the 'peacock' and caused a good deal of consternation as the barman rushed round with a cloth and tried to mop up the damage. It was however a good attention getter and after we had discussed the need to reduce the numbers I left for other city bright spots. I did make the mistake of mentioning this incident to someone and a few days later  my phone went with an exaggerated lisping voice berating me for ruining a good suit and threatening to sue but there was something slightly familiar in the tones. So I laid down the phone quietly and walked down the corridor, opened the door  and there was Peter Jones still lisping away and quite unperturbed when I said " Jones you b........ where did you learn to speak like that," he just said, "You put your tongue on the top of your mouth like this........"

# CHAPTER 18

## RETIREMENT..........
## FOR TWO WEEKS

After my last day of work I had exactly two weeks off. Neil had found a small offset printing and blueprinting business called Victoria Copy Services and we purchased this from Helen Lindo the owner. It was in the centre of Victoria on the second floor in the Exchange Building on Broad Street, an old building which had once housed the Stock Exchange and Y.M.C.A. in its time. None of us had any idea or any experience in printing or blueprinting, but there was some old equipment, an A.B. Dick press and a temperamental blueprint machine and the businesses downstairs on Trounce Alley had grown used to the noise transmitted through the floor. The rooms which we occupied were small and old and probably unsuitable for this kind of business and the customers had to toil up the stairs as did we when we had a paper delivery or were taking printed material down for delivery to customers. On the other hand it had something which was

priceless and that was its location close to the centre of the city.

This proved very convenient for the architects who had offices close by and brought their plans in for blueprinting. Some demanded 'background' which was a darker print whilst others did not like a lot of colour in the print. Some wanted mylars which are a heavier duty plastic kind of print when a lot of use is indicated but they all had one thing in common ... they wanted their prints right away!

The machine itself used anhydrous ammonia and had a large glass roll inside which was a powerful light. This burned the lines on the architects paper onto the light sensitive paper that we used and had to try to store carefully in a dark place. It had to be started up a few minutes before it could go to work and so it tended to be on all day with the gas turned on or off as required.

When there were dozens of prints in a set as in the case of a new hospital for instance, they had to be collated on a large table and these sets would then have to be given a binding strip to hold them with large staples from a big hand operated stapler. There was an automatic stapler for smaller sets.

The reason for the call from my short lived retirement was the need for someone to operate the blueprint machine, and so this is what I did during the day and sometimes into the evening, learning to adjust the speed and gas and feed the machine, collate the sets and bind them and deal with last minute insertions when some prints had to be altered. Working around this machine was sometimes hard on the eyes and the nose, but you got to meet your customers on a regular basis or the staff who had to carry the prints back and forth if we did not deliver them. There was often a queue at the machine with a lot of joshing as they waited their turn, however there was an elderly Chinese gentleman who always dressed in a three piece suit and shirt and tie and was the father of one of the architects Herb Kwan who would come right up to the front and say "You do my prints ... now!" and nobody seemed to mind because there were never very many.

There were parking meters in Broad Street outside so parking was a constant problem particularly for loading or off loading.

Neil had learned or was learning the business of printing very quickly. The principle of offset printing and the mechanics of the machine were a bit beyond Pat and I, although we could help to load and unload paper, make up the order and the Invoice, serve people who wanted photo copies, and keep an eye on the printing, keeping close to the switch which turned it off in emergency. Burton Cumming's wife came in once for photo copies.

Pat looked after the accounts, she used a 'one write system' which worked very well except that at the end of the month when Pat came to balance it there was sometimes a discrepancy and she would not leave it even if it was only a matter of a few cents, until she had found the error which generally proved to be a matter of addition on one of the invoices.

Pat and I were spending more and more time at the shop instead of playing golf or otherwise enjoying retirement. We did manage to get in an Alaska Cruise, and a couple of weeks in Palm Springs but not before Pat had to work hard to get the month end accounts done before we could go. Cash flow is always important in a small business and you have to get your bill into a customers hands as soon as possible after months end if you want to get paid.

Some aspects of the work were physical. There were boxes of paper to haul around printed or unprinted. We often joked that the fellows who made the deliveries from the paper companies Crown and Coast would buy us a dinner when we eventually left the premises. There was a piece of equipment called a guillotine which did the cutting in advance of printing to make paper a certain size, or after printing for the finished article. This was made of cast metal of some kind and was extremely heavy. It had a large blade which had to be very sharp and a large handle which brought the blade down on to whatever needed to be cut. Neil was a tower of strength in this kind of situation but I had to help sometimes to grab the large handle and almost hang on it some times to cut through the thickness of paper, particularly when we were cutting up hundreds of small tickets for instance.

We produced our own sales folder and with the permission of Victoria City Archives we used an old photograph of our location on Broad Street on the cover. A fair proportion of our printing was in the form of business cards so we produced our own with a background on the card to show what we could do and I used these cards in calling on local businesses to let them know that we were there and happy to look after their printing needs.It also seemed logical as we were a family business to change its name, so when we knew that our customers were familiar with the new owners our name changed to Hanson Printing Ltd and we adopted Tiffany as the font for the business logo which we started to use and for the sign which was hung outside the door at street level.

John Harris and I

Although any small business will give rise to some anxiety and make you reluctant to take your eyes off it for very long, we did have Neil there to manage it and this meant that Pat and I could get away for a holiday in the sun during the winter from time to time.

We went back to England and after a tour of the West country where we visited some of our old farm neighbours, and to Littlehampton where we saw Pat's old school friend and saw their old school house. We went to London for a very pleasant stay with John and Elizabeth Harris who lived close to the Thames.

One of these holidays saw us renting a unit in Thousand Palms just north of Palm Springs and on the way down we stayed at Reno for a few days. We were driving a Cadillac which was not new and just about affordable because a highway car was needed for a trip of that length and after we had got through the Siskyous without having to put chains on we could take side roads to Reno but as there was snow on either side of the road I asked the gas attendant in Weed if the roads were all right, and she told us that they were dry and clear.

We turned off the main highway and the further we went the higher the snow got on each side of the road and as night was falling the road became rutted ice. It was like driving down a luge track with the lights showing nothing but a canyon of snow and ice up ahead and what we would have done if someone came the other way I do not know. When we got to the final turn off for Reno the road improved considerably and the anxiety was lifted. When we resumed the trip from Reno to Palm Springs a few days later, the road which took us back to the I.5. had huge potholes, some of which you could have taken a bath in. There was a car overturned on the grass median to show how dangerous it was to drive too fast in those conditions.

Our second experience of Palm Springs confirmed why people enjoy and appreciate its climate in the winter months. I caught a glimpse of an unremarkable bird in the palms near the pool and shortly afterwards there was a succession of different bird songs which made me think that it was probably a mocking bird. We enjoyed the stalls and displays at an open air market held at the University at the weekends, however when we went to play golf at golf courses in the area there seemed to be a fairly hostile attitude towards visitors and in some cases they were downright rude.

The all day bus tour of Palm Springs and surrounding area was certainly worth taking. The bus driver was very knowledgeable about the film industry people who still lived in the area, pointing out their houses old and new with interesting anecdotes about some of them.

We spent two days at the Bob Hope Golf Tournament choosing two different courses one of which hosted the final day. The way in which everything was organised for the final was most impressive. Deputy Sheriff's waved you through intersections, course volunteers guide you into parking areas and buses took you into the course itself. The same arrangements worked in reverse afterwards as well.

The cable car was something that I wished I had never agreed to. Swinging around in a small observation car on a thin cable all that distance from the ground was not my idea of fun.

Our first cruise was to Alaska. Holland America provided a good showcase for the wonderful treatment that all passengers receive in the way of food and services. We were a little disappointed that we could not visit Sitka because sea conditions were too rough for the tenders. That was confirmed in the cabin because as I watched the curtain on a closet, it moved several degrees away from the vertical and then back again.

We cruised with Holland America again in 2002 and this time flew to Fort Lauderdale to board the Ryndam, which called at Half Moon Cay, Venezuela and Cartagena and then going through the Panama Canal and visiting more ports of call before disembarking at Victoria.

We did take some side trips but in Guatemala we contented ourselves with visiting the stalls of a market set up at the end of the harbour. It was very colourful with blankets and wraps, carvings and silver jewellery. I was fascinated by a stall which had wooden flutes that had been hand carved and the tunes that the stallholder could play on them, so I bought one for $5. When I got back to the boat I tried to play it but could not get even a squeak out of it. I marched back down to the harbour and found my flute player, gave him the one that I had bought and said, "play it" with our handicam poised. Well play it he did ... beautifully! showing that there was nothing wrong with my instrument ... just the player. I still have not been able to coax any sound out of it proving perhaps that it is very much an acquired art.

One of our most enjoyable holidays was certainly an earlier trip to New Zealand. The flight to Fort Lauderdale had been long and tiring for the Panama Cruise, but getting to and from New Zealand was a good deal longer and coupled with the time change, more exhausting.

Our decision to stay on the North Island and not to try to pack too much travelling into the month of February, was a good one. There were many opportunities to appreciate the Maoris, particularly when visiting Rotorua with its geysers and displays of their crafts. It was the singing of the Maori women and watching the men do a full length war dance the Haka that impressed me most.

There was an overall impression that the country was about twenty years behind the rest of the world when you watched television which had a large number of very old reruns and the laid back behaviour of everyone that you met. One thing however was an exception and that was their driving which seemed suicidal. The speed limits are set very high compared to what we are used to, and the roads have few stretches where you can see very far ahead. If you drive defensively they ride on your back bumper and overtake whether they can see the road ahead or not.

The volume of blueprints started to slacken off and gave me an opportunity to make some four wheel dollies to cart paper around and completed printing work. I put some shelves on wheels to hold the blueprint paper and try to keep the light from spoiling it. We kept our eyes on local auctions particularly where a print shop was closing down or selling up. The Credit Union in the centre of Victoria had its own print shop and when they decided to close this we picked up some equipment and a lot of tins of ink that were mostly part used but there were some full ones. I well remember piling things on to our wheeled dollies and pulling them through the streets back to Broad Street with some care having to be taken when going up and down kerbs.

When there was some time to give it some thought it was obvious that there was a gradual, not a dramatic change, taking place in offset printing and blueprinting..

In much the same way the small blueprint machines that architects were putting in their offices would provide them with one or two prints in the early design stages and they would only come to us when they wanted the long runs of the completed plans.

All this added up to a need to compete more aggressively for the remaining market, which might mean more modern equipment that we could not afford or a reduction in overhead which was equally impractical.

# CHAPTER 19

## TRUE RETIREMENT

The introduction of colour printers and the reduced price of photocopying and computer printers in many offices meant that the remaining professional printers would be competing for a shrinking market

There were other factors which helped us decide to sell the business when we received an offer in 1997, just about ten years after we started as business people with no previous experience where survival is the exception rather than the rule.

As we had found it difficult to be farmers with the knowledge that the animals would eventually end up on someone's table, so it was difficult to operate in a business sense when you came into close contact with your staff and their problems. For a business to succeed there has to be due regard for the well-being of employees, but you have to balance this against production and performance. Had we continued with increased overhead and uncertain sales volume I am sure that this would have been disastrous and we made the right decision just as we had when the earlier retirement issue seemed so difficult to make, but so obvious afterwards.

With an acre of garden to look after and the golf course just across the road at the top of my neighbour's garden there is always plenty to do.

There is the growing town of Sidney to shop for groceries about ten minutes away with the City of Victoria only half an hours drive and if we want a different walk than Sidney's waterfront, we have an annual pass to Butchart Gardens where there is always something to see at all times of the year.

Pat is a Sendial Volunteer and collects food orders for seniors or handicapped people who cannot get into the store. These are bagged and delivered to them later without charge.

There are many opinions given about Freemasonry, but I am pleased that my father encouraged me to join and have thoroughly enjoyed it. By joining one of the old Lodges, St. Andrews, which holds its meetings in central Victoria, it has meant travelling there for practices and meetings, but well worth it. Despite any criticisms of favouritism aimed at Freemasonry, I have never seen evidence to justify them, at least in Canada, and I am pleased to acknowledge that I am a Mason.

I have managed to continue playing golf on an infrequent basis, however Pat had to give this up when arthritis became too painful. This reduced our time out of the house and in 2002 we saw advertisements for two local Lawn Bowling Clubs who were holding open houses.

This proved to be an excellent opportunity for people like ourselves who knew nothing about the sport to have an opportunity to try it. As we had when joining Glen Meadows Golf and Country Club, we based our decision on the people rather than the facilities, because in joining Sidney Lawn Bowling Club we were joining a young club which had only started in 1998, and although it had an excellent green, the club house was only half built and subject to a mortgage loan. There were however some wonderfully enthusiastic members who were more than willing to share their knowledge and help us understand the rules and enjoy the game. It seems that we must have done the right thing because in that first year, Pat was the Ladies Novice Champion and I was the Men's.

Pat's brother David, his wife Sheila and their family live very close to us as do our children. My sister Gillian lives in the South of England and my brother Nicholas still lives in Kenya.

These then are my recollections, set down while I am still in full possession of my faculties. Memory however can be an elusive thing and I have I hope remembered things fairly accurately and not trespassed in areas which some would rather forget or not given enough prominence to those that they consider more important. Age may also have influenced my grammar and punctuation and any errors are strictly my own.

Perhaps there will be more important memories to come and once more I will have to sit down and write again.

ISBN 141200934-0

9 781412 009348